The Civilizing Machine

THE MEXICAN EXPERIENCE

William H. Beezley, series editor

MICHAEL MATTHEWS

The Civilizing Machine

A Cultural History of Mexican Railroads, 1876–1910

UNIVERSITY OF NEBRASKA PRESS

LINCOLN AND LONDON

An earlier version of chapter 2, "De Viaje: Elite
Views of Modernity and the Railroad Boom,"
appeared as "*De Viaje*: Elite Views of Modernity and
the Porfirian Railway Boom" in *Mexican Studies/
Estidios Mexicanos* 26 (Summer 2010): 251–89.

Library of Congress Cataloging-in-Publication Data
Matthews, Michael, 1978–
The civilizing machine: a cultural history of Mexican
railroads, 1876–1910 / Michael Matthews.
pages cm — (The Mexican experience)
Includes bibliographical references and index.
ISBN 978-0-8032-4380-4 (pbk.: alk paper)
ISBN 978-0-8032-4943-1 (pdf)
1. Railroads — Mexico — Social
aspects — History — 20th century. 2. Railroads —
Mexico — Public opinion — History — 20th century.
3. Popular culture — Mexico — History — 20th
century. 4. Mexico — History — 1867–1910. I. Title.
HE2818.M33 2014
385.0972'09034 — dc23   2013031269

Set in Sabon by Laura Wellington.

To my father, Charles Matthews, and to my mother,
Rossana Castagnetto

CONTENTS

ILLUSTRATIONS

Tables

ACKNOWLEDGMENTS

The completion of this book would have been impossible without the support and guidance that I received from many people. And attempting to acknowledge all the personal and intellectual debts that I have incurred along the way seems as challenging as writing this entire book, maybe more. That said, I will try anyway. My initial interest in Latin American studies and Mexico more specifically began at Simon Fraser University, where Richard Boyer provided incredible encouragement when I was an undergraduate and incredible feedback and friendship during my first forays into graduate work. Also, while I was an undergraduate, Edward Ingram and Terrance Ollerhead at the *International History Review* offered me a job as assistant to the editor, a job I was lucky enough to keep for five years and that piqued my interest in the study of history. I am thankful for their support at such an early stage in my academic career.

Research for this project began at the University of Arizona where my adviser, William Beezley, always provided unwavering support and invaluable advice. Kevin Gosner, Bert Barickman, and Linda Green all shared their vast knowledge of Latin America with me and, in so doing, shaped my approach to the study of history and culture. The Barbara Payne Robinson Research Grant from the History Department at the University of Arizona provided funds for archival research in Puebla, Zacatecas, and Mexico City, and the Tinker Foundation Summer Research Grant provided funds for archival research in Querétaro and San Luis Potosí. My graduate school compadres cultivated an intellectually stimulating environment and a profound sense of camaraderie and community. I would like to thank Ageeth Sluis, Amanda López, Jeff Bannister, Karin Friederic, Erika Korowin, Robbie Scott, Vikas Rathee, Ryan Kashanipour, and Sigma Colon for their support and friendship. *¿Cómo no te voy a querer?*

William French, Stephen Neufeld, Tracy Goode, James Garza, Victor Macías-González, and Áurea Toxqui offered wonderful advice while I was either researching or writing this book. Taking time out of his busy schedule to read the manuscript, Patrick Eberlein offered feedback from a refreshing perspective as someone outside the field, far outside the field. Ernesto Lundsford unwearyingly worked with me to translate numerous poems in this volume, although any errors in translation are mine and mine alone. I am thankful to Bridget Barry and many others at the University of Nebraska Press for their fine expertise, making it possible for this book to be published.

The archivists and staff at the Nettie Lee Benson, Archivo General de la Nación, Hemeroteca Nacional, Colección Porfirio Díaz at the Universidad Iberoamericana, Centro de Estudios de Historia de México, Archivo Histórico del Estado de Querétaro, Archivo Histórico del Estado de San Luis Potosí, Archivo Histórico del Estado de Zacatecas, and Centro de Documentación e Investigación Ferroviarias in Puebla were all extremely helpful and supportive, often demonstrating considerable enthusiasm for my project. Most of all I would like to thank Emilio García Teja, Carla Sánchez Gómez, and Magda Juanchi Gómez at the Biblioteca Lerdo de Tejada, who patiently catered to my (what I'm sure seemed like) endless requests and patiently endured my initial fumbling through the catalogues and document request forms. Also, while in Mexico City, Alma Bustamante helped me to navigate the city and showed me the routes to several archives. She also introduced me to the Pumas de la UNAM, and for that I am likewise truly grateful.

Elon University and the Department of History and Geography provided two things usually in short supply for young professors: time and money. The Hultquist Award and the Elon Faculty Research and Development Grant allowed me to undertake further research in Mexico City and Austin, Texas. Generous course releases offered me time to complete my writing and undertake the revisions that transformed my dissertation into a book. I thank my colleagues at Elon for promoting such a collegial environment, making it a superb place to work. At Elon I have benefited from the advice and support of David Crowe, Clyde Ellis, Mary Jo Festle, Charles Irons, Nancy Midgette, and Kirsten Ringelberg in preparing this manuscript.

Finally, I wish to thank my parents, to whom this book is dedicated. My unconventional upbringing offered me an opportunity to see a wider world at a young age, an experience that sparked my curiosity about different people and places.

The Civilizing Machine

INTRODUCTION

The nineteenth century, when it takes its place with the other centuries in the chronological charts of the future, will, if it needs a
symbol, almost inevitably have as that symbol a steam engine running upon a railway.

H. G. WELLS, *Anticipations of the Reaction of Mechanical and Scientific Progress upon Human Life and Thought* (1902)

Mexican newspapers and periodicals in the 1890s printed art,
poetry, literature, and social commentaries that revealed a fascination with the country's booming railway network. These
works exploited the symbolic power of the locomotive, a technological development closely associated with economic, political, and industrial modernization. Two poems published months
apart show the starkly different views that people held about
not only the railway but also a number of pressing issues regarding ideas about material progress, economic growth, social order, and national sovereignty. In 1894 Mexico City's *El
Mundo (Semanario Ilustrado)*, a weekly journal catering to
tastes of the well-to-do, offered readers a sonnet dedicated to
the marvels of the iron horse. The poet rejoiced at the locomotive's capacity to compress time and space as it dashed majestically across the landscape. His paean transformed the machine's
dark plumes of suffocating smoke into "vapors of incense" from
which the train emerged, allowing light to break through. Al-

lured by its relentless momentum, he boasted that the railway must either forge a forward path or find its grave. On its wings, the author concluded, it carried the fecund seeds of industry, art, and progress and convinced him that God's breath pushed the world forward.[1]

Months later, the critical firebrand *El Hijo del Ahuizote* offered readers a poem with a different take on railway travel, one that harshly questioned its capacity to carry the country into a better, more prosperous future. The cantos encapsulated the deep sense of animosity that many individuals felt against the foreign owned transportation network as well as their apprehensions about locomotive travel more generally. Targeting a wide range of readers—leftist and liberal intellectuals and popular and working-class groups—the poet described locomotive travel as a cataclysmic undertaking that killed as many people as typhus or cholera once had. The author branded engineers as "nihilists" with no regard for human life. Each stanza ended with the same line, sardonically repeating that passengers "paid in Mexican" (a double-entendre referring to their money and lives) only to be "killed in English" (referring to the allegedly reckless Yankees who operated the network). The author's venomous verses continued launching attacks at the foreign railway companies and their employees, tagging American engineers as "savages," "brutes," and "butchers."[2] By the end of the poem, the writer had transformed the railway into a symbol of disorder, death, and foreign domination, an image in stark contrast to the one provided by the newspaper's polite society counterpart.

As these poems suggest, in late nineteenth-century Mexico, H. G. Wells's observation that the railway would represent the ultimate symbol of the era seems patently prophetic. Yet as these verses also indicate, people failed to agree upon what exactly that symbol meant. These kinds of cultural expressions revealed deep divides about how people interpreted the impact of railway development on their society. The railway, the material incarnation of progress, became a commanding symbol used by politicians, intellectuals, artists, writers, and revolutionaries to express their visions of the role that modernization could play in gaining or undermining national salvation. The capacity of technological advancements to carry the country into a better, brighter future defined by the attainment of civilization dominated people's imaginations. It appeared as a panacea that could heal the wounds inflicted by the country's turbulent past. This study explores a critical, yet neglected, facet of late nineteenth- and early twentieth-century Mexico: the ideological and cultural milieus that shaped people's understandings about the role of technology in a developing country seeking to find its place among the pantheon of modern industrial nations.

Mexicans, after achieving independence in 1821, saw their new nation verge on national disintegration as external military threats and internal political conflict threatened to tear the country apart. In the 1830s, social and political turmoil abounded and undermined the recovery of the economy.[3] Bitter infighting between liberals and conservatives undermined organizing a united front against the United States' invasion (1846–48) that, after the signing of the Treaty of Guadalupe Hidalgo, left the country with half of its national territory.[4] The central government, during this period, lost control over the provinces that had fragmented into a plethora of self-ruling regional entities controlled by local leaders and *caudillos*.[5] The severed country almost lost its independence to the French, who installed a Hapsburg emperor who governed the country between 1862 and 1867.[6] Once free of the French, Benito Juárez and the Restored Republic, although suffering from bankruptcy, provincial revolts, and foreign threats, undertook the making of modern Mexico.[7]

Nearly everything changed when General Porfirio Díaz seized power under the banner of the Revolution of Tuxtepec in 1876, which ousted Juárez's successor, Sebastián Lerdo de Tejada, establishing a thirty-five-year dictatorship known as the Porfiriato (1876–1911). Despite inheriting an empty treasury, facing armed political challenges, and possessing an appalling international credit rating, by the end of his first term in office, Porfirio Díaz had succeeded in establishing the stability needed for material progress. The economy grew, political challenges ceased, and foreign powers officially recognized the regime. After handing over the presidency for one term to his longtime political ally, General Manuel González, Díaz returned to power and did not relinquish control of the presidency until 1911.

During his dictatorship, Díaz transformed the country and fostered a booming economy propelled by export-led development and buttressed by low tariff rates that revived the mining and agricultural sectors. The country experienced rapid adaptation of technological advancements such as steam, water, and electric power that replaced animal and human labor. Through a series of measures implemented to end political infighting and social upheaval, Díaz gave confidence to foreign investors to pour money into the country's various projects of national development. Railway construction, above all other infrastructural accomplishments, represented the most astonishing achievement sustained through the investment of massive foreign capital in the realm of material progress. The year that Díaz seized power, the country only possessed 640 kilometers of track that used 114 mules, rather than steam engines, to set trains in motion.[8] By 1884, the year of his first reelection, the grid had expanded to 5,731 kilometers and by 1898 to 12,173 kilometers. The year that Díaz left office, the country held 19,280 kilometers with another 8,000 in trunk lines.[9]

Most approaches to Mexican railway history have focused on the economic, political, and social aspects of transportation development. They have emphasized how the railroad played a crucial role in connecting local, national, and international markets and, in so doing, allowed for the growth of the economy.[10] Studies on Porfirian political and economic development have generally characterized the expansion of the railway network as coming at the expense of indigenous, agrarian, and labor groups while benefiting the export sector and foreign interests, thus undermining national sovereignty.[11] Revisionist studies have tempered these assessments.[12] Despite the considerable literature on the issue, the study of railway development in Mexico, and to a lesser degree Latin America, has yet to examine the cultural dimensions of the locomotive.[13]

This book examines how the Porfirian regime used its success in promoting railway development to secure and legitimize its rule. It argues that the development of the railway played a vital role, not only as a tool to unite the country and to link production zones to markets and ports, but also in the government's attempts to forge a modern, civilized citizenry with a unified national identity. Furthermore, it contends that having succeeded in bringing the internal stability needed for the growth and development of the economy, government officials repeatedly used the railroad as a symbol to highlight the accomplishments of Porfirian modernization and to justify the regime that had shed its liberal ideals and grown increasingly authoritarian. Boosters emphasized the ability of the government's railway project to bring civilization, to promote national unity, to increase commerce, and even to change the racial composition of the population. In so doing, they stressed Díaz's achievements and excused his heavy-handed tactics used to deliver on the regime's mantra of "order and progress."

At the same time, opposition groups, especially from the middle and working classes, although not contesting railway development per se, objected to the national costs and social hardships that resulted from the railway boom. Critics of the government often used the same rhetorical themes (civilization and progress, national unity, commercial development, and racial concerns) to challenge the manner in which the regime secured economic development. These competing discourses not only make known the contentious atmosphere surrounding the project of railway expansion but also reveal some of the fundamental weaknesses of the regime that led to its downfall. Opponents, many of whom put forward the first articulate challenges to the dictatorship prior to the 1910 Revolution, exploited the symbolic and rhetorical power of the railroad to underscore the more negative aspects of Porfirian modernization and to question the so-called universal truths that defined the regime's civilizing mission.

Cultural producers, both supporters and detractors of the regime, expressed their views regarding railway development as well as a host of related social, political, and economic issues in social commentaries, music, art, literature, and statecraft. These cultural representations and interpretations of the regime's policymaking played a crucial role in shaping people's attitudes about their government, their country, and their future. This considered, Porfirian railway development—traditionally analyzed in economic and political terms—must also be investigated on a cultural level as it influenced a range of artistic, literary, and intellectual works, all of which sought to uphold or undermine the legitimacy of Díaz as the country's indisputable leader. The railway represented the supreme symbol of "order and progress" as it connected markets, both nationally and internationally, and as it allowed for the rapid deployment of troops across the nation. This study, by examining the works of cultural producers that employed the locomotive as a symbol, explores these texts to help better understand the outlooks that different social groups held toward the processes of national development and modernization.[14] In so doing, it shows that these cultural productions reflected the deepening social divisions that existed during the Porfiriato, divides that would be made obvious in the tumultuous years of the Mexican Revolution.

Trains, Travel, and the Mexican Railroad System

A brief description of the country's four major railways provides a better geographic sketch of the reach of the network and offers a base for understanding the experience of those who journeyed across the region's diverse topography and territories. To leave Mexico City by rail, travelers needed to depart from either the Buenavista Railway Station northwest of the city's Zocalo or the San Lázaro Railway Station. Once at the station, they could take a tramway or a horse-drawn coach to their final destination. Coaches, like most railways, offered three classes of travel: blue (most expensive), red, and yellow (least expensive). Whether large or small, railway stations featured a similar design layout. The entrance—usually denoted by a tower with a clock in larger stations—housed the ticket and telegraph offices. Passengers would find a waiting area (sometimes two in larger buildings) and restrooms. A baggage room adjoined the ticket office. Express rooms stored mail, news rooms received information by telegraph, and news storage rooms were to be found. Outside, areas known as sheds with large awnings protected travelers from the elements. Railway stations, as described by writers and depicted by artists, were bustling and crowded areas with passengers waiting to depart, family and friends waiting for arrivals, and a host of vendors selling newspapers, books, and local foods such as *atole* and *tamales*, usually to third-class riders.

Of all the major railway lines across the country, the Mexican Central Railroad was the largest, stretching almost 2,000 kilometers from Mexico City to El Paso, Texas. Two important trunk lines, one to Guadalajara and one to Tampico, made the Central the most important line in the country in terms of size (5,000 kilometers or 25 percent of the entire national grid) and freight (carrying 30 percent of all cargo). Trains leaving from the Buenavista station in Mexico City to El Paso cut through the middle of the country, crossing the Federal District and ten states: Mexico, Hidalgo, Querétaro, Guanajuanto, Jalisco,

Aguascalientes, Zacatecas, Coahuila, Durango, and Chihua-hua. Thus travelers experienced a diverse and changing land-scape as the train snaked through the mountainous regions of the old mining centers of Querétaro, Guanjuanto, and Zacate-cas before slowly descending into the deserts of the northern states. Crossing through Coahuila and Durango, passengers would observe the showcase of Porfirian modernity: the La-guna region and its main town, Torreón, a city built after the arrival of the railway in 1884 (originally called Estación de Torreón) that spurred a boom in the establishment of large cot-ton-growing estates. In 1880 the Atchison, Topeka, and Santa Fe Company starting building its main line connecting Mexi-co City with the United States and completed it in 1884. After leaving the Federal District, passengers would view the entire Valley of Mexico, the immense precipice at Nochistongo, and the Querétaro ravine. In all, the trip took about sixty hours. Trains left the Buenavista station heading to El Paso once a day, usually in the evening. Trains from El Paso also arrived once a day, usually at noon. The company offered riders three classes of travel. First-class featured a Pullman buffet, drawing room, and sleeping cars with private compartments and beds. Third-class passengers, in contrast, traveled together in a public com-partment, often in cramped quarters. For shorter excursions, third-class passengers often traveled in open-aired cars used for livestock. Although prices varied throughout the Porfiriato, companies based the cost of tickets on distance traveled. Rates for the Central, as with the other major lines, were as follows: three cents per kilometer for first class; two cents per kilome-ter for second class; and one and a half cents per kilometer for third class.

The next largest line provided the shortest route between Mex-ico City and the United States. The Mexican National Railroad connected the Federal District with Laredo, Texas. Starting at the San Lázaro station, it measured 1,700 kilometers that included three trunk lines that crossed seven states. James Sullivan and William Palmer's railway company started building the line in 1880, finally inaugurating it in 1888 in San Luis Potosí. Crossing through San Luis Potosí, Coahuila, and Nuevo León, the National offered travelers an impressive panorama of the Valley of Mexico before descending into the Valley of Toluca. After passing through Celaya, San Miguel de Allende, and San Luis Potosí, the line cut through the desolate deserts of the Sierra Madre leading to the town of Saltillo. Going further still, the appearance of textile factories and grain mills notified travelers they had reached the northern industrial town of Monterrey. Leaving the Sierra Madre, the National's trains crossed the Río Salado on an impressive international bridge before reaching the Laredo station. Trains departed to Laredo once daily, at night, and trains returning from the U.S. border arrived in the early morning. The National, like the Central, offered three classes of travel.

The oldest of all railway lines, the Mexican Railway, most often referred to as the Veracruz (Mexico) Railway, first received a concession in 1837, during the presidency of General Anastasio Bustamante. Political turmoil, foreign threats, and a lack of capital hindered its completion. In 1865, during the French Intervention, Emperor Maximilian attempted to complete the line by granting a concession to the Imperial Railway Company, which indeed accelerated construction until the pretender's fall from power in 1867. The emerging political stabilization of the Restored Republic allowed the government to complete the line in 1873. Leaving the Buenavista station, trains proceeded to Veracruz via Orizaba. Of all the country's railways, the Mexican represented the most popular among foreign travelers as it provided extraordinary panoramas. Leaving the capital, trains would descend 1,200 meters in a distance of 40 kilometers. The immense drop in elevation offered travelers drastic changes in scenery from orange groves and coffee plantations with a backdrop of snowy volcanoes (Popocatépetl and Ixtacihuatl) to tropical jungles signaling the proximity of the coast. The rugged topography and sharp descents pitted engineers and builders in a fight against nature, leading to spectacular feats of engineering such as the bridge over the Barranca de Metlac (the Metlac Ravine) made famous by José Maria Velasco's painting. The Barranca del Infiernillo (the Little Hell Ravine), a semicircular viaduct clinging to the side of a mountain, offered travelers breathtaking, if not terrifying, vistas. Tourists could also take the Mexican Railway for excursions to view the pyramids of San Juan Teotihuacan, a trip that took just over an hour from the capital. The Mexican provided riders with first-, second-, and third-class compartments, costing customers three cents per kilometer, two cents per kilometer, and one cent per kilometer, respectively. It left the Mexico City station twice a day, once in the morning and once in the evening. Trains arrived from Veracruz twice a day.

This route was originally intended to connect the port cities of Acapulco and Veracruz. The Interoceanic Railway's planners hoped to connect Mexico City to both oceans, a goal that its Mexican promoters and London backers never accomplished. Completed in 1891, the line connected the capital to Veracruz, although it took a different route than the older Veracruz (Mexico) Railway. Leaving the San Lázaro station, the Interoceanic passed through Texcoco and Puebla before reaching Jalapa and eventually Veracruz. A branch line that skirted Lake Texcoco offered travelers the opportunity to visit Amecameca, Cuernavaca, and Jojutla. For Mexican travelers, especially religious pilgrims, the Interoceanic allowed quick passage to the popular Shrine of Sacromonte at Amecameca. Like the Veracruz (Mexico) Railway, the Interoceanic undertook a sharp descent into *tierra caliente*, relying on a series of bridges, tunnels, and viaducts to reach the port city. Trains left Jalapa in the evening and arrived in Mexico City in the morning.

Railroads, the Mission of Civilization, and
the Phantasmagoria of Progress

The Porfirian regime's most ambitious project of national development and material progress—the construction of a nation-wide railway system—provided officials with a powerful symbolic and rhetorical tool to promote their civilizing mission.[15] A growing literature on the cultural history of the Porfiriato has inspired this book. These works have explored an array of issues including state formation, tensions and overlap between traditional (rural) and modern (urban) identities, and the outbreak of the Mexican Revolution. They demonstrate that the ruling elite and their supporters used cultural practices and values to establish their legitimacy and to attempt to remake society along modern European guidelines.[16] These studies have helped explain the success, span, and problems of Porfirian rule.

By its achievements at advancing the civilizing mission, the regime endeavored to establish its legitimacy as the government grew increasingly authoritarian and disregarded the hallowed Constitution of 1857. Díaz and his backers repeatedly took advantage of public rituals, civic ceremonies, and the subsidized (hence pro-government) press to highlight his achievement at civilizing the country. Such an accomplishment was demonstrated by securing peace and bringing progress and thus establishing the necessary conditions for the population to enjoy a level of material culture equal to that of Europe and the United States. In this regard, for the elite, cosmopolitanism represented an essential component to the formation of a modern national identity.[17]

Officials understood technological progress as an essential component to the civilizing of individuals. Railway development demanded a series of proper behaviors such as self-constraint against the use of violence (banditry, for example, had perpetually undermined the safety of travel before Díaz ascended to the presidency) and a reliable work ethic among the labor force that would build the national transportation grid. Railway travel, likewise, demanded proper behaviors such as punctuality and etiquette. Norbert Elias, in his classic study, *The Civilizing Process*, posited that in the transition of European society from feudalism to modern nations, personal behaviors such as table manners, bodily propriety, and housing conditions played a central role in the middle class's attempt to create its own standards as opposed to those of the Middle Ages. He traced how European courtly society used these codes of conduct to distinguish themselves from inferior ranks and how acts of etiquette made clear the social hierarchy. He also showed that patterns of self-restraint become intertwined with the concept of civilization. Only through the establishment of societies with a centralized monopoly of power did self-restraint become an essential aspect of the civilizing process. The growing complexity of societies and the growing interdependence between individuals within a society, coupled with a central authority's monopoly of force, fostered a sense of stability that made self-restraint a decisive trait of the civilized individual.[18] In Porfirian Mexico, government officials and their boosters worked to promote the "civilizing process" that extolled these types of proper behaviors — expressed and defined in art, literature, pageantry, social commentaries, and political rhetoric — to make clear their political legitimacy while, at the same time, demonstrating to foreign audiences their ascendance to the pantheon of civilized countries.

In the context of European imperialism, nineteenth-century colonial officials and policymakers used the idea of a "civilizing mission" to justify their economic and political ambitions in Africa and Asia, often couching their objectives in humanitarian terms. European advances in technology provided them with tangible proof of their superiority, further validating their global outlook.[19] These assumptions about superiority — sometimes expressed as racial supremacy — came to represent in the

minds of Europeans universal truths about the relationship between so-called traditional and modern societies. This book argues that late nineteenth-century leaders of Mexico, an independent yet underdeveloped country, promoted a self-civilizing
mission, through the use of the railway as the supreme symbol
of national development, as a means of attaining social order,
political stability, and material progress. The discourses that divided between the "civilized" and the "barbaric" proved powerful in government attempts to create boundaries differentiating
elite and popular identities. Furthermore, since railway travel
demanded behaviors such as timekeeping and precision, it also
became a symbol of the new demands of an emerging capitalistic society.[20]

For elite Porfirians, especially in the early years of railway
construction (roughly 1880 to 1888), the civilizing capacity of
technology found its most intimate expressions. Writers, artists,
journalists, and government officials interpreted railway expansion as a phenomenon that would allow the once war-torn and
socially divided country to unite and move forward toward a
better future. A near religious fervor emerged regarding the importance of technological modernization and its ability to transform the country and its citizens. Inspired by Comtean positivism, a philosophy emphasizing scientific politics that viewed
society as a natural organism that went through stages of evolution,[21] technology and progress assured Porfirians that their
country verged on reaching the so-called final stage of history.
Comtean positivism, much like its Saint-Simonian predecessor,
represented a near-utopian outlook insofar as it offered a vision
of social development without the emergence of class conflict
envisaged by Karl Marx's theory of historical materialism.[22]

Walter Benjamin challenged such Panglossian views of social
development, arguing that the utopian promises offered by capitalist modernization and technological progress had created a
collective dream consciousness among Europeans that viewed

machines as alleviating human misery while they ignored how modern technologies had fostered the greater exploitation of individuals.[23] This dream consciousness denoted an example of what Marx referred to as the fetishism of commodities—that is, the process by which people transformed consumer products into objects with ambiguous meaning divorced from understandings of the human labor and exploitation that created these goods.[24] The only meaning held within these commodities was what the consumer or observer projected upon them. For Benjamin, the process of fetishization could be understood by examining how people experienced commodities sensually. This transformation of commodities, a phenomenon he referred to as "phantasmagoria," emphasized the ways that consumer goods became magical objects unable to show how they came into being.[25] While Marx and Benjamin focused on how commodities came to have an intrinsic value to people, this study highlights the ways that middle- and upper-class literature during the early years of railway development—and especially during railway inauguration ceremonies—expressed encounters with the locomotive—a capital good—as emotive, sensual experiences that confirmed the utopian promises of modernization and so too the regime's civilizing mission. But the euphoria that the railway inspired among individuals masked the social, economic, and political sacrifices made in order to secure its arrival.

The regime's organization of civic ceremonies celebrating the inauguration of railways provided important opportunities for officials to justify their power through symbolic acts. Officials symbolically and rhetorically associated their rule with the country's ceaseless drive into the future. Inaugurations, and the regional expositions that showcased local products that often accompanied these events, revealed a fetishism of not only local commodities and the railway but the government as well. In ceremonies, political leaders appeared as autonomous figures magically bestowed with power, not as individuals whose status stemmed from the authority that people invested in them.[26] During the Porfiriato, these types of celebrations repeatedly highlighted Díaz as the country's indisputable leader, linking him symbolically to the railway as the only person capable of securing the necessary conditions for material progress.

These ceremonies allowed the elite to demonstrate civilized behaviors and values that they believed all groups should aspire to—whether dressing properly, demonstrating etiquette, or enjoying European art and music. In largely peasant societies, such as nineteenth-century Mexico, ruling groups placed civilized behaviors on a pedestal that few could aspire to achieve as they lacked the material or cultural means to do so.[27] Indeed, lavish celebrations for railway inaugurations allowed the elite to flaunt their sophistication as a way to separate themselves from common society. Such events also connected them to foreign countries regarded as sophisticated and civilized. Railway inaugurations played a crucial role in establishing a cultural framework that justified government authority and that sought to provide guidelines for the moralizing and civilizing of the citizenry. These frameworks allowed the ruling elite to draw on moral values to define legitimate political practice.[28] Civic rituals provided an opportunity for supporters of the regime to highlight the indispensability of Díaz and the absolute necessity of his perpetual reelection.

The arrival of the locomotive, as demonstrated by the works of writers, artists, journalists, and politicians, evoked strong emotional and sensual reactions among its audience as trains seemed to materialize and vanish in a cloud of smoke.[29] A wide range of sources reveal that social commentators viewed railways as the cornerstone to national redemption after years of economic and social turmoil. Yet, as years passed and railway development proved incapable of ending the hardships that people faced, opposition groups used cultural mediums to highlight the human and national toll behind the government's infrastructure project, including the loss of sovereignty, the people's loss of land, the draconian implementation of laws, the frequency of train wrecks, and the poor treatment of native workers by foreign companies. These sources worked to undermine people's approval of the regime, especially its brand of authoritarian modernization.

This book examines the changing dynamic between the Porfirian regime and opposition groups through an analysis of the diverse and conflicting representations of the railway program in elite and popular culture. Its perspective owes a debt to the insights of Antonio Gramsci's concept of cultural hegemony. For Gramsci, all governing bodies inevitably face a difficult juggling act, namely, maintaining the delicate balance between consent and force in legitimating rule.[30] Ruling groups, to gain consent from subordinates, must attempt to obtain their acceptance through the social and cultural order. In other words, dominant culture requires consent from subordinate groups in the realm of values, beliefs, mores, and prejudices that define existing social, economic, and political relations.[31] This idea holds that while any given government might face political or social opposition, most groups find it difficult to translate their experiences into ideologies that challenge the hegemonic culture. Nevertheless, Gramsci maintained that through a "war of position," opposition groups could undertake practical activities in civil society that worked to erode the legitimacy of those in power and provide a vision of a better and more just future.[32]

In Porfirian Mexico, relations between ruling and popular groups were not only established through Díaz's manipulation of local, state, and national governments and his reliance on coercion. His rule also depended on fostering a shared language and ideology among various groups that stressed an unwavering belief in modernizing the country by any means necessary. While not all people agreed on the exact approach that this project needed to take, competing and complementary discourses nevertheless agreed on the essentialness of attaining material progress, serving to create a sense of social consensus about the need for modernizing the transportation system. Yet a growing number of reinterpretations of how the railway had failed to promote modernization and civilization began to challenge the ideas that the regime and its followers had upheld. Indeed, the consensus established by Díaz and his supporters proved shallow and underdeveloped as a result of the administration's narrow alliance of elite groups and reliance on government-sponsored violence to maintain order. The voices of opposition examined in this study reveal one important line of attack that worked to erode the hegemony of the regime.

Challengers of the Porfirian regime used popular culture—the opposition press, artwork, stories, poetry, and ballads—to draw people's attention to the failures of the regime in regard to an array of social, economic, and political problems. In all these works, the railway, as the supreme symbol of the regime's accomplishments in the realm of material progress, played a central role in framing critiques against the government. These expressions of oppositional and popular culture helped to expose the fetishism of material progress—embodied in industrial commodities, luxury goods, and even railways—that allowed much of the government's policies to go generally unquestioned.[33] Indeed, especially after 1895 or so, the elite cultural representations of the railway proved too narrow, allowing opposition groups to provide their own symbolic meaning over the successes and failures of government policy, a strategy that likewise exploited the railway's iconic power. In so doing, the regime's challengers crafted a counter-nationalism that contested a national identity based on cosmopolitanism and that appropriated the discourse of civilization and savagery to their own ends.[34]

This book pays considerable attention to the role of the press in producing the cultural representations of technological development. It shows that Porfirian newspapers offer scholars more than a source of information showing what events occurred and when, but also provide understanding of how people interpreted these events thus shaping their worldviews.[35] A wide range of newspapers, dailies, and weeklies were published in Mexico City, offering readers 576 periodicals throughout the Porfiriato. In Mexico City, the literacy rate improved from 38 percent to 50 percent during the Díaz era. In the rest of the country, the literacy rate improved from 14 percent to 20 percent. The circulation of periodicals throughout the era increased with the largest presses running 20,000 copies per day. Nevertheless, the average circulation of newspapers amounted to 6,000.[36] Don Coerver has assumed that low literacy rates and low circulation of newspapers lessened the press's influence on society.[37] Yet as E. P. Thompson argued, political ideas articulated in the press could be disseminated to illiterate audiences through public readings at social gatherings as well as through popular culture such as ballads and cornerstone parodies.[38] While the printed word could only reach a relatively small population, the opposition and popular press's frequent use of images to attack government policies allowed these periodicals to reach a far wider audience than their counterparts targeting literate society.[39] Furthermore, Díaz's harsh treatment of dissident reporters—arrests, beatings, and the destruction of printing presses—reveal that the regime viewed the press as a threat, attempting to quell the printed opposition.[40]

While traditional and revisionist studies of railway development offer valuable insights regarding policymaking and the economic effects of new transportation technologies, they nevertheless reduce its role in society to its success or failure in producing backward linkages (its capacity to promote industry) and forward linkages (its ability to move economic units to markets) in the economy. Few have considered the symbolic or metaphorical dimensions of the railway and how it molded social and cultural relations. Scholars have ignored the ontological and epistemological power of the railway: how it shaped people's experiences, emotions, mentality, and material culture as well as their social, political, and intellectual outlooks or how elite groups used it to prove the efficacy of developmentalist ideologies and their version of the universal benefits of Western-styled modernization.[41] In Porfirian Mexico, the railway provided a metaphor for the goal of the regime: the uninterrupted, relentless, and at times violent drive forward into the future, a future denoted by technological sophistication, social order, material progress, and above all, cosmopolitan civilization. The railway's capacity to bring the country into closer communication also made it a powerful icon affirming nationhood. Yet the railway also moved people to discuss their fears and fascination with what the future might hold and with what appeared to be the cold, indifferent nature of modernity.

The chapters that follow integrate these ideas to explore the ways that people understood the railway's capacity to save the country and carry it into a future denoted by limitless progress. It examines moments of celebration and crisis when people's emotional and sensual reactions to the locomotive reached a climax, seeking to investigate how these experiences evoked either confirmation or contempt for the Porfirian modernization program. Chapter 1, "The Discourse of Development: The Railroad Debate of the Early Porfiriato," examines the early years of the railway debate in the Mexican Congress and in the press during Díaz's first presidential term. It sketches the rhetorical strategies used by boosters and opponents of Díaz's transportation policy and argues that both groups viewed railway development as a near-utopian goal that would revitalize the country after decades of social, political, and economic backwardness. Politicians and the press described the diverse ways that railroad construction promoted movement, energy, commerce, immigration, unity, and civilization. It explores the reasons why opposition groups, although not contesting railway development as such, nonetheless questioned Díaz's choice to offer concessions to U.S. companies and to build a north-south line connecting the capital to their northern neighbor before an east-west line connecting both coasts. It shows that although Díaz enacted controversial measures—such as giving the executive branch full power to grant concessions thus bypassing Congress—when he left office in 1880, he received a warm farewell, even by longtime opponents. Much of this praise was openly based on his success at securing important railway contracts and spurring construction.

Chapter 2, "De Viaje: Elite Views of Modernity and the Railroad Boom," turns to how the middle- and upper-class press represented the arrival of the railway in poems, literature, cartoons, and social commentaries. It demonstrates that elite groups expressed optimism at the locomotive's ability to spur national regeneration. It explores the often emotional language used by writers to describe their encounters with the railway to reveal the sensual impact of it on people enthusiastic about the locomotive's civilizing potential. These narratives, and the emotional and sensual experience they evoked, offered readers tangible proof about the accomplishments of the regime as they often expressed devotion to Díaz and his policies promoting "order and progress." But it also shows that these groups shared anxieties about the social and cultural changes spurred by modernization, especially what seemed the loss of the familiar.

Chapter 3, "Festivals of Progress: The Railroad Ceremony," investigates how government officials used railway inaugurations, as well as other civic ceremonies that featured the railway, as a means of promoting new values that corresponded to a liberal, capitalistic, and civilized country. It reveals that organizers exploited pageantry to create an aura of sacrality around Díaz and the regime he headed. In so doing, these celebrations helped foster a cult of personality dedicated to the dictator that aided his triumph in securing repeated reelections. It also shows that these ceremonies played an important role in disseminating

ideas of national unity across the country, a development closely associated with Díaz's indispensability.

The following two chapters provide counterpoints to the previous two. Chapter 4, "The Price of Progress: Popular Perceptions of the Railroad Accident," maintains that while many individuals understood the locomotive to represent the pinnacle
of modernity, the experience of train wrecks undermined this
belief for many sectors of society. The frequent newspaper coverage of accidents fomented a growing opposition to the country's foreign owned railways and exposed the false promises of
technological progress and of the capacity of modern machinery to improve people's lives. These critiques make known a
counter-nationalism that attacked the government's pandering
to outside interests, calling for a nationally owned and operated
transportation system. Popular perceptions of the railway and
the limits of its utopian potential were expressed in a wide range
of cultural productions such as *corridos* (popular ballads), penny presses, popular art, and oppositional newspapers.

Chapter 5, "La Loco-Matona: The Railroad in the Popular
and Opposition Press," looks at the representations of the railway in newspapers that were most critical of the government,
arguing that while the regime used the railway symbolically and
rhetorically to legitimize its rule, Díaz's detractors employed
the symbolic power of the locomotive to highlight the cold nature of modernity as well as to make a series of attacks on policymaking decisions. The opposition press sought to highlight
the national costs and human toll that buttressed railway development. Moreover, they often used it symbolically to represent
other economic, political, and social issues they viewed as detrimental to national development. This chapter maintains that
these sources helped expose the fetishization of railway expansion, seeking to make known the country's loss of economic sovereignty, the draconian laws that underpinned progress, and the
violations of the Constitution of 1857.

Together, these examples reveal that the regime's exploitation of the symbolic power of the railway as an icon of social order and material progress proved to be a double-edged sword. While government boosters and officials closely associated Díaz with the railroad and his success at securing the trappings of modernity, others began to associate railway development with issues they viewed as detrimental to their country. Thus the connection that the regime fostered, associating the dictator with the railway's utopian potential, in the end helped to undermine people's confidence in the future envisioned by Díaz and his supporters. Yet opposition groups did not altogether abandon the belief in the efficacy of modern technologies to improve people's lives. Utopian beliefs about the benefits of civilization and modernity, while perhaps tempered, continued to drive the political aspirations of many individuals who, although not opposed to development per se, sought more nationalistic and socially equitable policies in their attempts to capture progress.

ONE

The Discourse of Development

The Railroad Debate of the Early Porfiriato

Let us become the doctor of this extremely sick patient, of Mexico
. . . there is in this great organism a state of alarming prostration;
its advanced stage does not correspond with the capabilities at its
disposal; its constitution is that of an athlete that cannot lift even
the tiniest object; . . . in this inferior organism the diagnosis is anemia. The lack of activity, the lack of circulation, the lack of movement. There is blood, there is vitality, but it is completely motion-
less, and if it does move, it is with a hopeless sluggishness.

And fine: now having made the diagnosis, science has for this
case of an anemic human race one infallible cure:

—Iron! the medic would say to his patient.

—Iron! we would say, taking this analogy to its conclusion.

—Invigorate the blood cells to trigger its circulatory potential.

—Let us propel its powerful vitality by creating arteries so
we can move freely and swiftly, circulating that activity that
is heat, and heat that is light and life.

La Patria, March 13, 1880

By the end of his first term in office (1876–80), Porfirio Díaz
had worked effectively to foster the stability needed for economic development, an accomplishment demonstrated most clearly by the success of the railroad project. Policymakers believed
the railroad would promote national integration and guaran-

tee prosperity through export-oriented economic growth. The railway project allowed for the rapid transport of agricultural products and mineral resources to ports, invigorating the economy as well as allowing for the mobilization of labor needed for those sectors. It encouraged political stability and social peace by integrating isolated regions, where local *caudillos* often held sway rather than the federal authorities and by allowing government officials to mobilize the military against any potential armed political challenges. Thus the railroad helped the Porfirian government build the modern nation.

Yet railroad development represented more than a national program to integrate the country and foster economic growth. The debate surrounding its construction also opened up a discussion in which both the Porfirian administration and its opposition defined their own versions of civilization, patriotism, and commercial development. By examining this aspect of the railway project, it becomes evident that transportation development was a cultural project, not just an economic and political one. Few historians have examined the discursive aspects behind national railway programs in Latin America. Paulo Roberto Cimó Queiroz examined railroad promotion in Mato Grosso, Brazil, and argued that the railway secured both political and symbolic interests. The São Paulo elite promoted railway development in an attempt to incorporate a vast group of planters far from Brazil's center of power — many of whom had fostered separatist ideologies — into the national economy.[1] In so doing, the Brazilian elite hoped to promote a sense of national identity through railroad construction.

Kim Clark's study of railway development in Ecuador also explored the discursive aspects that underpin state-building projects. She argued that a discourse of movement, energy, and connection emerged in the national railway debate that appealed to a wide range of social groups. Clark examined these debates using Raymond Williams's interpretive framework of keywords, that is, words that call attention to struggles over meaning and that are obscured through common use. For Williams, keywords do not have a fixed meaning because people voice and transform them through conflicts over political, economic, social, and cultural projects. Clark, using this framework, revealed that the keywords used concerning the Ecuadorian railroad plan had an ambiguous enough meaning to help secure support from various elite groups, allowing government officials to undertake the project.[2]

This chapter builds on these studies by examining the discourses that surrounded railway development during the early Porfiriato. The symbolic dimensions of this project, in some cases, paralleled the examples from Brazil and Ecuador. Nevertheless, the rhetorical strategies used by both promoters and opponents of the railway project were shaped by their country's historical development and peculiarities. Decades of political strife, warfare, and foreign interventions and invasions that had racked the nation since Independence framed the debate that emerged around the country's need to expand its railway system. Politicians and the press argued, for example, about how much foreign capital should be used, whether an east-west line should be constructed before a north-south line, and what role U.S. companies would play in such a project. The multitude of opinions demonstrates that while all groups recognized the need for the construction of a nationwide transportation system, the manner in which it would take place was hotly contested.

Discussions about the necessity of railway development revealed that politicians and the press viewed their nation as one that needed to be conquered in order to civilize its people. In this way, the locomotive would play a central role. The arguments made by those individuals promoting the expansion of the transportation system mirrored those used by European colonial officials in Africa and Asia regarding the capacity of science and technology to bring an end to superstition and ignorance and to promote the expansion of production and commerce.[3] The

Mexican elite discussed railway development in a similar fashion, emphasizing its potential to transform Indians into modern
citizens that, through the exploitation of resources and land and
integration into the economy, would allow for their prosperity
and social uplift. They also maintained that the railway, as civilizer, could put an end to the country's backwardness and the
cycles of violence that had undermined economic development
since Independence, likewise reflecting European beliefs about
the locomotive as an agent of social change. As the upper class
stressed their whiteness — they did so on the global stage, for
example, at world's fairs[4] — they also emphasized their responsibility to bring science and technology to the country's Indian and peasant communities as a way to demonstrate their capacity to be modern and also to make known the government's
goal of civilizing the nation.

Boosters of the regime, especially the liberal press and liberal
policymakers, emphasized the railroad's ability to energize the
country, foster national unity, encourage a heightened sense of
patriotism, increase commerce, promote immigration, and secure peace. As such, railway development represented a near-
utopian goal for liberals who strongly believed in its potential to
remake society. They stressed the achievements of Díaz's rule,
especially his successful promotion of national "order and progress" during his first term in office. Supporters also lauded his
achievement of securing the first large-scale railway contracts
with a national scope.[5]

Conversely, political opponents and anti-Díaz newspapers
often used the same rhetoric to challenge the manner in which
economic development had been fostered. These competing discourses not only revealed the contentious atmosphere of early railway expansion, but also called attention to the symbolic power of the railroad. They show that all groups shared the
belief in the railway's power to promote civilization and progress, although they differed over the manner in which govern-

ment officials should advance railroad development. Despite a significant opposition, the range of discourses in which various groups debated this development proved to be quite narrow. The administration's supporters and its critics both promoted railway development for the same reasons, although they differed on the method of executing this project. While a vociferous opposition challenged the strategies used by the administration to promote development, pro-Díaz liberals forged a sense of consensus concerning the need for railway expansion.

Díaz's success at promoting railway development in his first term contrasted with Sebastián Lerdo de Tejada's (1872–76) apparent failures at securing railway concessions. Often ascribed to Lerdo's nationalist concerns and fear of U.S. economic domination, a belief encapsulated by the famous phrase attributed to the ousted president "between strength and weakness, the desert,"[6] scholars have shown that these views of his failures have been exaggerated. While Lerdo showed himself to be cautious in granting railway contracts, his inability to secure significant and successful railway contracts related more to congressional opposition and lack of capital. An obstructionist and nationalist Congress pressured Lerdo, for example, to promote the failed north-south railway concession to "Los Catorce," a group of Mexican investors headed by stockholders such as Antonio Escandón and Sebastián Camacho. After failing to secure the needed Mexican and European capital for the project, Lerdo annulled the contract, transferring it to American promoter Edward Lee Plumb's International Railroad Company. Mexico's terrible financial reputation in Europe scared away would-be backers who demanded settlement of past debts before investing in infrastructural projects.[7] Despite claims of anti-Americanism, of the eighteen concessions granted during the Lerdo administration, eight went to U.S. promoters.[8]

Nevertheless, supporters of Díaz cultivated a memory of Lerdo that emphasized his failures at railway promotion as a primary justification for his ouster. Justo Sierra and Francisco Bulnes, for instance, both characterized Lerdo as fearful of American investment, a disposition they plainly linked to the lack of railway development during his presidency.[9] Francisco Bulnes chose the exceedingly inappropriate moment of Lerdo's 1889 funeral to take that claim further. Delivering the eulogy, Bulnes vehemently exclaimed that the 1876 Revolution of Tuxtepec resulted from the former president's failures in the realm of railway expansion, an accusation that simultaneously bashed Lerdo while exulting Díaz.[10] The existing belief that Díaz had risen to power because of his plans and capacity to secure important railway contracts was further enhanced by the pro-Díaz newspaper, *El Ferrocarrilero* (The Railroader), and by the moniker "Railroaders" self-applied by Díaz's boosters.[11] Díaz's ability to secure the first major railway concessions provided the president, as well as his supporters, with an effective symbolic tool to underscore the accomplishments of his administration, solidifying his reputation as a proven promoter of economic development.

Movement and Energy

Previous administrations had failed to promote a sustained period of railway expansion. Between 1837 and 1873, various governments had attempted to secure railroad contracts, only to be undermined by persistent armed conflict between liberals and conservatives and by foreign occupation. Since the central government, during this period, only controlled the area between Mexico City and Veracruz, and since it had been a chief trading route since colonial times, several administrations sought to improve transportation between the two cities to boost international trade and customs revenues.[12] Aside from the Veracruz (Mexico) Railway, the country lacked any substantial railway network outside the central region. When Díaz took power, the country's inadequate railway system made the expansion of a national grid one of the primary, and unmistakably important, goals of his government.[13] Railway development took on added importance because the nation's railroad construction lagged far behind other Latin American nations.[14] For Díaz, railroad expansion was the linchpin of his economic and nation-building program. In 1877, the Treasury's annual report stated that, for Díaz, railway construction represented the chief goal of his administration, as it would allow the nation's agricultural production to be more easily and cheaply transported and, in so doing, revive the economy.[15]

In the early years of the Porfiriato, newspapers supporting Díaz's, and later Manuel González's, presidency repeatedly emphasized the railway as the cornerstone of an economic, political, and social transformation. Often they emphasized its capacity to promote progress and civilization through its regenerative qualities. One Mexico City newspaper, *El Boletín de la Cooperación*, clearly articulated this idea in its discussion of the inauguration of a rail line between Mexico City and Morelos, celebrated on September 16, the day of Mexican Independence. In it, the author could hardly withhold his exuberance regarding the railway's potential to inject energy and revitalize the nation:

> Mexico regenerates. Mexico grows. Mexico will soon occupy a distinguished place among the nations that march at the vanguard of civilization. . . .
>
> We will soon have a place to enumerate or discover one by one our improvements: for today, we are happy to mention the indicated and to state that the construction of the railway, destined to change the face of our Republic, has commenced under the best possible auspices that could have been imagined. . . .
>
> Energized by this hope, we conclude this article how we began it, repeating: Mexico regenerates. Mexico grows.[16]

Railway building, however minor, stimulated the hopes of pundits that the country, through increased transportation and interconnectedness, would usher in a new era of growth and prosperity.

Many members of the press promoted the Porfirian brand of modernization—which in this case meant offering contracts to U.S. companies—and repeatedly stressed the railway's ability to regenerate and transform the country after a long period of economic backwardness and political infighting. Boosters often depicted any opposition to railway development as archaic or savage, contrasting these opinions with the civilizing aspects of modernization. In an article criticizing some congressional opposition to contracts handed out to the future builders of the Mexican Central Railroad, *El Heraldo* condemned such challengers as the "enemies of progress" and their ideas as those of a "foolish civilization" impeding national progress. The author characterized any opposition to railway development as unthinkable, since the locomotive crossing the country's deserts had even captured the imagination of "savages" about the absolute need for national progress.[17] The press frequently juxtaposed the civilizing quality of the railroad against the savagery that liberals believed characterized the country's remote regions. This type of discourse remained potent as nearly a decade later a provincial newspaper again highlighted the locomotive's capacity to civilize. In Coahuila, one reporter, discussing the benefits of building a railway through the Sierra Mojada desert, speculated that it would create new towns in the desert where before only savages and wild animals had dared to live.[18] The railroad promoted order, in this argument, where before only chaos existed. In this way, the railway represented the goal of the Díaz administration: to bring peace and progress to a country that had been dominated by wild, unruly social and political strife. Liberals viewed their own nation as one to be conquered and civilized through the arrival of the locomotive, sentiments that paralleled the ways that Europeans justified their colonial ambitions.[19] Through the promotion of modern projects, the nation could transcend its uncultivated, savage condition to become a refined nation at the vanguard of the civilized world. The contrast of the civilizing capabilities of the railway with the country's untamed environment offered the liberal press a powerful symbol of modernity.[20]

The press linked the juxtaposition of savagery and civilization to notions of race, especially what social commentators viewed as the country's racial character. The railway, they argued, would transform the Indian into a modern, productive citizen. *El Monitor Republicano* told readers that building a national railway system connecting the isolated interior of the country to the coast would help to reach Indian populations whose "backward traditions," "deficient civilization," and "helpless isolation" led them to underproduce agricultural products that could be exported to foreign markets.[21] Similarly *El Hijo del Trabajo*, a workers' newspaper that claimed to speak on behalf of the people (*pueblo*), congratulated the 1,000 Indians who had found work building the Mexican National line to Toluca. The reporter compared the nation's indigenous peoples to "savage Hottentots" who once having lived in degradation as a result of their barbarous ways now demonstrated their dignity through work. The author claimed this as definitive proof that the Indians no longer viewed the laws of the nation as something used to suppress them; instead, they saw the laws as tools to be used to articulate their rights as citizens.[22] In the same manner that liberal intellectuals believed that incorporation into the national market would allow Indians to become more active citizens,[23] contrasting the perceived inertness of indigenous communities with a future where they would become engaged citizens—both commercially and politically—revealed their belief in the locomotive's power to transform the country's peoples.

This sentiment also found expression at the inauguration of the Morelos Railway line in 1880. The event organizers had a young Amecameca Indian boy give the inauguration speech. He told the crowd the history of great inventors from Johann Gutenberg to James Watt. He also said that communication between regions spurred by railroads allowed for the mixture of not only

ideas and customs but races. He went on to state that the locomotive would transform his nation as it had the United States
and Europe and declared that Mexico must follow in their path.
A reporter for *El Periódico Oficial*, which published the speech,
maintained that the boy's words represented the transformation
of a pueblo once lost in snowy volcanoes and fantastic traditions
into a commercially oriented society being brought back to life.[24]

High-ranking politicians could even become the targets of ra-
cialized attacks if they appeared to impede railway development.
When supporters in Congress of the presidential candidate Justo Benítez stalled the negotiations with the Sullivan and Palmer
company to build a line that would connect the capital to the Pacific coast because they feared too much U.S. economic control
over Mexico, *El Monitor Republicano* cited a U.S. newspaper
that attacked Benítez, charging that he had "pure Indian blood"
and that he "hated Americans" to such a degree that he sought to
sabotage the whole project.[25] By emphasizing Benítez's indigenous
background, pundits associated his fears regarding national sovereignty with a refusal to move the nation forward. Here, then,
Indianness was discursively linked to stagnation and idleness,
the antithesis of what the locomotive symbolically represented.

The press often discussed the railroad's importance for national development in evolutionary terms, characterizing it as a
regenerative force that would usher in a new era of modernization and capitalist development. Indeed, the evolutionary context
in which individuals discussed the need for railway expansion
fit well with the Comtian positivist logic shared by members of
the Díaz administration, many of whom viewed their country
as being on the brink of becoming modern. Also influenced by
ideas of social Darwinism espoused by Herbert Spencer, liberal intellectuals viewed societies as social organisms that evolved
over time.[26] The railway project, it was hoped, would represent
a major milestone in this process. One Mexico City newspaper
maintained that the country's evolution from "demagoguery

and oligarchy" to "progress and civilization" resulted from the railway's regenerative power, which had transformed the country into a "Lazarus figure that had broken its bonds, shaken the dirt from its tomb, and prepared to move forward."[27]

Liberal newspapers also used the language of revival and energy, often characterizing the country as a body that the railway would infuse with life. One reporter, in his article "What Mexico Needs to Live Actively," compared the nation to a sick, anemic body that needed to be revitalized through the construction of railroads. The author's metaphor maintained that a lack of activity and movement had drained the nation of its energy. Continuing the metaphor, he offered readers an account of a medical examination where a doctor recommended to his patient (Mexico) that iron (railways) would solve his problem of prostration.[28] The pseudoscientific rhetoric espoused in his article provided valuable insights into Porfirian ideals of human progress shared by many liberal intellectuals. One year earlier, Justo Sierra had put forward a similar argument stating that the nation suffered from anemia and that only iron (railways) and new blood (foreign colonization) could cure it of its lack of energy.[29] *El Monitor Republicano*, similarly, described railroads as the new blood injected into the arteries of the social body, allowing it to reinvigorate and develop.[30] Here the emphasis on movement and circulation intersected with nineteenth-century ideas about the body. Through the physical activity and movement that the railways spurred, the country would refashion itself as a modern nation, a transformation that could be paralleled by its citizenry. William Beezley has demonstrated how nineteenth-century officials sought to encourage physical activity, in the form of sport or exercise, to foster a healthy, modern, and productive citizenry.[31] Through the discussion of railroad development, Porfirians simultaneously argued that national progress meant delivering the country and its citizens from the economic and social stagnation that had persisted since Independence.

These ideas were not only those of the metropolis but also promoted in the provinces. *El Coahuilense* boasted that the locomotive, bringing with it the seeds of civilization, crossed one extreme of the Republic to another, awaking the *pueblos* that slept in the arms of ignorance.[32] Echoing the belief that the nation found itself in a state of lethargy, Félix Romero, a congressman and Oaxacan railway promoter, argued that the building of train tracks and telegraphs was absolutely necessary because Oaxaca's youth needed movement, active communications, and broader horizons to accomplish their loftiest desires.[33]

The emphasis on movement and energy proved to be an especially enduring discourse. Even twenty years into Díaz's dictatorship, provincial newspapers continued to confirm the railway's analeptic qualities. In 1899, *El Correo de Chihuahua* boasted that railways, the ultimate symbol of progress, now dominated the Chihuahuan landscape, proving that the state had moved forward, empowered by energy, honor, and industry. This belief, he maintained, was not only that of the government but also of all the state's inhabitants.[34] As these examples make clear, liberals incorporated the discourse of movement and energy into discussions about political, social, and economic reform. By doing so, they advanced their claim about the absolute necessity of railroad development. And when the government successfully established railroads throughout the country, it appeared to validate the policies of the Díaz regime, the export market thrived, and foreign investment poured into various sectors of the economy. Thus for Porfirians, the railway propelled the nation into the future denoted by energy, movement, and growth, a future that was often contrasted against a past associated with inertia, ignorance, and backwardness.[35]

National Unity and the Patriotic Debate

Politicians and the press closely tied the idea of movement and energy to the railway's capacity to connect the country and, in so doing, forge a sense of national unity. By eliminating the physical distance between regions and compressing time and space, the railroad would unite Mexicans into a tight-knit family, a feat that previous administrations had failed to accomplish. Before railroad development, the lack of traversable highways and navigable waterways had encouraged the regionalism and local *caudillismo* that persisted throughout the nineteenth century.[36] *La Industria Nacional* recognized this problem, referring to the railway as a "lasso of salvation" that would tie the nation together economically, socially, and politically.[37] One extremely self-assured journalist from *El Sufragio Libre* declared that the railroad represented the great civilizer and social reformer of the nineteenth century as it destroyed distances, offered new conveniences, and converted the nation's peoples into a close, happy, and hopeful family.[38] The liberal press highlighted how a nation, separated by difficult topography from the Atlantic to the Pacific, could be unified internally and then, in turn, connected to the rest of the world.

Creating a united country, for the liberal press, represented more than commercial expansion and linking distant regions. It also revealed the hope that this interconnectedness would foster a deep, shared sense of nationalism among the country's citizenry. Through a successful and far-reaching railway program, people would gain a sense of pride in their country. In this way, support for the railway project became a patriotic act. Both policymakers and the press repeatedly equated railway development with patriotism. *La Patria*, for example, noted that all the political factions agreed on the "patriotic idea" of connecting the nation with railways whose establishment would bring betterment for all sectors of society.[39]

Similarly, other Mexico City newspapers sought to convince readers of the connections between railway expansion, patriotism, and economic and political well-being. The *Express Mercantil Mexicano* maintained that a "patriotic vision" shaped their firm conviction that railway concessions would produce a beneficial transformation of the economic and political problems of the Republic.[40] During the early years of railroad construction, liberals viewed optimistic expectations regarding the efficacy of railroads as a patriotic act in itself. Liberal newspapers portrayed opponents to railway expansion as "the enemies of progress" and often questioned their patriotism. In San Luis Potosí, where some members of the government and press had expressed reservations about the costs of building the Tampico trunk line off the Mexican Central Railroad, one daily condemned opponents' criticisms as "unpatriotic and affected by indolence." Furthermore, it branded critics who opposed the government's transportation program as malcontents always grumbling and never contented.[41] Journalists equated railway development with patriotism and cast anyone who even questioned the manner in which it took place as a disloyal citizen, undermining the good of the nation.

Nevertheless, members of the press who questioned the ways that the regime promoted its railroad project, especially the government's apparent favoring of U.S. companies, also framed their arguments through the ideals of patriotism. Writers often used nationalist sentiment when discussing the treatment of Mexican workers by U.S. railway managers. *El Correo de la Tarde* criticized the Sullivan and Palmer interests, builders of the Mexican National Railroad, for compromising national dignity by the deplorable treatment that their workers received from U.S. bosses.[42] The press often charged that native workers suffered as a result of poor pay, unsteady employment, and managerial racism. These allegations continued throughout the Porfiriato, reaching a fever pitch in the final years of the regime, especially before the nationalization of the country's railway system in 1908.

During the first term of the Díaz administration, a lively and heated debate arose in the Congress about whether or not land grants and favorable concessions should be used to entice U.S.

capitalists to invest in the nation's railway development. The debate, more specifically, revolved around the issue of patriotism and national sovereignty vis-à-vis U.S. interests. The Sullivan and Palmer company, who courted the administration to build the Mexican National Railroad, which theoretically would bring the rail network to the Pacific coast through one of its trunk lines, unleashed an intense debate in Congress between supporters of Díaz's transportation policy and two of his most powerful political rivals, Justo Benítez and Felipe Buenrostro. The minister of economic development, Vicente Riva Palacio (1876–80), favored offering land grants and concessions to the Sullivan and Palmer company, arguing that railroad expansion represented a patriotic duty to save the nation from the precarious situation in which it found itself. He maintained that it was not its history of civil war that destined Mexico to be a lesser country but its failure to keep up with the progress of civilized nations. The lack of foreign commerce would doom the country.[43] The majority of members of the Congress agreed. In the same session, Congressman Francisco Menocal supported the minister and urged fellow congressmen to follow Riva Palacio's recommendations, as voting against the measure would only undermine the "honor" and "future" of their country.[44]

Some concerned members of the Congress feared such concessions would give U.S. companies control over the country's commerce and, as a result, would threaten national sovereignty. Congressman Buenrostro, opposed to handing over the contract to the U.S. company, maintained that he entered the debate with a refined spirit of patriotism. This forced him to conclude that the United States' railway monopolization would harm the country by allowing it to cede territory and money for the benefit of foreigners and not for his fellow countrymen. He adamantly defended his loyalty to the *pueblo*, stating that it was not that he opposed railway development per se but that he opposed the manner in which the government sought to handle it. He defiantly asked his fellow congressmen who were the real patriots: those members who legislatively sought to rush such an important project or those who demonstrated patience and calm when considering the vital interests of the country.[45] Those in Congress who challenged Díaz's strategy of railway promotion wanted a more homegrown approach that would encourage native companies to incorporate and then build a national grid. They maintained that this would protect the country's sovereignty from foreign, especially U.S., ambitions.

Other members went so far as to argue that offering U.S. businesses the opportunity to build railways connecting both nations could lead to a second invasion that would result in further loss of territory, if not total annexation. Opponents not only cited the U.S.-Mexican War as a justification for denying the Sullivan and Palmer contract but also harkened back to other attacks against national sovereignty such as the Pastry War.[46] Congressmen argued that ambitious imperial powers had stabbed Mexico in the back. For them, the favorable concessions offered to companies such as Sullivan and Palmer opened the door for the nation to be subjugated to U.S. expansionist ambitions. The rhetorical strategies employed by the opposition centered on their misgivings about the political and economic objectives of their northern neighbor. Especially vocal against the administration's strategy of railroad promotion was a group of congressmen who supported Justo Benítez as Díaz's presidential successor.[47] Felipe Buenrostro, a *benitista*, challenged the minister of economic development, arguing that the Sullivan and Palmer concession amounted to providing an enemy with the weapons to invade their nation.[48] The debate over whether or not to offer concessions to the Sullivan and Palmer company had transformed a debate about railways into one about the nature and vigor of Congress's patriotism. On the one hand, supporters of Díaz's railroad project, and the favorable concessions offered to foreign companies, emphasized that true patriots sought to pull the country out of the economic turmoil it had experienced throughout the nineteenth century. On the other hand, opponents sought to demonstrate their patriotism by defending the country from a possible U.S. economic invasion or, worse yet, an outright military takeover. Opponents thus questioned why the government did not attempt to promote the organization of national companies that could develop the transportation infrastructure.[49] Congressman Alfredo Chavero voiced his concerns regarding U.S. ownership of the vital railway lines, stating that he preferred an "impoverished liberty over an opulent subjugation."[50]

Even *El Monitor Republicano*'s journalists, ardent supporters of railway development and often critical of members of Congress that stalled concessions, demonstrated trepidation when they argued that Sullivan and Palmer's Mexican National line should first be built to the Pacific and then to the northern border as a strategy to mitigate the "filibustering ambitions of the ogre to the North."[51] *El Express Mercantil Mexicano* suggested a similar concern when it stated that uniting the Pacific and the Atlantic by rail would allow the nation to trade goods with the markets of Asia and Europe, something that would protect national autonomy and territorial integrity.[52] The author's comments revealed his hope that connecting both oceans would provide a counterbalance to U.S. economic ambitions by promoting trade with Asia and Europe. While liberals that supported Díaz's transportation policy argued that their nation needed to be colonized through railway development, opponents also considered matters related to conquest, but in a different light. The prospect of allowing U.S. companies to crisscross the nation with railway lines kindled concerns that their nation would become the target of imperial ambitions, whether economic or military.

In response to these kinds of critiques, Congressmen Eduardo Arteaga maintained that the construction of railroads did not represent the only way that the United States could undertake expansionist ambitions.[53] Industrial boosters stated that their northern neighbor would gain more by tapping into their rich agricultural and mining economies than by attempting to annex their country.[54] The United States' emerging philosophy of dollar diplomacy, not political domination, ultimately proved those groups correct. Opposition groups, especially the Catholic press, eventually recognized this development, identifying the flood of U.S. capital as the *invasión pacífica* (the peaceful invasion).[55]

These critiques, for the liberal and pro-Díaz press, represented an assault on the government's attempts to move the country forward. Díaz viewed the nation-building project of railway development as far too important to be bogged down in debate. In the early months of 1880, he replaced *benitista* cabinet members to ease the ratification of railway contracts. Moreover, in that same year, Congress passed a law giving the executive branch full control over the granting and revising of railroad concessions.[56] Díaz secured Congress's approval by incorporating a series of guidelines for railway concessions that placated concerns over national sovereignty. The guidelines stipulated that the executive would oversee tariff and freight rates, that two executive appointees, in charge of overseeing financial and technical reports, would sit on the companies' boards, that companies would hand over concession rights to the national government after ninety-nine years, and that the government would officially consider all companies as Mexican and subject to the nation's laws.[57] Despite the nationalist rhetoric that Díaz used to make railway concessions an executive decision and despite the fact that most newspapers viewed railway development as absolutely necessary, *El Monitor Republicano* disapprovingly compared the president's centralization of decision making to Louis XIV's infamous statement: I am the State.[58] Likewise, *El Hijo del Trabajo* interpreted Díaz's centralization of power as opposed to the promises made in his famed proclamation of La Noria that criticized the Lerdo de Tejada government for the overreaching of federal power exerted on state and local governments.[59]

Despite these measures, congressional debates had stalled the administration's efforts to finalize the Sullivan and Palmer concessions as well as the Atchison, Topeka, and Santa Fe Company represented by Robert Symon. *La Tribuna* lambasted congressional opposition to the project and rejoiced at their political marginalization, calling their resistance unfounded and useless and motivated by a political circle that, fortunately, had lost all political credibility.[60] Indeed, Benítez's opposition to Díaz's railway project proved to be his downfall. Until 1879, just months before the presidential election, Benítez, campaigning under the standard of the *Partido Liberal Constitucionalista*, appeared to most political observers to be the logical presidential successor. But with his followers dismissed from cabinet and high-ranking administrative positions, and his public rift with the president over the railway issue, Díaz instead chose Manuel González to be his successor.[61] In a decision that presaged his priorities, Díaz chose the developmentalist candidate over Benítez, who campaigned on the platform of upholding the provisions of the 1857 Constitution.[62]

The administration's handling of the railroad issue also foreshadowed the authoritarian tactics that Díaz willingly used in his policy of forced modernization. At the same time, it revealed, at least in his first presidential term, Díaz's need to negotiate with Congress, as his approval of congressional guidelines for railway concessions demonstrate. The railway represented the most important national project that the administration had undertaken, and Díaz would not allow the opposition to undermine that goal. He understood that U.S. investment was the easiest way to secure rapid and widespread railway construction.[63] Years later, the issue of American owned and operated railways and the loss of national sovereignty would resurface as a forceful critique used by opponents to challenge the legitimacy of the regime.

In the face of congressional opposition apprehensive about the possibility of heightened U.S. influence over Mexico, many government officials and members of the press anticipated that railway development would benefit the nation by promoting immigration, especially from north of the border. *El Cronista de México*, a conservative religious weekly, argued that the construction of a railway across the state of Veracruz would make that state the first to enjoy the benefits of foreign colonization.[64] The following week, the publication continued to express its support for railway expansion, but this time by discussing the country's northern states. It dismissed fears of U.S. dominance and argued that U.S. immigration would strengthen the country. Its writers suggested that their fellow countrymen needed to trust the United States despite its past aggression, arguing that the White House's judgment could not be so bankrupt as to entertain such evil intentions as conquest. In fact it argued that the injection of U.S. capital ensured that they would avoid conflict with Mexico in order to protect their investments.[65] Through immigration and investment, policymakers and the press believed the nation could attain the often ill-defined concept of "civilization" and, in so doing, reap the rewards of material progress. But as Congressman Pedro Collantes reasoned, the benefits of civilization did not necessarily have to take place through immigration. He claimed that the railroad would bring moral progress to the nation when people from other countries crossed their lands, leaving behind their money, their ideas, their enlightenment, and their civilization, which, as he opined, his country so desperately lacked.[66] The railway would allow for the penetration of modern civilized sensibilities and tastes by bringing foreign travelers who would share these values with fellow countrymen. These sentiments reflected the belief among politicians and pundits that railways could also transform the country to become more cosmopolitan. Again, much like European colonial officials, it is clear that liberal politicians believed that by bringing individuals from so-called civilized countries to Mexico, the railway would spur intellectual, moral, and material betterment.[67]

While some government officials and members of the press viewed too much foreign influence negatively, most supporters of railway expansion eagerly anticipated foreign immigration that would result from faster transportation connections between the United States and Mexico. Indeed, many newspapers viewed successful railway development going hand in hand with foreign immigration.[68] Some maintained that railways would create a more secure environment for immigration and foreign investment.[69] Newspapers that highlighted the railway's efficacy in promoting U.S. immigration at times used a nationalistic discourse, underscoring the country's beauty and appeal that would entice U.S. immigration. *El Sufragio Libre* argued that vast numbers of U.S. immigrants would establish themselves south of the border, lured by the country's pleasant climate and healthy environment.[70]

One liberal daily asserted not only that the railway boom promoted immigration, something it viewed as desperately needed for the commercial advancement of the country, but also that it specifically promised to bring more European and American immigrants to Mexico. A reporter for *La Industria Nacional*, an ardent supporter of both Díaz and González, contended that railway development would whiten the country, producing better patterns of production and consumption. The reporter estimated that within four years a quarter of the population would be white, adding five million pesos in national income per year.[71] The reporter made clear a connection between what he called the whitening of the country and commercial progress. White immigrants from the United States, some officials believed, offered Mexico a group of consumers who possessed the level of sophistication to appreciate and purchase foreign products and, as a result, yield more tax revenue for the government. This sentiment mirrored many officials' ideas about the necessity of foreign immigration. Justo Sierra, for instance, would later argue that more superior peoples needed to be incorporated into their society in order to help the evolution of less developed sectors. Such a project would allow those lesser groups to reach the "vanguard of human development" and ensure their "self-preservation."[72] Yet despite these lofty predictions, in the end, significant immigration failed to take place in the numbers envisioned by journalists and policymakers.[73]

While the opposition's fears of the United States might have been justified, especially with the memory of the U.S.-Mexican War, supporters of the concessions to U.S. companies interpreted their decision as choosing between the lesser of two evils. Mexico, viewed by many as financially incapable of promoting homegrown railroad development, would have to advance improvements to the transportation network by any means possible, even if that meant offering extremely favorable concessions to U.S. investors. Legislators maintained that linking the two economies, through the establishment of interconnecting railway networks, would quash any attempts by the United States to invade militarily. The railway project represented such an important step in the path toward civilization that policymakers accepted taking on a large foreign debt and opening their borders to their powerful neighbor, despite the fact that the lessons from the past weighed on the minds of many liberals like a nightmare.

In the nationalist debate over U.S. railway concessions, contradictory arguments emerged not only between supporters and opponents but also within each group. Supporters of Díaz who had hoped to attract U.S. investment for railroad construction often found themselves walking a high wire. For example, they dismissed the opposition's concerns about allowing too much U.S. economic influence or giving the United States too much military access to the nation as anti-patriotic. Thus they needed to find new ways to define what constituted patriotism, choosing to emphasize economic development and the expansion of modern infrastructure and industry as the foremost nationalist cause. The words "patriot" and "nationalist" held different meanings for different groups, but in the dispute over the railway question, Porfirians sought to transform those meanings to promote their own versions of economic development. Yet, as Richard Weiner has argued, liberals often articulated contradictory impulses, on the one hand, about the necessity of foreign investment and immigration and, on the other, about the fear of undermining national sovereignty.[74] These contradictory tendencies also revealed themselves in the railway debate. A journalist at *El Sufragio Libre* demonstrated this conflict over meaning when he argued in favor of the Sullivan and Palmer concessions, asserting that the clearest proof of the country's need for railways lay in the sad reality that if war's alarms did again ring between the nations, the United States would be able to mobilize a powerful army to the Rio Bravo in a matter of days. His country, he gloomily concluded, would take two months to deploy an army to confront the invaders.[75] While this journalist recognized the possible threat that the United States posed, because of their advanced stage of railway development and their technological superiority, he simultaneously argued that the construction of American owned and operated railway systems represented the best way to mitigate that danger.

While Díaz and his supporters did indeed demonstrate less alarm in offering contracts to U.S. investors, a position that allowed for exponential railway development after 1884, apprehension about U.S. economic control continued to loom large among policymakers throughout the Porfiriato. As we will see in chapter 4, government officials, especially at the start of the twentieth century, came to identify the nation's railways with foreign domination. Indeed Finance Minister José Limantour would justify the 1908 nationalization by invoking claims of political and economic sovereignty.

Commercial Development and Political Stability
The railroad's unification of the country integrated people previously separated by vast distances and difficult terrain. It also

linked the country's productive zones with the world market as well as internal markets.[76] Those politicians who wanted to develop the railroad through foreign, especially U.S., investment used the proposed commercial advantages that the country would gain as a result of expanded transportation networks to support the government's favorable concessions to U.S. companies. By emphasizing the commercial returns and material progress offered by rapid railway development, pro-Díaz newspapers and politicians could downplay what seemed to many a political position that undermined the nation's sovereignty. One journalist emphasized the importance of making the United States a principal trading partner, stating that rapid and cheap lines of communication between both nations would foster a close alliance based on commercial reciprocity.[77] Members of Díaz's government expressed these sentiments and considered the establishment of a commercial partnership with their northern neighbor as absolutely essential for national economic well-being. Manuel María de Zamacona, the foreign minister who engineered U.S. recognition of the Díaz government in 1878, told industrialists in Chicago that the Díaz administration believed railways to be the most important development needed to foster friendly commercial relations.[78] The Díaz administration clearly viewed the establishment of strong commercial ties with the United States as a way to enhance the relationship. If the United States had permanent investments in Mexico, it would dissuade the former from undertaking any kind of military intervention that would disrupt mutually beneficial commerce. The opposition press, especially Catholic newspapers, did not always share this vision for the future. La Voz de México, for example, argued in favor of using railway development to promote the growth of internal markets. In so doing, its writers questioned the value of export-led economic expansion and foreign domination over the economy.[79]

The liberal press boasted about the commercial boom that would take place as a result of improvements in the transportation of raw materials and consumer goods. First, it would revitalize the nation's agricultural and mining sectors. Second, the building of railways would provide labor for a large number of workers, raising their standard of living and providing new opportunities for social advancement. Mexico City's *La Tribuna* made clear that railroad building would regenerate the nation by giving people work, by developing industry and agriculture, and by spurring commerce, referring to the locomotive as a "powerful life-giving element."[80] The press regularly credited railroad construction for employing masses of idle hands. Both politicians and journalists argued that the colossal task of laying track would generate exponential growth in the amount of jobs available. One newspaper, discussing the construction of the Interoceanic Railway, argued its vital importance to the people who clamored for the opportunity to work and make a decent wage. The nation's citizenry, he continued, understood that in work rested the solution to the majority of the social and political problems that faced the nation.[81] *El Hijo del Trabajo* reported the inauguration of a railway line to Morelos and congratulated the country's workers whose growing numbers and diligent labor had contributed to the betterment of the nation's communication networks. The journalist rejoiced that the future of the working class looked bright, predicting that the construction of a national railway grid would guarantee steady employment for the nation's workforce.[82]

Work, for middle- and upper-class Porfirians, represented a redemptive, and almost sacred, activity that would bring peace and progress.[83] *La Tribuna* made explicit the connection it saw between work and political stability, suggesting that working people did not have the desire or need to undertake seditious acts against the government.[84] The creation of steady work for the country's citizenry, for this and many other journalists, would advance the cause of internal stability. If citizens had employment and kept their families well fed, they would have little incentive to take part in sedition and undermine the peace so urgently sought by Díaz and his followers.

Thus railway development also offered the hope for the establishment of political stability, a goal the citizens long awaited. *El Sufragio Libre* made the connection explicit, predicting that only the construction of railroads and development of banking would transform the nation into one at the vanguard of civilization and that would occupy a place in what he quixotically referred to as the "golden temple of progress."[85] Peace would not only allow liberals the political stability needed for everyday governance; it also placed Mexico in the pantheon of civilized nations, making it more attractive to foreign investors put off by the pitiful international reputation the country held because of its past political chaos.

Díaz and the Railroads

Together, the various discourses used by the liberal press and policymakers stressed how railway expansion would create a new nation and complete a break from the past, a past characterized by economic stagnation, internal divisions, and constant threats from abroad. In their promotion of the railway project, boosters began to identify railway development with Porfirio Díaz. His administration's success at securing concessions and drawing the blueprint for national railway development, something that other presidents had failed to do, became an important marker of Díaz's early achievements.[86] The railway seemed to offer all the solutions: it would invigorate the economy, promote foreign colonization, foster political stability, and provide an effective means of communication across the country. Connecting Díaz's presidency to railway development—indeed, the first major concessions of the Mexican Central and Mexican National took place during his administration—helps explain why, during his 1884 reelection bid, supporters described him as the "Savior of the Nation."[87]

During the first Díaz administration, newspapers regularly contrasted the president's success at promoting railway development with Sebastián Lerdo de Tejada's apparent failures.[88] *El Monitor Republicano*, for example, chided the old regime's naiveté when negotiating with foreign railroad interests. It claimed that Lerdo had allowed the Mexican Railway to charge excessive freight rates and forge a monopoly in the transportation of goods between Mexico City and Veracruz.[89] Beyond that, critics also charged that Lerdo's administration handed out railway contracts to anyone who solicited them and, in so doing, had killed the possibility of promoting native industry.[90] *El Monitor Republicano* went so far as to argue that the people had supported the Revolution of Tuxtepec because of President Lerdo's failures regarding railway policy, especially the granting of a monopoly to the Mexican Railway, which used this control to thwart the development of competing companies in order to keep freight rates artificially high.[91] Ironically, Díaz's transportation program would end up looking strikingly similar to Lerdo's insofar as it granted concessions to foreign interests.

While Díaz's opponents questioned the way that the government pursued railway investment, giving it a shellacking in the press, most newspapers and politicians supported railway expansion as the nation's main priority. Reporters regularly made Benítez, as well as his supporters in Congress, the target of scorn for what they viewed as their misguided opposition to the Mexican National Railroad. *El Monitor Republicano* questioned Benítez's loyalty to the country, asking whether or not he recognized that the nation's poverty could be alleviated by a railway project that would create jobs and promote industry.[92] *El Monitor Republicano* told readers to consider his interference in the completion of railway contracts as the principal reason to oppose his presidential ambitions.[93] In sharp contrast, while often a critic of Díaz and his administration, *El Monitor Republicano* stated in an article about the Mexican National Railroad that

Díaz and his minister of economic development, Riva Palacio, could not have their patriotism doubted, a criticism repeatedly expressed by Benítez supporters in Congress.[94] As Díaz prepared to leave office, even some of his most vocal opposition expressed gratitude for his success in railway development. *La Voz de México* stated that even opponents must recognize the good intentions of their adversaries and applauded Díaz for overcoming congressional opposition in signing the Symon and the Sullivan and Palmer contracts, which set in motion the construction of the Mexican Central and Mexican National companies.[95]

Liberal newspapers praised the Díaz administration's nation-building policies, especially his efforts to spur considerable railroad construction. A journalist for *El Sufragio Libre* lauded the president and credited his administration as the most dynamic promoter of progress. He told readers that Díaz's presidency would be associated with the sounds of the pickaxe, the whistle of the locomotive, the clatter of the rails, and all the obvious benefits those developments brought to the Republic.[96] The railway was not only the clearest example of the success of infrastructural and transportation development; it also became the most dominant symbol of modernization. By the end of his first term, Díaz had become synonymous with railroad expansion and, as such, Mexicans came to identify his presidency and policymaking with development.

In 1880, when Díaz was set to hand over the reins of government to Manuel González, governors, *ayuntamientos* (town councils), and citizens wrote the president congratulating him for his promotion of better communications and transportation between the states. During the congressional debates regarding the Sullivan and Palmer contract to build a line connecting Mexico City with the Pacific and the northern border, governors from all over the country wrote James Sullivan either pleading with him not to lose faith in the railway project or thanking him for his work with the president on the railway issue. These letters reveal how provincial leaders understood railway development as central to the betterment of the nation and viewed the railway project as inextricably linked to Díaz's first term in office. In fact, so many officials and reporters submitted letters that Ireneo Paz, an old supporter of Díaz from the days of Tuxtepec, published them.[97]

Letters to the outgoing president emphasized the same themes that the press and Congress repeatedly articulated. Díaz's supporters used the language of national regeneration, national unity, fervent patriotism, and commercial development in praising him, demonstrating the ubiquitous nature of the often repeated discourses that advanced the cause of the railway project. An official from Puebla wrote the president suggesting his term would be defined by the success of the railway project. He credited Díaz with uniting the country and bringing the benefits of civilization to all regions. Furthermore, he predicted that if Manuel González followed the model of Díaz, people from all nations would immigrate in search of a better life offered by his country's benign climate and sky.[98] Toluca's governor likewise wrote the president as he prepared to leave office. He thanked him for the railway construction his policies spurred, telling him that the people of his state had experienced national integration, progress, and civilization as a result of the transportation development undertaken.[99] The Oaxacan intellectual who would become minister of public education, Demetrio Sodi, also wrote to the president immediately after he left office. He expressed thanks to Díaz for his success in the railroad program that he attributed as the root of the nation's happiness. He noted that he looked forward to the presidency of Manuel González, hoping that he could lead as well as Díaz and continue construction.[100]

The *ayuntamiento* of Merida, Yucatán also commended the president as he left office for the success of the railway program to promote energy and movement throughout the country, an accomplishment it identified as his legacy.[101] But it was not only urban centers that congratulated the president's efforts. The small town *ayuntamiento* of Motul, Yucatán, wrote the president and thanked him for demonstrating, through the establishment of railroads and by adhering to the sacred principles of no reelection, the nation's aptitude for morality and patriotism.[102] Another Yucatán *ayuntamiento*, officials from Villa de Temax, congratulated the president for his unwavering leadership demonstrated most clearly in the railway development that had, according to its officials, given the country energy, movement, and prosperity.[103]

The small municipality of Mazatepec, Morelos also wrote the president immediately after leaving office. In the letter, Adrian Ortega, on behalf of the municipality, stated that the Republic had never witnessed such peace, a development proved by Díaz's decision to allow Manuel González to ascend to the presidential chair. The author continued telling the outgoing president that the nation's people could never deny the shadow cast by his administration's activity in terms of railway expansion.[104]

Considering Díaz's success at securing the first major railway concessions across the country, he seemed a logical choice to serve as minister of economic development. This sentiment was also highlighted in several letters that reached his desk. One well-wisher stated that he was contented to know that Díaz would take over as the minister of economic development and that his work securing the railway line to Toluca made him an ideal candidate.[105] Similarly, Manuel López Leon, who worked for that ministry, thanked the president for improving the condition of the nation's railway lines and for his decision to remain in government as the minister of economic development.[106]

In Díaz's final months in office, he received a warm farewell from the liberal press and local, state, and national policymakers. Above all other accomplishments, people acknowledged his success at securing large-scale railway contracts as his crowning achievement. Their letters demonstrated that the language of movement, energy, and revitalization permeated the discourse of officials from state governors to small-town *ayuntamientos*.

Conclusion

Between 1876 and 1880 Díaz's administration, like no other government before it, aggressively sought to develop the nation's railway network. Surrounding the railway project, people drew on various discourses to promote or challenge the way that this nation-building mission would be realized. Groups that either supported or opposed Díaz's brand of economic modernization, despite their differences, agreed that the railroad represented an important undertaking that would transform the country. Whereas Mexico's past was characterized by political instability, regional isolation, economic backwardness, and foreign intervention, its future, with the successful development of a national transportation network, would be something much greater. Awakened from decades of lethargic progress by the whistle of the locomotive, Mexico would refashion itself as a modern nation where presidential succession would be bloodless, where citizens would feel a patriotic connection to their national community, where export-led economic development would generate wealth, and where foreigners would invest and not invade.

This considered, Díaz's return to the presidential chair in 1884 is not surprising. During the González interregnum, no viable candidates had emerged, and the pro-Díaz press repeatedly touted his achievements in terms of maintaining stability and promoting progress. *La Libertad*, for example, noted that Díaz was the only logical candidate in the upcoming 1884 election, since he had a track record in achieving what no other Mexican had, namely, "securing peace and material progress, something that had seemed impossible."[107] Likewise, in the months leading up to the election, the *Mexican Financier* opined that it was "important to the peace, well-being, and prosperity of the nation that Díaz be elected." It evidenced this statement by Díaz's success at courting U.S. investment and showing the world the "precious opportunities" that existed for investment in Mexico.[108]

The discourses used by the elite to foster economic modernization provided an idealized, although vague, view of the future that all groups could, in one way or another, agree upon. While various sectors of the press and policymakers often quarreled about the manner in which railway expansion should be undertaken, they often discussed the need for railway expansion in the same ways. By repeating ambiguous notions about the railway's ability to regenerate the country, to unify the people, and to promote commercial development, political opponents smoothed over disagreements regarding railway expansion and conveyed the appearance of consensus, at least in terms of the utopian promises the locomotive offered. The multiple visions of how exactly railway development should be advanced were incorporated together, creating a more or less unified outlook about the locomotive's potential to regenerate the country and, in so doing, achieved a degree of hegemony. The discussion of the railway program demarcated the boundaries for dissent and of the possible political alternatives to Díaz's vision of railroad development. In this way, any alternative strategies for railway development—and, for that matter, economic and political development—were pushed aside, through political manipulation or personal attacks in the press, for example, if they did not correspond with Díaz's program of modernization. The following chapter explores how the rhetorical themes expressed by policymakers about the civilizing and revitalizing potential of railway development found articulation in art, poetry, literature, and social commentaries in the elite press.

De Viaje

Elite Views of Modernity and the Railroad Boom

All of a sudden, the curtain is lowered abruptly on the sun, on beauty, on the thousand scenes of life and nature which our mind and heart have savoured along the way. It is night and death and the cemetery; it is despotism — it is the tunnel! Nothing but beings that dwell in the shadows, never knowing the bright wing of freedom and truth! . . . Nonetheless, after hearing the cries of confusion and dismay from passengers on the train as it enters the gloomy archway, and their exclamations of joy on quitting the tunnel, . . . who would dare maintain that the human creature was not made for light and liberty?

BENJAMIN GASTINEAU, *La Vie en chemin de fer*
(cited in Walter Benjamin, *Arcades Project*)

Due to Díaz's success at securing railway contracts during his first term in office, the 1880s and 1890s witnessed an extraordinary railway boom that captured many people's imaginations. No other nineteenth-century technology reshaped the public and private spheres and the relationship between city and countryside as did the steam-powered locomotive. In particular, it inspired artists and writers to contemplate its capacity to reshape people's understanding of time, space, and social relations and how the railroad represented the embodiment of the age of progress. Porfirian weeklies that targeted middle- and upper-class audiences offered readers an array of poems, stories, cartoons, and social commentaries about railroad development that highlighted these themes. The nation's burgeoning transportation network stirred up a great deal of interest among imaginative writers, a development in sharp contrast to Europe during its early years of railway expansion.[1] The arrival of the railway compelled elite members of society to examine and articulate their views about the nature, possibilities, and consequences of modernization. Women's journals especially played a central role in celebrating a vision of how railways would make real the redemptive promises of modernization as well as how Porfirio Díaz's regime succeeded in securing the prerequisite conditions of peace and order needed for national development. While the expansion of the railroad system inspired elite writers to praise and publicize their country's success at securing the utopian promises of modernity,[2] the social transformations spurred by modern travel also awakened anxieties about the railway's capacity to alter familiar understandings of time and space as well as social and gender relations.

To explore the cultural representations of the railway among elite circles, this chapter examines high-society periodicals that published an array of artistic and literary works on the subject of the iron horse. The railway was a common subject in several of Mexico City's leading literary publications of the late nineteenth and early twentieth centuries such as *El Mundo (Semanario Ilustrado)*[3] and *La Revista Moderna*.[4] *El Mundo (Semanario Ilustrado)*, an illustrated weekly published by the editors of *El Imparcial*, the government-subsidized and most widely distributed newspaper in the nation's capital, was launched by *científico* Rafael Reyes Spíndola, the so-called father of modern Mexican journalism.[5] These publications offered readers an array of texts including national and foreign news, art and science chronicles, and a literary section that printed novellas, short stories, essays, and poetry. *La Revista Moderna*, published fortnightly by Jesús E. Valenzuela, who was also a regular contributor to *El Imparcial*, sought to promote exclusively modernist literature, although in time its editors became less rigid and allowed a wider array of literary styles to reach its audience. Some of the era's most prominent writers contributed to its publications, including Amado Nervo, Federico Gamboa, and Luis Urbina, among a host of other prominent authors. According to Adela Pineda Franco, *La Revista Moderna* appealed to elite audiences invested in the nation's material progress and urbanization. As such, the publication's contributors—especially in their writings on history and literature—emphasized the progressive development of society and promoted a "triumphalist vision" that rested on a depiction of the past that served as the foundation for a "utopian future."[6]

Although less expensive than *El Mundo (Semanario Ilustrado)* or *La Revista Moderna, El Mundo Cómico* was also a relatively expensive illustrated weekly, costing five centavos. It offered humorous depictions of current events.[7] Railway literature was also published in *El Cronista de México*, a popular independent illustrated Catholic weekly with a distribution of 8,000 copies per week.[8]

Women's journals such as *El Correo de las Señoras* and *Las Violetas del Anáhuac* shared a similar fascination with the locomotive, printing poems and travel chronicles that featured railways. The latter, edited by Laureana Wright de Kleinhans, gained distinction as the first periodical to discuss female suffrage and equality of the sexes during the Porfiriato.[9] All of these publications clearly targeted well-to-do audiences as the prohibitively expensive cost of the journals, between five and fifty centavos an issue, allowed only those individuals with disposable incomes to subscribe.[10] Although available through monthly subscriptions in the provinces, these periodicals were most widely circulated in Mexico City.[11]

In the 1880s and 1890s, the railway surged in popularity among the writers, poets, journalists, and artists of these periodicals. This literature reflected the ways that elite groups experienced and interpreted modernity as well as their attitudes toward the nation, its government, and its future; it also draws attention to the connections between discourses that the elite articulated in their political rhetoric and those favored in popular venues, commonly premising both upon hailing the railroad as the harbinger of civilization and progress.[12] Literature about locomotive travel represented more than lighthearted tales published solely for amusement. The publishers and contributors to these periodicals often had direct connections to the Díaz government and the *científicos*, especially *El Mundo (Semanario Ilustrado)* and *La Revista Moderna.*[13] They were printed for consumption among elite audiences and used to celebrate the efficacy of the regime's program of establishing "order and progress." The emphasis on the civilizing potential of railways matched well with the positivist ideology held by many politicians and intellectuals of the era. Writers and artists often used the utopian promises offered by the railway to highlight its capacity to reinvigorate their country after a half century of civil wars, foreign invasion, and economic stagnation. The positivist belief that society represented a natural organism was often espoused by *científicos* who viewed railways as arteries pumping blood and life into the moribund nation.[14] For *científicos* such as newspaper mogul Reyes Spíndola, as well as leading female intellectuals such as Wright de Kleinhans, material progress would help establish political peace and end the cycles of violence that had characterized the country since Independence, a crucial factor in the establishment of "civilization."[15]

Writers extolled the government's accomplishments of transforming the nation along modern Western guidelines and, in so doing, generated enthusiasm among those groups most loyal to Díaz. Yet these sources also presented a shared sense of fear and distrust about the consequences of modernization and the shifting social relations that resulted. Furthermore, these works highlighted changing attitudes among the elite toward

the growing divide between rural and urban society, a development discussed in both positive and negative terms. Together,
these works illuminate an ambiguous and ambivalent response
to the process of modernization, a process most clearly represented by the railway boom.

The Experience of Modern Travel

Literary magazines, women's journals, religious publications,
and illustrated weeklies all regularly published accounts of railway travel. These chronicles, often titled "De viaje," described
the nation as experienced through the first-class carriage windows, and travel writers described the flora and fauna of the
changing countryside, the emerging provincial metropolises,
and the delights, displeasures, and dangers of locomotive travel.
This literature offered readers a chance to experience their nation through the writings of journalists who used the expanding railroad network to tour the country. Writers described in
detail the changing landscape: the vast deserts of the north, the
mountainous terrain of the Sierra Madre, and the rainforests
of the southern littoral. They emphasized the evanescent quality of railway travel, marveling at its speed. The annihilation
of time and space became a common theme.[16] *El Mundo (Semanario Ilustrado)* frequently printed poems about the railroad that emphasized the civilizing and revitalizing qualities of
these "centaurs of progress." One poet displayed his exhilaration when recounting the speed and movement of the locomotive that seemed to be flying across the countryside, exclaiming:

> Look at it! It goes along chewing up the distance;
> It hardly seems to touch the ground;
> And devoured by desire,
> It spews clouds out of its burning mouth![17]

The speed of railway travel was often expressed by writers
through descriptions of their visual experience while watching

the landscape roar by. The intimate relationship between traveler and landscape that existed during preindustrial forms of travel such as the mule, horse, or stagecoach, as a consequence, was
destroyed. What appeared to the traveler as the loss of scenery,
fostered by the rapid movement of the railroad, created a new
form of sensory experience not permitted by older forms of travel where every detail of the environment could not only be perceived but closely analyzed. Using Newton's theory of mechan-
ics that maintains that size, shape, quantity, and motion are
the only qualities that can be discerned objectively, Wolfgang
Schivelbusch argues that this experience created a mechanization of perception, creating a sensation for the traveler that the
landscape was disappearing since the passenger could no longer
experience the smells, sounds, and so-called synthetic perceptions that were part and parcel of older forms of travel.[18] Writers
often described the sensation of the vanishing landscape. This
experience was pointed out in another poet's musing about locomotive travel:

> Where do the grey fields go
> At such a frantic pace?
> They go to distant places
> Where Man awaits![19]

The early experiences of rapid movement on the railway described in nineteenth-century European accounts tended to stress
the negative psychological aspects of mechanized motion. In
their accounts about railway excursions, passengers often conveyed a sense of fatigue and boredom when describing the experience of travel, a sensation caused by their inability to adapt
their mode of perception to the rapidity of the railroad.[20] Mexican travelers' accounts rarely described the perceptual effects
of rail travel. When travel writers did take the time to discuss
the emotional and psychological impact of their journey, they
evinced no such ill effects. Instead, travel chronicles emphasized

the exhilaration felt as a result of the sensation of flying across the countryside or being projected through space. In one travel journal published in *El Cronista de México*, titled "Cartas a mi Prima," a young man wrote to his cousin about the experience of locomotive travel as wings carrying him over the seas, forests, plains, and mountains.[21] In the women's weekly *Las Violetas del Anáhuac*, a journalist traveling to Veracruz described the sensation of crossing the bridges over ravines such as la Cañada de Metlac as that of a bird flying over a great chasm.[22] The impression of flight described by passengers resulted from the visual experience of the traveler looking out the train's window. The mechanization of the passenger's perception fostered a sense that the landscape disappeared, producing a feeling that the locomotive was not embedded in space but soaring through it.

Detailing the emotional effects of railway travel, while a frequent practice among writers, did not represent the most common subject matter of their accounts. Above all, the literature about modern travel emphasized the civilizing qualities of the locomotive, a theme especially common in railway poetry.[23] The railway's domination over the landscape and its capacity to reshape it offered elite Porfirians a powerful symbol with which to represent the mission of the Díaz regime.

Railroad Poetry

The civilizing qualities of the railway were often addressed through poetry, stories, and travel literature published in the elite press. These works stressed similar themes when focusing their artistic vision on the railway, especially those of national regeneration, patriotism, and social peace. Descriptions of the railway's potential to spur social, economic, and political transformations represented the artistic equivalent to the positivist philosophy espoused by intellectuals and politicians that viewed material progress as definitive proof of Mexico's evolution into a modern, cosmopolitan country, a sentiment that often evoked great national pride. Poetry offered a commanding medium to express both the personal and national hopes regarding the transformative capacity of modernizing projects. As Carlos Monsiváis notes, poetry during the Porfiriato represented not only the era's highest form of artistic expression but a barometer of individual and collective sensibilities.[24] Railroad poems stressed the regenerative qualities for societal uplift that in one case took on a deeply emotional, at times even romantic, tone. Rosa Navarro, writing for *Las Violetas del Anáhuac* from her home in Guadalajara, produced a twenty-three-stanza paean to the railway. Her poem, "Á la locomotora," described the railway as the vanguard of civilization and highlighted many of the ideals shared by middle- and upper-class Porfirians about the importance of national progress. She narrated her first encounter with the railway:

> Hail, blessed
> Messenger of progress,
> And I welcome you
> Harbinger of prosperity.
> Before I knew you
> How often I saw you in dreams!
> And how I longed for the day
> That I could look at you.
> Three years I have dreamt
> In seeing you with such determination,
> My lovely dream came true,
> And what bliss to awake![25]

Navarro detailed a deep emotional connection to the railway and the possibilities of prosperity it offered. The emotive language used to discuss the locomotive, whose arrival the author declared she had only dreamt about, revealed an intense conviction about the betterment of the nation made possible through railroad development. This assurance, not surprisingly, was most often expressed by the middle- and upper-class groups that most

benefited from the regime's attempts to promote peace and prosperity. After the decades of political upheaval and economic
stagnation, most Porfirians shared a profound sense of the absolute necessity of modern nation-building projects to break the
cycles of chaos that had bogged down the country's progress.

She continued, describing her first encounter with the railroad in near-romantic terms:

> On the banks of Irapuato
> I saw you for the first time,
> And it seemed like a Chimera
> That you would come to my city.
> I longed to see you here
> So ardent was the desire,
> That today in my home I see you
> I am dreaming again . . . !
> My tears of joy
> With which I greet this day
> Of such sacred bliss
> Tell me that I'm awake![26]

Here the author welcomed the railway as she would a romantic interest. The dreaming and longing used to describe her emotional state suggested more than a feeling of simply delighting
in the novelty of the locomotive; it revealed a subjective, sentimental side of modernity that tempered the cold, scientific discourse that so often characterized discussions of railway expansion, a discourse from which women were excluded.[27]

Navarro then shifted her attention to how the people of Jalisco celebrated the arrival of the locomotive:

> The thousand "Long Lives" to Jalisco,
> The murmurs of enthusiasm,
> The praises of progress,
> Welfare and peace.

The emotion that is portrayed
On the faces of the people,
And this great gathering
Bring me to reality. . . .
Grateful day of memory
That conquers honor and laurels,
To the progressive government
That brings us industry and peace.[28]

She explored common themes about the railway's potential
to transform the nation. *Tapatías* (residents of Jalisco), according to the author, recognized the interconnections among patriotism, good government, industriousness, and peace, all important themes extolled by policymakers. This poem, while not
mentioning Díaz directly, nevertheless demonstrated that Porfirians, especially the well-to-do, shared a belief in the successes
of the government's policies promoting national development.
And through its celebration in the literature published in journals, they provided an important base of support for the regime.
Indeed, women's journals such as *Las Violetas del Anáhuac* often displayed intense support for Díaz's government because of
its success at establishing peace across the country.[29]

Beyond that, this railway poem evinced a romantic tone and
invoked an emotional connection between the writer and locomotive. Targeted to female audiences, on one level it demonstrated that some elite women assumed a public role in lauding the accomplishments of the regime in securing the material trappings of
progress. On another it suggests that her use of romantic tropes
not only clearly targeted women but also utilized romantic mo-
tifs to describe an object that was in many ways anything but romantic. Navarro, focusing on technology and progress—issues
associated with the public realm and thus from which women
were excluded participation—drew on romantic language as a
bridge between rationality and science and the aesthetic of emo-

tion that might resonate with other upper-class women's sensibilities and tastes. This allowed female writers such as Navarro to actively engage the discussions of modernization as well as mobilize other women to do the same. And, like her male counterparts, Navarro made a fetish of the railway by highlighting its redemptive and utopian potential, describing it as an object imbued with near-magical powers to alleviate the social and economic dislocations that the nation had experienced since Independence.[30] By emphasizing the railway's ability to transform the nation and its people insofar as social habits, political structures, and material wealth, this journal, an early crusader for women's suffrage and rights, fashioned a female subjectivity that allowed for a meaningful engagement with the broader national discourses of progress and the attainment of civilization. Yet her celebration of the railway allowed Navarro to express a sincere nationalism while demonstrating that women's patriotism could be expressed through technological interests and civic engagement, not only through maternity and motherhood.[31]

Even satirical poems that sought to point out the problems of the Porfirian regime recognized the railway as a potent transformative device that could revitalize the nation and its people. *El Coyote*, a weekly that regularly critiqued the government, published poems and stories in which the railway played a central role. One such poem, "A Tlalnepantla," contrasted the nation's material advancements with the backwardness and inefficiency of its legal system. While condemning the corruption and incompetence of the town judge, and the national government that allowed such officials to be placed in positions of power, the poem also praised the arrival of the railroad as an invigorating force that would bring life to the moribund town of Tlalnepantla, a once great Aztec city:

> Once sad and dejected
> By the ravages of time:

Now again it rises
On the wings of progress,
Serving the iron road
As a station and as sustenance
It dreamt that it revived.
It dreamt that it took breath.[32]

Literature relating to the importance of railway development often drew connections between revitalization and movement.[33] As in Europe, the railway's capacity to compress time and space was the most common description made about locomotive travel. Writers used this concept as a central metaphor about the importance of movement and national revival. This sonnet, "La locomotora," clearly attempted to confirm the connections between the compression of time and space, movement, and revitalization:

Sister of the sun and the dark night,
With space and time at war,
The hills pressing on the earth,
It advances majestically across the plain.
Amongst the incense of the vapor it gleams
Rays of light, and with the rocks it closes upon,
It sinks into the heart of the mountains,
Seeking there a path or a grave.
Today it parts from the western coasts,
Tomorrow the Indian Ocean in its grasp
It will go to temper the red horizon.
On its wings it carries the fertile seeds
Of industry, of art, of progress. . . .
Make way for the breath of God that drives the world![34]

Another poem published in *El Mundo (Semanario Ilustrado)* demonstrated the compression of time and space as a prominent theme among writers. Here the author described the locomotive as a steed galloping over the countryside:

Beating to the rough rhythm
Of its powerful veins,
And the rough bronze warp
Of its creaking muscles,
Deliriously through the fields
It crosses and erases distances,
And its round wings
Dizzyingly go and go.[35]

The dizzying speed of the railway, as these two poems illustrate, destroyed the distances between destinations and, in so doing, created an impression that regions were brought into nearer proximity. Also, allusions to vertigo and dizziness indicate that writers sought to convey the disorienting quality of railway travel that altered previous ways that people experienced the natural world. No longer could travelers express a profound relationship with objects of nature, as the speed of locomotive movement transformed them into panoramas at once distant and distancing.

The notion that towns and peoples were being brought into closer intimacy as a result of railway expansion was, likewise, a common subject matter in literature. Provincial publications, especially for railway inauguration festivities, produced poems that considered how the railway brought once distant regions into contact. This segment from a poem published for the inauguration of the San Luis–Tampico line, a trunk line of the Mexican Central Railroad finished in 1890, demonstrated this theme:

In Tampico! I'm here
Recalling now that yesterday
I was watching the burning sun
Back in San Luis Potosí!
Could the vastness before me
Perhaps get narrow

Closing the distance
For the crossing? . . . Not at all:
In one stride . . . of progress:
Blessed be that great step![36]

This writer's emphasis on the railway's capacity to compress time and space also produced a counterpoint, namely, that by bringing regions together, the locomotive created new spaces by allowing people to visit regions that were once prohibitively distant.

As this literature reveals, Mexicans were eager to take advantage of railroad development to travel across their country. It also suggests that long, esoteric newspaper articles about the need to unify production zones with national and foreign markets may have done little to stimulate readers' enthusiasm compared with the imaginative writings fueled by the railway fever that hit the nation in the 1880s and 1890s. The connections made by writers between the diffusion of modern technology, economic development, and the aspirations to realize civilization were a central theme in Porfirian developmentalist ideology.[37] *Científicos* such as Reyes Spíndola viewed economic and material progress as the vital component in resolving the social and political problems affecting the country.[38] Studies have demonstrated that discourses linking western technology and the civilizing of non-Western peoples were central to the rationalization used for colonial projects in Asia and Africa, although often couched in humanitarian terms.[39] In the case of Mexico, we see a self-civilizing mission undertaken by middle- and upper-class Porfirians that highlighted their own sensibilities and beliefs while, on the other hand, attempted to convince themselves about the necessity of promoting railway development as a way to transform their country along progressive guidelines. Poems, stories, and travel literature all played an important role in diffusing elite beliefs about the ontological necessity of large-scale transportation projects in securing the rewards of civilization.

Travel Literature and "Order and Progress"

Travel writers, especially those who wrote for periodicals that targeted middle- and upper-class audiences, took pride in relating what they viewed as the government's success at securing "order and progress" in all corners of the nation. Journalists provided their readers with detailed descriptions of the material improvements achieved in provincial cities. While perhaps not conscious attempts of pro-government propaganda, these sources nevertheless lauded the efficacy and success of the Díaz administration's commitment to modernizing the country.

Laureana Wright de Kleinhans, the editor of the women's journal *Las Violetas del Anáhuac*, recounted her train excursion to the port city of Veracruz. Strolling through the city streets, she applauded the town council's success at delivering on the promises of order and progress. She reported her utter surprise about the material advancements made in that city, such as the extreme cleanliness and hygiene that the city's leaders promoted as well as the complete safety that reigned in all corners of Veracruz. Moreover, she couched her travel narrative in racist language as she marveled at how the town's Indian population had been transformed into a diligent, hardworking people who were no longer affected by the "cancer" of immorality and vagrancy. She concluded by telling her audience that in the eight days she spent in that port city she did not once encounter a drunk, vagabond, or thief.[40]

While Wright de Kleinhans's description may have used at least some hyperbole, it nevertheless demonstrates that travel literature was a genre that could be used to convey and promote the ideals shared by elite Porfirians. In this case, the city's leaders had managed to promote hygiene and secure its streets from criminals, and they had also succeeded in promoting middle-class values of work and sobriety—a feat that the author plainly linked to the city's new sense of peace and security. The modernization of provincial cities meant, at least for members of high society, that their nation was becoming more European and less Indian in its character, an idea that corresponded to positivists' beliefs about the necessity of racial fusion.[41] Furthermore, Wright de Kleinhans's locomotive travels provided the opportunity for her to connect issues of progress, science, patriotism, and morality. In so doing, she legitimized female participation outside the confines of the domestic sphere in a manner that simultaneously displayed concern regarding matters of morality, a subject commonly associated with women's roles as moral guardians.

In the same year, *El Correo de las Señoras*, an ardently pro-Díaz weekly, printed a series of travel narratives from *El Diario del Hogar*, where Manuel Caballero had published his account of visiting Guadalajara for the Jalisco Exposition and noticing how the city had developed in recent years. He boasted to his readers that the city had a European appearance in its elegant buildings, its orderly streets, and the decent conduct of its citizens.[42] Ironically, Caballero had been a vocal opponent of Díaz, writing for antigovernment newspapers such as *El Diario del Hogar*.[43] He not only emphasized the importance of modern city planning as a vital aspect to becoming more European but likewise stressed the value of decent, orderly behavior in securing the trappings of civilized society. Scholars have demonstrated the interest of elite Porfirians in portraying their nation as modern, peaceful, and civilized as a means of securing foreign investment in Mexico.[44] But as these narratives make evident, elite writers also sought to prove these ideals to themselves. As William French notes in his discussion of moral reform, these types of discourses were central to middle- and upper-class attempts at class and self-definition.[45] The general sense of enthusiasm prompted by the arrival of the locomotive and its civilizing qualities, a feeling also clearly shared by Díaz's opponents, helped to highlight the regime's success at establishing nationwide peace and progress the very same year that the *caudillo* sought his first consecutive reelection, an act that flew in the face of the Constitution of 1857. Through sanguine representations of the country's development, journalists and social commentators, even those writers opposed to the president, drew connections that inextricably linked Díaz to national progress.

More than ten years later, using travel literature to demonstrate the triumphs of the regime remained a common practice. Alberto Leduc's travel series titled "De viaje" for *La Revista Moderna* narrated to his readers his adventures touring the nation from Oaxaca to Chihuahua. Getting off the train in Monterrey, he boarded a streetcar on which he toured the city's ample and clean red-bricked streets. He visited the city's numerous factories, where he marveled at the production of silver ornaments, matches, and beer and gleefully described the columns of smoke spewing from their flues as definitive proof of his country's successful modernization. After enjoying a cold pint of beer in the Alameda, the very act a symbol of modernity demonstrated by the industrial production of beverages and their refrigeration, the contented tourist headed back to the station where he reflected on the success of General Bernardo Reyes, Nuevo Leon's governor, in transforming Monterrey into the nation's first industrial town, before boarding another train to Saltillo.[46] Likewise, while visiting Chihuahua City, he described the city's edifices, highlighting the hospital, the governor's palace, the mining bank, and the Hotel Palacio as examples of the modern architecture that the city's leaders embraced.[47] The connection among the development of railways, industry, and the construction of modern buildings was a common motif in these journals, as the locomotive represented the industrialization of travel. This link was illustrated in one cartoon's jest regarding the confusion created by the similarities between both forms of industrialization, an association clearly implied through the image of the smokestack as a connotation of industry.

In another segment of Leduc's series of travel narratives, he applauded the safety and security in the country's provinces.

1. Optical effects — "Let's hurry, the train is going to leave us." *Cómico*, August 20, 1899.

Visiting Pachuca, the author informed his readers that visitors had no reason to fear thieves in the streets.[48] He boldly touted to readers that travelers should not worry about losing their watches or wallets, since the thief had become an "exotic plant" in that city.[49] Traveling across the states of Chihuahua, Coahuila, and Durango, the journalist boasted that the northern provinces were no longer characterized by the "killers, cadavers, and mobs of assassins" who had hindered the region's attempts to secure peace and order. Instead, he noted that his generation now comfortably traveled the railroads unaffected by crime, since

the miseries of hunger, thirst, and persecution no longer affected his fellow countrymen.[50]

Printed in some of the leading literary journals, these examples show that travel literature disseminated ideas about the
country's modernization program. While these travel accounts
surely reveal a general sense of enthusiasm toward the railway,
they also lauded, whether as acts of conscious propaganda or
not, the government's achievements in promoting industrialization, work ethic, sobriety, hygiene, and social order. At the
same time, the promotion of the regime by *La Revista Moderna* was not surprising, since its editors had close ties to the Díaz
administration, so much so that one of the journal's founders
and contributors, the poet Amado Nervo, served as a representative of the government at the Universal Exposition in 1900,
becoming an important tool of the government's campaign to
improve the country's international image.[51]

Published accounts of railway travel provided writers with the
opportunity to share their beliefs with readers about the benefits of modernization realized under the leadership of President
Díaz. In these accounts, writers emphasized how the nation's
newfound peace and prosperity had allowed for the promotion
of modern values. Yet these accounts also gave middle- and upper-class groups the chance to call attention to the tensions between rural and urban society that they viewed as resulting from
rapid modernization. City-dwelling citizens undertook railway
excursions to visit provincial towns, and provincials likewise
undertook excursions to the city. As a result, urban individuals
encountered traditional behaviors and pastimes they considered
backward or barbaric. Writers of various genres stressed the divisions between urban and rural society in their portrayals of
the *provinciano* (provincial yokel), a stereotyped character used
in the poems, stories, and journals about locomotive travel, who
came to Mexico City in search of adventure and entertainment.

In "Cartas a mi Prima," the author joked to his cousin about the rustic provincial travelers getting off their second-class trains to spend more in fifteen days than they could spend in fifteen years in their own *pueblo*, a statement that plainly connected material culture, consumerism, and civilization. The writer described provincial visitors to the country's capital as they marveled at their first surprise: electric light. The author scoffed at the provincials who compared the glow of the light bulb to that of the moon, stating that their assessment failed to recognize how the moon's luminosity paled in comparison and suggesting the rustic visitors' inability to appreciate the splendors of modernity.[52] The fictional account not only implied an inability to appreciate electricity but also insinuated that the rural traveler could not even comprehend modern technology as he was forced to rely on the natural world to describe his experience.

Next, the provincial traveler hailed a coach to take his family to a hotel and received a second surprise: the high cost of services in the city. Mistakenly boarding a "blue flag" coach, the city's most expensive taxis, the provincial visitor argued over the price of the ride with the driver, who nonetheless managed to take advantage of the trusting family.[53] The visitors proceeded to their hotel room, where they were shocked at the substandard quality of the Turco Hotel. The rural tourists, expecting varnished pine furniture, floral patterned sofas, and oil lamps from the times of Emperor Iturbide, instead suffered with a bug-infested room made worse by its stained carpets and curtains and a hard bed. Finally, attending a production at a theater, the family was again disappointed to find that the second-class balcony had seats as dusty as the "road between Mexico City and Guadalajara." The experiences in the capital forced the provincial traveler to think of his village and how the train had brought home to his memory, making him feel the full intensity of his abandonment.[54] The description of the rural traveler in the metropolis, as depicted by the urban observer, portrayed the provincial visitor as incapable of effectively negotiating the modern city. The provincial traveler, in the end, dreamed of returning to his *pueblo* where the journal's writer implied he belonged.

The misplacement of the rural traveler in the city was likewise narrated in tales about women. *La Broma* published a story that told readers about a provincial girl taking the train to the capital in search of a gentleman of good standing. This tale also highlighted the perceived differences between rural and urban sensibilities. The author told his readers that girls from small towns, not having met more than the town druggist and the good-looking but unworldly boys of their village, enjoyed traveling to the city in the hope of meeting possible suitors. The author suggested that the smooth movement of the train and the whistle of the engine made it much easier for young women to get caught in the "web of locomotive romance."

The story continued with the main character, Albertina, looking for love after arriving in Mexico City. While there, the author underscored the differences between urban and rural outlooks. Nowhere was this more apparent than the three failed love connections attempted by young Albertina, tales she recounted to her friends back in her provincial town. First, Albertina came across a fine suitor whom she liked but who became too brazen. After he asked Albertina to show him her heart, a euphemism for sexual relations, she left the lustful lad. Then she met a young cavalryman who had taken coffee several times with Albertina and her mother. He appeared to be a respectable man, yet Albertina discovered him on his knees making an amorous proposition to the servant girl. Finally, a young man began to court her, but after he borrowed five pesos from her father, he never returned. In the end, Albertina gave up on finding love and returned home.[55]

This story demonstrated the divide that Mexico City's writers understood to exist between provincials and city-dwellers. Rural peoples, as this story shows, were portrayed as conservative, traditional, and naïve about urban life. Moreover, they

2. People of good faith — "I told you we were going to be late. Now the train is going to have to return and pick us up." *Cómico*, August 6, 1899.

were unable to cope with the behaviors and expectations that city life seemed to demand. The story suggested that while the railway might awaken sexual desire in young women, they were not prepared to deal with rapacious young men and their forays into urban life would be ultimately unfulfilling.[56] Yet the tale of Albertina's ordeals also implied another view, one that highlights the ambivalent outlook that some writers held toward the processes of social and cultural change spurred by modernization. In this case, Albertina, with a little help from her family, successfully handled the compromising situations that she encountered. The story also draws attention to the lesson that young women should be as distrustful of the modern city as Albertina was of the predatory men she encountered. In so doing, the writer cast a cold eye on urban life, stressing moral decay as a predominant feature of modern society.

The rural traveler, typically referred to as a second- or third-

—¡En qué peligro tan grande estaría yo si viniera el tren!

3. "What trouble I would be in if the train were coming!" *Cómico*, September 24, 1899.

class passenger in the literature, also carried objects that symbolized rural life. In one story published in *El Mundo Cómico*, provincial travelers became inebriated on pulque and, as a result, allowed their roosters and hens to run amok on the train as it pulled into the station.[57] Writers characterized the rustic traveler as the antithesis of the modern, urban citizen, a passenger whose tastes and proclivities have rendered him or her incapable of responsibly dealing with the tools of modernity. Figure 2 shows two provincials ill-prepared to deal with the demands of modern travel.

This idea was furthered in another cartoon's portrayal of a mule driver whose lack of knowledge regarding the railway schedule placed him in certain peril.[58]

Together, these sources reveal that the railway, although limiting the spatial and temporal distance between the capital and the provinces, at the same time made the social and cultural divide between them more visible, a development that allowed urban writers to define themselves as the vanguards of modern life against provincial inhabitants typically portrayed as uncouth and backward. Elite writers dialectically connected past and present, rural and urban in a manner that defined modernity through the traditional and vice versa.

While travel literature targeting middle- and upper-class audiences often celebrated the progress attained by Porfirian rule, they were not always paeans dedicated to the success of the regime. Although travel writers praised what they saw as the successes of modernization, they also criticized transformations they viewed as detrimental to their society. *La Revista Moderna*'s Alberto Leduc did not always agree with the changes he witnessed sweeping the country. Arriving in Torreón, the showcase of Porfirian modernization, the author grumbled that he could only tolerate a couple hours in what he referred to as an unpleasant and Yankee-phile town where his fellow countrymen had fallen into the *gringo* custom of charging high prices and being inhospitable.[59] Dealing with the unpleasantness of U.S. citizens was a common theme in the travel literature of the elite press. Writers most often complained about having to share their train compartment with ill-mannered Yankees, whether they were unrefined passengers or rude workers. In the chronicle "Cartas a mi Prima," the writer composed a poem about his journey on the Mexican Central Railroad, the first line to connect Mexico and the United States, bringing many Mexican travelers in contact with their northern neighbors. In it, the self-styled poet carped about the uncivilized behavior of the railway company's employees:

> The conductors are
> Some Yankees so rude,
> Traveling inside the wagon
> Chewing black tobacco
> And with their feet raised up
> On top of the seats.[60]

Writers from all political leanings frequently criticized U.S. conductors, machinists, and other railway employees. The most common complaint was their rudeness toward Mexican passengers and their failure to learn Spanish. While more radical elements of the press used these issues to call for a nationally run railway system, pro-Díaz journals rarely called for such measures, choosing instead to poke fun at the *gringo* workers. Moreover, the government's success in promoting railway expansion had come at the cost of giving U.S. firms a lion's share of the nation's transportation network, something that resulted in an increased presence of U.S. citizens on the railway and in railway towns.[61] While observers appreciated locomotive travel as a modern and civilized endeavor that demonstrated, in a positive sense, the increasing influence of foreigners over Mexico, they were nevertheless vociferous in their hostility toward foreign, particularly U.S., actions and attitudes they deemed distasteful.[62]

The experience of railway travel also allowed urban travelers to criticize the customs of their fellow countrymen, whom they viewed as uncivilized. The popularity of the bullfights in Toluca,[63] an event so well liked that the Mexican Central and

Mexican National railroad companies offered discount fares for spectators to attend, gave *El Cronistas*'s travel correspondent the opportunity to juxtapose what he viewed as the tensions between traditional society (represented in the bullfight) and modern society (represented in the railroad). The writer questioned how the railway, the most powerful advance of the era, could transform itself into a vehicle that lured travelers away from civilized society. He chided the violent spectacle as a catering to people's "dark passions" and "blood lust." Such gory displays of violence, he concluded, convinced him that the heart of man was made of mud and that his virtue was little more than refined hypocrisy.[64] This account, while suggesting a binary conception that separated the traditional and the modern, also demonstrates that the railway disrupted attempts to neatly divide these categories, pushing each upon the other. The travel writer, in order to convince himself or to prove to the reader that civilization was engendered through material progress and proper tastes, needed to travel back in time (or, in this case, to the provinces) to make that argument possible.

These descriptions of the provinces indicate that modernity, in the formulation of Peter Fritzsche, constitutes more than the necessities of the present, "but sustains the desire to explore a strange and remote past."[65] This exploration of the past allowed writers and readers to use literature about locomotive travel to define themselves as the vanguard of modern civilized society against an uncouth rural population with antithetical sensibilities. By traveling back in time, so to speak, these accounts defined the modern present as the perpetual distancing from the past, a past they were forced nevertheless to explore.[66]

Together, these sources also support Mauricio Tenorio-Trillo's claim that notions of modernity represented a contradiction of forces and ideas that encompassed both optimism in progress and concerns over decadence and moral decay.[67] While the railway offered people a window on the possibilities the future might offer, outlooks understood through a teleological world-view of limitless progress, it also forced them to peer back into their pasts to find a means to identify the possible problems that modernization might spawn. And, in this way, this literature also emphasized a fear of losing national identity, in the case of Leduc's discussion of Torreón, or proper moral values, in the case of Albertina's story, associated with a past that was recognizable and comforting.

Railroads and Notions of Egalitarianism

While literature about locomotive travel accentuated the differences between rural and urban society, it also fostered a sense among some travelers that it represented egalitarianism and democracy. Most railway companies divided their passenger trains into three classes, so the experience of locomotive travel clearly drew attention to the differences between social groups traveling in the same convoy. Nevertheless, literature published in polite society weeklies and periodicals attempted to show that since the same vehicle and the same power took passengers to the same destination, the railway was a permanent symbol of people's equality. Miguel Ramos Carrión's sonnet published in *El Mundo (Semanario Ilustrado)* makes evident this idea:

> The pleasant view of life
> Is the train on which I'm whisked away,
> Seeing passionate people at my side
> So many beings I encounter in my travels.
> I travel in a first-class seat,
> From the heat and the wind I'm sheltered,
> And in the same train there's a poor wretch
> Who's occupying a hard seat in third class.
> But although we suffer or rejoice
> The two of us separated, anyone can see
> That we travel the same distance.

And when all is said and done our fate is still the same

For we'll both unfortunately end up

At the final destination: DEATH.[68]

Writers used the railway as a marker of democracy and egalitarianism, associating it metaphorically with the understanding of death as the ultimate social leveler. The poem nevertheless also offers another reading quite different. While writers might have imagined the locomotive as a symbol of idealized values of egalitarianism, these verses demonstrate that, for this author, although death might represent his equality with poorer passengers, in life the train clearly divided people into classes. In another poem published in the same weekly, the author recounted taking a train with his two children. Before the train pulled out of the station, the writer, sitting comfortably in his first-class compartment, compared the railroad to a destiny that all passengers, whether in first or third class, must face:

The happiness that arises in the path

Like a shadow disappears; such is fate. . . .

What train so deceitful is the one of Destiny!

Will her most beautiful destination be death?[69]

These writings also hint at a melancholy view of modernization, associating the railway with death. These writers, even those that sang the praises of progress, also tinged their works with verses that tempered the enthusiasm of material progress and emphasized, at least in these cases, a frightening reality that technology could not cure: the ephemeral nature of life in the grand scheme of things. This theme corresponds to Claudio Lomnitz's conclusion that the rapid changes spurred by modernization drew people's attention to how the increased pace of life seemed to hurry people toward death.[70]

At the same time, elite Porfirian periodicals such as *El Mundo (Semanario Ilustrado)* did not want to push the metaphors of democracy and egalitarianism too far. Other works published in *El Mundo (Semanario Ilustrado)*, sometimes imported from Europe, used the railway as a metaphor to condemn ideologies that promoted more radical forms of egalitarianism. While printing literature from France and Spain allowed editors to cut their costs by not having to pay Mexican writers for original works, they nevertheless chose materials they believed would resonate with Mexican audiences. Editors chose literature that they felt demonstrated a cultural affinity between themselves and Europeans regarding issues of aesthetics, morals, didactics, and recreation.[71]

One such story, originally published in a French journal, was translated for *El Mundo (Semanario Ilustrado)*'s readers. "La rebelion de la máquina" (The machine's rebellion), a tale of pseudo–science fiction, told the story of an inventor, Doctor Pastoureaux, and his assistant, Jean Bertrand, an old factory worker, who built a train that could think and had a soul. One night the train overheard workers discussing how machines had taken the place of men, causing laborers to lose their jobs and capitalists to get richer. After hearing insults made by workers upset at the machine that had supplanted them, the intelligent yet innocent engine began to ponder the moral quandary of whether or not it was created only to take away people's jobs. Jean Bertrand, like the machine, began to develop concerns about the locomotive he had helped Doctor Pastoureaux to build after workers verbally attacked him for creating a monster that undermined the livelihoods of the working class.

The story then shifted to Doctor Pastoureaux, who held a banquet to introduce his new machine to a group of industrialists. He told the audience that he had invented a machine that would free all people from the drudgery of work. In response, the group lifted their wine glasses and toasted the inventor. Doctor Pastoureaux then took the group to a balcony where they could observe the machine in action. Jean Bertrand reluctantly let the train loose for the eager crowd, but not before hurling insults at the train, calling it the "devil's machine" and a "slave to capital." The train, unable to cope with the vitriol, went mad and decided to rebel. At first the machine leisurely toured the area where the spectators watched. Then it began to gain more speed, belching out a whistle as menacing as the "howls of war." Doctor Pastoureaux, realizing that something had gone wrong, commanded the machine to stop, but the machine, stirred by Jean Bertrand's calls to go faster and to ignore the Doctor, launched itself over a cliff into the ocean, ending in a "gigantic iron suicide."

The final part of the tale took place in a post-apocalyptic world covered in the ruins of what was once civilization. The author explained to his readers that, following the train's example, all machines had rebelled against humans and created a world where people were forced to revert to hunting and gathering and were often prey to larger beasts. The author concluded by telling his readers there were no more *castas*, nor scholars, nor bourgeoisie, nor workers, nor artists, and that all people now possessed a definitive equality after the destruction of everything.[72] Here the author asserted that societal divisions were not only natural but necessary. The railway, often a symbol of democracy and egalitarianism, in this case was used to dismiss radical forms of equality and antidevelopmentalist, luddite behavior. Furthermore, it suggested that a world without technology and class hierarchy would descend into barbarism, a sentiment that matched positivist beliefs that related material progress and social evolution.

Despite shared notions of the railroad's inherent potential to promote social equality, elite audiences could identify with the story's principles, which emphasized the importance and necessity of social hierarchy and the ability for technological innovation to improve the lives of the poorest sectors of society. These sensibilities resonated with middle- and upper-class readers who were regularly informed by newspapers about attacks against the railroad undertaken by communities threatened by its incursion into their lands.[73]

A similar theme was articulated in a colossal poem published to celebrate the arrival of the twentieth century. Miguel Bolaños Cacho praised the familiar subject matter of order, progress, civilization, commerce, democracy, and the important strides his nation made toward modernity during the Díaz administration. The poem, likewise, made connections between the futility of radical philosophies of egalitarianism and the value of modern technology to improve the plight of workers. The author wrote:

> And Fouriér and Saint-Simón forward:
> Confronting the feared voice of Karl Marx,
> The magnificent, radiant creation
> Pouring out heat and light and life,
> —From the unknowable infinity to our lips;—
> The universal brotherhood of the righteous,
> Aguste Compte [sic] and his inspiring maxim:
> LOVE, ORDER, PROGRESS! . . .
> —You—"worker" in the shadows who spent
> Your youth deep in a grave
> And, at the sound of the same beat, night and day,
> Beneath the earth in which you buried yourself
> As though in your own tomb;
> Hear the immense roar
> Of the steam that moves the machine,
> To exhume you: burn your incense
> On the altar of the nineteenth century![74]

While imaginative writers viewed the railway as inherently promoting democracy and equality among passengers, it was also used as a symbol to express the limits of egalitarianism. In this way, the locomotive worked well as a metaphor for not only the liberal authoritarianism of the Porfiriato but also the conservative-liberalism that had dominated politics in Mexico since the 1870s.[75] While policymakers and elite groups might pay lip service to liberal beliefs of equality, they viewed the country's need for modernization as superseding any attempts to establish a more democratic, less socially stratified society.

The Compartment

Notions of intimacy, etiquette, and gender relations found profound expression in the close quarters of the railway compartment. Accounts of railway travel in stories, cartoons, and social commentaries discussed the annoyances that passengers experienced as a result of traveling in close quarters with strangers. Often satirical in nature, these accounts provided readers with examples of what constituted proper behavior in the railway coach. *El Cómico* published one such satire about a traveler taking the first-class train to Puebla. While waiting for the train to leave the station, an overweight sixty-year-old man sat next to the narrator, taking up three seats with his luggage and not using the storage compartment. The boorish traveler proceeded to inspect his teeth in a mirror, cut his nose hairs, spit out the window, and then clean his fingernails and his spectacles, all of which led the narrator to avoid all conversation with his unwanted travel companion. Nevertheless, the traveler chatted up the narrator, forcing him into a guessing game of what his occupation might be. After several guesses—ranging from *hacendado* to philosopher—the narrator gave up and the irritating traveler, delivering the story's punch line, informed him that he was a contractor for the Ministry of Sanitation.[76] While perhaps not a hilarious tale of the annoyances of railway travel, this account presented readers with clearly defined expectations of how first-class passengers should and should not behave in the railway car. In this case, notions of etiquette clearly involved the policing of the body and suggested that hygienic maintenance, while an important public project, should be undertaken in private.

The annoyances posed by fellow travelers were a constant theme in railway literature. In one narrative, a travel writer told his readers about the types of passengers that one could unfortunately encounter on the train. He described the ill-mannered traveler who refused to allow anyone to take a seat next to him and who glared at any person in his compartment who dared to open or shut a window. Rude travelers were also characterized by stretching and spreading their legs without consideration of their fellow passengers and by snoring whenever they slept. Bad-mannered eating habits were also frowned upon in the railway car. The author chided passengers who used their fingers to eat and who took swigs out of bottles.[77] Much like the tale of the intoxicated third-class provincials who let their roosters loose in the train, these stories gave writers and readers the opportunity to define acceptable civilized conduct.

Polite society periodicals emphasized other important types of behavior essential to locomotive travel. Most notably, publications stressed punctuality as an essential practice to be learned by travelers. Indeed, railway travel fostered a new importance on time and timekeeping as the transformation into an industrializing society required a new set of cultural values.[78] Newspapers published any incident of trains arriving ahead or behind schedule as well as the schedules of their arrivals and departures. Middle- and upper-class journals and weeklies, likewise, stressed the importance of punctuality. *El Mundo Cómico* warned readers that the traveler who did not find a seat in good time ran the risk of being left behind on the running board or on the platform of the station, contemplating the train as it roared away.[79] Similarly, illustrations published in weeklies wanted to impart to their audience the value of timeliness, especially in regard to railway travel. *El Mundo (Semanario Ilustrado)*, for example, printed a cover illustration of an upper-class couple arriving late at the train station with the caption: "Better hours early than minutes late."[80]

EL MUNDO.

TOMO. II   MEXICO, OCTUBRE 24 DE 1897.   NUMERO 17.

Más vale horas antes que minutos despues.

Por Villasana.

4. Better hours early than minutes late. *El Mundo (Semanario Ilustrado)*,
October 24, 1897.

Railway travel was used discursively and symbolically by
newspapers, journals, and weeklies to stress the ideals of mid-
dle- and upper-class society. Values such as politeness and punctuality were showcased in the literature of locomotive travel.
These accounts also reveal that Porfirian writers and artists were

not only concerned with inculcating these principles among the lower classes,[81] but that these values were also highlighted in publications targeted at primarily elite audiences. Elite groups sought to shape *all* Mexican citizens through the promotion of so-called modern, civilized, and capitalistic sensibilities while also allowing writers to reaffirm their own class and self-definition. Considering the portrayals of provincial and third-class travelers, these works sharpened the distinction between classes and placed the elite as moral and behavioral models for the rest of society.

Despite all the discussion about the railway's redemptive capacity to reshape behaviors and values, travel literature at times demonstrated a deep sense of fear toward the social and cultural changes spurred by modernization. The experience of traveling in close quarters with strangers was sometimes portrayed as a dangerous activity that could put unsuspecting, innocent passengers in harm's way. While there were no highly publicized murders on Mexico's railways as there were in Europe,[82] the emergence of both satirical and serious literature on the dangers of locomotive travel were published nonetheless. Moreover, most tales printed in journals about the risk of encountering nefarious characters in the train compartment were European imports, usually from France or Spain. Despite the fact that these were foreign narratives, their publication in Mexican periodicals suggested some of the same concerns about the close proximity of strangers in the railway compartment.

El Mundo (Semanario Ilustrado) published a French import about a man traveling on the Lyon railway. Riding in a first-class compartment, the passenger found himself trapped with a gun-wielding lunatic who confessed to murders he had committed. The lunatic, convinced he could fly, disrobed and prepared to jump out the train window. The passenger, realizing that the train was only eleven minutes from reaching the next stop, stalled the crazed man until it pulled into the station. There the lunatic, not having realized where he was, jumped out the window, only to land in the arms of medics who awaited the escaped patient.[83] This story found its Mexican counterpart in El Buen Tono's cigarette advertisement, which played on the fear of fellow coach passengers. Printed in *El Mundo Ilustrado*, it suggested to readers that a fine quality of smoke might save one's life.

Strangers were forced to share space in a way that older methods of travel did not allow. Older forms of travel such as the stagecoach or horse were usually done in groups with acquaintances, friends, or family as a way to mitigate the dangers of highway travel. The railway journey changed the intimacy of travel, especially for the middle and upper classes, who could afford to travel alone in first-class compartments, both as a result of their economic means but also because of the inherent safety of the railway itself that mitigated the need to travel in groups. Thus a contradiction emerged where the safety of the railway journey that allowed for individuals to travel alone was undermined by the traveler's forced confinement with strangers. Moreover, the tale discussed above suggested to readers that a keen sense of timekeeping might save passengers from dangerous situations.

The fear of strangers did not always put the protagonist of stories in immediate danger. The protagonist might share the train compartment with a nefarious individual while not experiencing any threat whatsoever. Nevertheless, these types of narratives reveal similar fears regarding the unknown fellow traveler. In one such tale, imported from Spain and published in *El Mundo (Semanario Ilustrado)*, a man found himself sharing a railway carriage with a young woman whom he described as elegant and alone. Looking out the window, he examined the changing landscape while he contemplated how he might gain the attention of the young woman across from him. Debating a variety of ways that he could strike up an exchange, the man failed to muster the courage to speak to her. Then, breaking the awk-

5. El Buen Tono Company plays on fear in the compartment to sell cigarettes. *El Mundo Ilustrado*, December 11, 1904.

ward silence between them, the woman addressed him, asking whether he would be willing to pick up a package for her at the next station. He obliged and retrieved her parcel at the next stop. As they chatted, she asked him about the approaching tunnel. He explained that it would be extremely dark and would take about a minute to cross. The woman appeared frightened and asked the man to open the window, and again the young man obliged. Just before they passed through the tunnel, the woman took out a baby wearing exquisite diapers from the parcel, kissed it on the head, and, as the train roared through the dark tunnel, threw it out the window to its death. The man, seeing what had happened, initially thought of denouncing the young woman to the authorities before he realized that he would have no proof against her and that he was the only witness of the baby in the parcel. The story ends in a cloud of mystery with the man sitting in silence for the next thirty minutes until both passengers reach their final destination.[84] While the story was vague about the exact relationship between the woman and the child—although it seemed to suggest that she was an upper-class woman who had a baby out of wedlock—it offers some valuable insights about the fears of shifting social and gender relations that emerged with modernization.

This story offered readers a negative view of the consequences of a world turned upside-down through the reversal of gender roles, a reversal that took place in, and was allowed by, the privacy and close quarters of the railway compartment. The tale evoked a fear that modern life, as symbolized through railway travel and gender reversal, broke down the known rules of social interaction. The mysterious woman was not a passive sexualized object. She engaged the man in conversation, made him the subject of her bidding (picking up the package), and even turned him into an accomplice in the child's murder (opening the carriage window). This story, while an exaggerated narrative, nevertheless surely hoped to elicit a strong reaction from readers about the possible consequences of modern life. It suggested some of the fears about the changing roles of women—in this case, the independent woman who by traveling alone had entered into the public realm—that undermined established relations between the sexes as well as a weakening of the family structure. Furthermore, the man could not rely on the usual indicators of social position based on her outward appearance—she was well dressed, polite, and wealthy. In the era of mass consumption and mass transportation, these older and, for men, comforting assumptions needed to be jettisoned.[85]

Railroads and Sexual Desire

Publications stressed how the railway compartment undermined traditional notions of female prudence, especially regarding sexual desire. The privacy of the railway compartment was characterized, again both satirically and seriously, as a space where social norms could be ignored by both men and women. It provided travelers with a private space where sexual desire could be acted upon without the fear of public scrutiny. Yet, in this way, the railway compartment introduced travelers to a new kind of space, one that linked both public and private realms. While the compartment—that is, of course, the first-class compartment—could be isolated from public view, it was also clearly situated in the public realm insofar as it brought together strangers who traveled alone. When writers discussed this phenomenon, especially the close confinement of members of the opposite sex, it either aroused humorous depictions of male sexual desire or dark anxieties about female sexual awakening.

La Crónica Mexicana published a story in which travelers discussed the differences between stagecoach and railway travel. In the railway compartment two men discussed the fear of derailment, a misfortune that concerned people new to industrial travel. One traveler lamented that railroad accidents created human hecatombs that made "tortillas" out of passengers.

Then the conversation suddenly turned to a racier topic. Another passenger told his companions that he missed the intimacy of the stagecoach that allowed male travelers to take advantage of being in close quarters with women. He explained the stagecoach's advantages vis-à-vis the railway:

> Above and beyond making good and solid masculine friendships, one can enter into equally enjoyable relationships with women. It was common then to travel packed into the carriage. . . . Even the most inexperienced and least advised chap came out a master in the matters of love as a result of the inevitable and regular contact made with the female companions that shared the limited confines of the stagecoach and its constant gyrations.

To which his fellow traveler replied:

> Don't fool yourself, friend. . . . In the locomotive ones can enjoy themselves in the same manner . . . and when there are two willing participants they do so . . . in the end, there are tunnels . . . and there can even be acts of foolishness committed without risk, acts that in the stagecoach would have come at a cost.[86]

The traveler suggested that the railway journey allowed for a more fleeting romance between men and women. While stagecoach travel might provide a favorable environment for courtship because of the amount of time spent in the carriage—not to mention the opportunities to take advantage of bumps in the road to catch a falling woman or to fall upon a woman—the railway's speed, as well as the privacy and darkness provided by the tunnel, was understood as giving men and women the opportunity to engage in less serious, ephemeral forms of romance, relationships made possible by the railway's compression of time and space. The scene ends with the speaker noticing that his friend, as well as another elegantly dressed young man, had shifted his attention to a pair of beautiful women who shared the compartment where they conversed.

The use of the tunnel by men and women to undertake acts of sexual transgression was another common theme among writers and artists. One cartoon indicated that while men might be the aggressors, women also took advantage of the complete privacy offered by the darkness of the tunnel.

The connection between locomotive travel, especially the experience of mechanical agitation, and sexual arousal emerged as a subject of analysis for nineteenth-century psychiatry. Sigmund Freud and Karl Abraham, for example, argued that the passengers' experience and fear of unstoppable motion out of their control was paralleled with the sensation of their own sexuality racing unrestrained.[87] The story from the *Crónica* discussed above demonstrates that Mexican authors viewed a connection between sexual arousal and locomotive travel. Like Freud's theories regarding industrial travel, which emphasized the stimulation of prepubescent male sexual longing,[88] the literature regarding railway travel portrayed males as the most common subjects of sexual arousal on the railway. Concurrently, in the United States, physicians debated about whether or not railway travel's supposed capacity to induce orgasms in women should be used to heal female hysteria.[89] Women, at the same time, were often portrayed as targets of men's sexual advances, making railway travel a dangerous activity insofar as it might jeopardize their respectability, suggesting that good, virtuous women should not travel alone.[90]

But the theme of sexuality and railway travel was not only discussed in terms of the arousal of male desire. Literature about railway travel also portrayed young woman as susceptible to sexual awakening on the locomotive. "La niña se transforma en mujer" (The girl becomes a woman), another story published in *El Mundo (Semanario Ilustrado)*, related to its readers the possible socializing effects of the railway journey on young women. The author told the story of Emma, a teenage girl who, taking the train for the first time, witnessed her cousin, the locomotive's

6. In the train. "Hands to yourself, friend, at least wait until we reach the first tunnel." *El Mundo Cómico*, May 29, 1898.

engineer, saying a sad good-bye to his newlywed wife moments before he pulled the train out of the station. The young couple embraced and kissed in the engineer's car as the wife, with tears welling in her eyes and trying to hide her sorrow with incoherent words and smiles, failed to conceal the sadness she felt because of her husband's departure. Emma, almost voyeuristically, could not take her eyes off the scene. Later, as Emma rode in her comfortable first-class coach, she spent day and night thinking about the moment shared between the young couple at the station. Emma, obsessed with the scene she witnessed, could not sleep and was constantly awakened by agitating and feverish dreams about the embrace and kiss she observed. In her dream she envisioned that she too had formed a blessed nuptial and that her beloved husband was also about to embark on a long journey away from her. Like the sad wife at the station, Emma also exchanged amorous kisses with her beau immediately before the train pulled out of the station. Then, after the account of her dream, the author immediately shifted his description to the movement of the train that soared and, as he explained, put Emma's life in imminent danger. Suddenly, the young woman awoke alarmed and screaming. Emma's mother, finding her daughter trembling and crying, questioned her about what had happened. Emma, lying to her mother for the first time, said she had had a nightmare. For the rest of her journey, she was racked by guilt. The story ends with the author stating that the "caterpillar had transformed into a butterfly."[91]

Again, literature about railway travel targeted to elite audiences emphasized the interconnection between the passenger's sensation of an inability to control sexual desire and an inability to control the train's movement as described by Freud's theories. The story hints that the hurried pace of modern life, represented by locomotive travel, could even accelerate the development of a teenage girl into womanhood. These stories crafted by middle- and upper-class writers suggested not only that the railway accelerated conventional notions of time but that it could also accelerate personal time, prematurely transforming individuals into sexual beings. Moreover, while the awakening of sexual desire in men tended to be described as taking place with little repercussion, the story of Emma implied that the arousal of sexual desire in women could have more harmful consequences, a theme likewise articulated in the Spanish tale of the mysterious woman's infanticide published in that same journal three years earlier. In this case, the lie she told her mother, and the guilt she experienced as a result, undermined the family bond through her sexual awakening. These stories make known the gendered understandings of sexual desire that accepted, and at times encouraged, men to fix their gaze on women in public, viewing men's libidinal awakening with amusement while women's was seen as unsettling or dangerous. Women's presence in the public realm, outside the boundaries of the home, threatened the idealized unity and hierarchy of family life.

Conclusion

During the 1880s and 1890s, a surge in the production of literature about railways and railway travel took place in Mexico. Fictional and nonfictional writings—stories, poems, editorials, travel journals—published in periodicals that targeted middle- and upper-class readers demonstrated the elite's attitudes about the rapid modernization experienced under the leadership of Porfirio Díaz, a period of unprecedented political peace and economic growth. The railway, the ultimate symbol of progress, proved to be a powerful icon used by a wide range of publications, including government-subsidized, independent, Catholic, and women's journals, to discuss the delights and displeasures that people viewed as resulting from the economic, social, and cultural transformations taking place around them. The often contradictory responses that elite writers expressed toward railway development in poetry, fiction, and popular art reveal an ambivalent response to the societal transformations spurred by modernization.

These writings allowed elite, urban Porfirians to define themselves as modern citizens and to diffuse ideas about the benefits of progress, the success of the governing regime, and the ways that civilized individuals should behave. In so doing, they sought to inculcate—or, perhaps if we consider the emotive language used in much of these works, seduce—modern values such as proper etiquette, hygiene, and punctuality not only to the lowest orders of society but also among themselves. The stories, poems, and travel journals printed in elite publications reveal that the middle and upper classes sought to convince themselves about the necessity of promoting social and economic development along European lines as much as they tried to push these values among the working and lower classes. At the same time, these discourses allowed elite groups to legitimize their own sense of moral superiority and, in so doing, confirm their own social status.

Literature about the railway represented it as a tool capable of constructing a civilized society where economic expansion would lead to social peace and national unity, a theme that fit well with the positivist philosophy that shaped government policymaking. Not surprisingly it was frequently *científico* and pro-government publications that stressed this subject matter. The general sense of enthusiasm and self-confidence about the strides the country had made toward becoming modern, discussed by both supporters and detractors of the regime, especially in the genre of travel literature, highlighted the successes of Díaz's presidency. As has been shown throughout this chapter, women's journals played an important role in this project, bringing to light an underexplored topic of Porfirian history—that is, an examination of the ways that bourgeois women, commonly excluded from participation in national discussions about science and technology, endeavored to engage with, and contribute to, debates about how those issues related to economic and national development. Moreover, the use of poetry and artwork to celebrate the railway's utopian capacity to reform society reflects the role of cultural communications in decimating ideas about political and economic projects such as transportation development. These cultural works reveal people's emotive, sensual reactions to the arrival of the railway that transformed it into a magical object able to cure a wide range of national ills that had plagued the country for a half century.

These sources also allowed writers and readers to discuss the aspects of modernization that they found distasteful or frightening. The increased presence of Americans, the arrival of provincials to the city, the persistence of so-called backward pastimes, the annoyances and fears posed by strangers, and the appearance of women in the public sphere all represented topics that writers tackled in their works. In so doing, they often exhibited a sense of ambivalence, and at times anxiety, toward the consequences of modernization. Yet the notable exception to this trend was women's journals that consistently interpreted the arrival of the locomotive in exceedingly positive and even romantic terms. Railway poetry allowed elite women to participate in public discussions about science, technology, and national development, discursive arenas clearly outside the domestic realm. For men, in contrast, the arrival of the railway and the transformation it seemed to spur in their understandings of public and private, time and space, and past and present, generated angst among sectors of middle- and upper-class observers who acknowledged the redemptive and utopian potential of transportation development while simultaneously expressing apprehension about the social and cultural ambiguities that emerged as a result. The intimacy of the railway compartment, to many writers, appeared to foster the collapse between public and private and feminine and masculine spaces as well as the relationship between past and present. Writers often described the railway journey into the provinces or the arrival of provincials to the city in a manner that isolated the past as remote and distant while relying on it to define the sensibilities of the modern present and possibilities the future might offer. Together, and above all, rather than reveal an unbounded enthusiasm for the railway as a symbol of economic and material progress, these accounts demonstrated the contradictory impulses of fear and allure that people held toward the sociocultural changes spurred by modern life. While the cultural productions examined in this chapter make known some of the elite's conflicted feelings toward modernization, official statecraft offered a much more consistent discourse that celebrated the utopian promises of the railroad. These sentiments were expressed most clearly in government-sponsored pageantry, the topic discussed in the following chapter.

THREE

Festivals of Progress
The Railroad Ceremony

Hail to Progress! Hail to the powerful
Century of Reason, which ignites and fills
The cosmos with its brilliant breath!
From the clean, blue, vast and calm
Expanse of astral spaces,
To the bed of sand
Where the seas sleep in silent solitude.

It floods everything with a divine flash,
The omnipotent and sovereign power
That has showered with laurels the path
Of this century: human intelligence!
Hail to the steep mountain ranges,
And the deserts and the ocean deep,
The word and the voice, there are no more boundaries!

> JUAN DE DIOS PEZA, *La inauguración del
> ferrocarril de San Luis Potosí*

On November 20, 1892, the polite society periodical *México
Gráfico* covered President Díaz's participation in the inaugural
run of the Durango-Oaxaca Railway. The reporter declared that
the recent inaugurations of several railway lines pumped new
blood into the nation, incubating national strength through the
development of commerce and industry. He detailed people's sin-

cere, unbridled enthusiasm for the "festivals of progress" that proved the country's civilization and bright future. This sort of exuberant sentiment expressed about the arrival of the locomotive was a common phenomenon during the Porfiriato.

Railway expansion represented the most important infrastructural development to take place during the Porfiriato.[1] As such, the inauguration of new lines generated great fanfare. National and local leaders took advantage of the ceremony, as well as other civic festivities that featured the locomotive, to celebrate the progress that their country had made.[2] Railway inaugurations and other public celebrations provided elite groups with opportunities to use symbolic rituals in an attempt to secure and legitimate the rule of Porfirio Díaz and to impart didactic lessons on observers about the values and mores they believed individuals should cherish. Above all, event organizers, and the press that covered these festivities, celebrated the success of the government in making its mantra of "order and progress" a reality.

Organizers typically ordered the inauguration ceremony into four parts employed to evoke popular enthusiasm: the arrival of the inaugural train, usually carrying the guests of honor; a civic procession across the city's principal streets and to important buildings; a lavish banquet dedicated to the guests of honor; and a gala ball that often carried on until the early morning hours. *Ayuntamientos* (town councils) often coupled these events with regional expositions that showcased local products and commodities. An essential aspect of the railway inauguration, as well as civic ceremonies that involved the locomotive in one way or another, was the invitation extended to the press. Reporters routinely rode on the inaugural train, covering the events for readers of the government-subsidized press and elite periodicals.

These events allowed middle- and upper-class Porfirians to celebrate the values they believed had lifted their country out of the political turmoil and economic backwardness that had characterized it since Independence in 1821. They presented and lauded ideals that they felt corresponded to a liberal, capitalistic, and progressive nation. The railway inauguration allowed the governing regime to disseminate these values through symbolic acts of pageantry and to justify the government's growing authoritarianism and its violations of the Constitution of 1857, especially the article of no reelection. This considered, it is not surprising that railway inauguration ceremonies became more spectacular as well as more didactic after 1888, the year of Díaz's first consecutive reelection.

Public celebrations created a sacred aura around liberal, positivist values as well as around the regime itself. The railway inauguration represented a modern form of liturgy that extolled the virtues of material progress and social order.[3] In the formulation of Mona Ozouf, a new order seeking to institute itself must make the very act of its institution sacred.[4] Public rituals allowed rulers opportunities to reshape people's basic beliefs and cultural values.[5] During the Porfiriato, railway inauguration organizers coordinated processions and appropriated religious language and imagery as a way to secure this connection. The association of the civic ceremony with religious symbols and metaphors represented a transfer of sacrality to social and political values in a manner that leaders hoped would resonate with ordinary people who attended and participated in these events.

While public festivals had long been used by dominant groups to express their beliefs regarding social organization and values,[6] the arrival of the railroad offered government officials and event organizers a dramatic new occasion to emphasize ideas of political stability, material progress, and national unity. Policymakers and the press exploited the symbolic power of the locomotive as an icon to represent the beginning of a new era and a new order. Yet despite their efforts, the signs and symbols used by the ruling elite could be manipulated and reinterpreted by social critics to highlight contradictions within the official discourse as well as perceived policy failures.[7] By using pageantry and symbols to draw attention to the successes of the regime, officials and organizers also heightened people's expectations of the government's responsibilities in terms of national development.[8] This chapter examines how railroad inaugurations helped to promote a cult of personality around Díaz that highlighted the *caudillo* as the nation's indispensable leader; a pervasive sense of national identity; an expression of conspicuous consumption and cosmopolitanism used to advance the country's image both nationally and internationally; and new values that the regime hoped to make sacred: social order, progress, and industry.

The Cult of Díaz

Governing officials actively sought to promote the image of the president as the nation's uncontested, and incontestable, patriarchal leader. This was not necessarily new. Before Díaz had ascended to power, Benito Juárez and his cabinet members had used the inauguration of a railroad line between Mexico City and Puebla to celebrate Independence in 1869. The festivities symbolically highlighted national progress, national unity, and Juárez's commitment to civilian rule and liberalism.[9] But railway ceremonies took on an added importance during the Porfiriato, as boosters of the regime employed them in an attempt to forge a "cult of personality" around Díaz.[10] The speeches and symbols deployed by organizers were framed within the discourse of patriotism and republicanism that advanced notions of citizenship and national identity. Through the construction of national monuments and the celebration of civic ceremonies, elite Porfirians hoped to foster a national character defined by modern values of social order, work ethic, and material progress.[11] The development of a national railway system provided ample opportunities for the regime to demonstrate its capacity to uphold these values as the railway both tangibly and symbolically linked all three. It promoted order through the government's ability to deploy troops to regions in rebellion, work ethic through its construction and new job opportunities, and material progress through the stimulation of the economy, connecting local and foreign markets. Members of Díaz's cabinet, state governors, local leaders, prominent businessmen, and the press all drew on railway inaugurations, as well as the *fiestas presidenciales* (presidential festivals) and the president's travels across the nation, to promote the cult of personality around Díaz. These events tied Díaz's career as a military hero and civilian leader to the country's turbulent history as he had allowed the nation to overcome its past economic and political turmoil, a success story where the railway's redemptive power played a central role.

Attempts to promote a cult of personality around Díaz first began during his second term as president in 1886 when an organization, the Society of Friends of the President, began preparations for his birthday. Then, in 1888, the National Porfirian Circle was formed to secure the repeated elections of the president.[12] These groups used national holidays to celebrate the successes of Díaz's presidency and honored his birthday on September 15 so that it could be combined with the commemoration of Mexico's independence from Spain. As Daniel Cosío Villegas noted, Díaz became "the flag of Mexican nationalism."[13] Symbolic acts such as the construction of monuments and the organization of elaborate state funerals for high-ranking officials became increasingly important to legitimate a government seeking to implement constitutional reform—in 1887—that allowed for the president's repeated reelection.[14] Railroad inaugurations throughout the country shared the symbolic linking of Díaz and the locomotive.

Yet before 1888, more often than not, railroad inaugurations received little fanfare. The 1880 inauguration of the line built between Mexico City and Amecameca received little coverage in the press and was not attended by any prominent politicians. Indeed, the only person of note to attend was Archbishop Pelagio Antonio de Labastida y Dávalos, who came to bless the railway as well as take part in the religious festivities at the Shrine of Sacromonte.[15] The only events planned were bullfights and cockfights.[16] Similarly, the 1882 inauguration ceremony organized for the arrival of the Mexican Central Railroad in Querétaro received little national attention. A short commemorative book made no mention of Manuel González, Porfirio Díaz, or the national government's accomplishments in securing railway development. Instead, it praised the state government's sincere patriotism and desire for progress.[17] The event proved to be in sharp contrast to the lavish ceremonies that took place years later.

The completion of the Mexican Central Railroad on March 8, 1884, that took place in Zacatecas likewise received little ceremony despite the fact that its completion represented a major accomplishment, linking the nation's capital to the United States for the first time. The track's builders, organized in four divisions starting at four points along the planned route,[18] finally met in Zacatecas, where they laid the last spike. Although some celebrations had been planned to correspond with Cinco de Mayo (May 5, a commemoration of the 1862 victory over the invading French army at Puebla), when the momentous occasion arrived, no major celebrations took place.[19] Instead, on May 10, a small group of U.S. railway investors were received by government officials for a banquet at Chapultepec Park in honor of Thomas Nickerson, president of the Mexican Central. Speeches made by participants made no mention of the work of either current president Manuel González (1880–84) or former president Díaz. The banquet also received little attention in the press. The only significant news story regarding the affair lambasted Nickerson for failing to attend the banquet. In it, the writer stated that Nickerson and his "stupid colleagues" had behaved like "true Yankees," failing to express any gratitude.[20]

In the few celebrations that did take place during the presidential interregnum of Manuel González, a period of major railway construction, Díaz often received as much praise as the sitting president during the inauguration ceremonies. The completion of a railway between Mexico City and Cuautla, Morelos, in 1881 prompted a celebration in which President González and Díaz (recently having resigned his position as minister of economic development to be elected governor of Oaxaca) were invited as the guests of honor. At the climax of the event, the master of ceremonies offered both González and Díaz a ceremonial crown on behalf of the people of Morelos. The crowd erupted into a frenzy of applause.[21]

One year later, during the inauguration ceremony celebrating the Mexican Central Railroad's arrival in Guanajuanto, the governor ended his speech by lauding Generals González and Díaz for working to realize Alexander von Humboldt's prophecy that Mexico would become the bridge of the world's commerce.[22] Díaz's success at pushing forward railway contracts despite considerable congressional opposition eventually received acclaim from local and state leaders as the most significant achievement of his presidency, especially taking into account Sebastián Lerdo de Tejada's failures in that aspect of policymaking.[23] Even during the presidency of González, people continued to associate Díaz with the success of the railway program. Díaz cultivated his image as a railway promoter during his brief governorship of Oaxaca (1881–82) during the interterm presidency of González, setting in motion the construction of the Tehuantepec Railway, his so-called pet project.[24]

The federal government's lukewarm participation in railway inaugurations changed during Díaz's second presidential term. The two most extravagant and didactic opening ceremonies—in Guadalajara and San Luis Potosí—were organized during the last year of Díaz's second presidential term and the year he would seek his first consecutive reelection. Officials took advan-

tage of the symbolic power of the inauguration to garner support for Díaz, a project that had become all the more important with Díaz's flouting of the 1857 Constitution's no reelection
clause. The railway inauguration provided a prime opportunity
for members of the governing regime to highlight the necessity
of reelecting Díaz in order to secure continued national development. Indeed, by his third reelection in 1892, he would become known as El Necesario (the indispensable one).

The public enthusiasm generated by railway inaugurations
often prompted outpourings of support for Díaz. At the 1888
inauguration for the Mexican Central line reaching Guadalajara, 70,000 people gathered at the train station not only crying
out "Vivas!" (Long Live!) to Jalisco, to Mexico, and to the locomotive as the "messenger of progress," but also to Díaz and the
government.[25] Likewise, that same year, at the San Luis Potosí
inauguration for the completion of the Mexican National Railroad, Díaz's presidential train arrived to throngs of enthusiastic
supporters as well as a triumphal arch decorated with flowers
and reading: "Viva el Gral. Porfirio Díaz" (Long live General
Porfirio Díaz).[26] Another reporter noted that, even in the dead
of night, at every station on the way to San Luis Potosí, crowds
of people, accompanied by military bands playing the national
anthem, awaited the president's locomotive shouting "Vivas" to
Díaz, repeatedly waking the sleeping passengers.[27] Reverence to
Díaz represented a central aspect of the inauguration ceremony. The name and image of Díaz were invoked—even when he
was unable to attend—in an effort to harness popular enthusiasm for railway development in support of the regime.

The Porfirian press's coverage of inauguration ceremonies
proved a serviceable tool in disseminating the belief among Mexicans that national development would be impossible without
Díaz and, in so doing, helped promote the cult of personality
around him. El Partido Liberal, a newspaper that received subsidies from the administration,[28] covered railway inaugurations

with greater depth and zeal than any other publication, suggesting that editors for the pro-government organ recognized the symbolic power of these events. Through civic celebration and then its coverage in the press, boosters of the regime—both event organizers and news reporters—reached a wide audience. Indeed, considering the country's low literacy rates, news reports mainly targeted middle- and upper-class audiences. Yet the dramatic visual expression of the inauguration ceremony could reach a broader group of people.

For the 1888 inauguration ceremonies in San Luis Potosí, *El Partido Liberal* produced a month of coverage.[29] The journalist, who traveled with the entourage that accompanied Díaz, reported on the enthusiastic crowds that the presidential train received at every stop, the generous *hacendados* that provided lavish lunches, and the various events planned in San Luis Potosí. The climax of the celebration, for the reporter, came when a banquet was held in honor of Díaz and the state's governor, Carlos Díez Gutiérrez. There Díez Gutiérrez stood and toasted the president, dedicating to him a long, laudatory speech. The governor praised Díaz's patriotism to the nation, as a hero in both war and peace, demonstrated by his civic virtues and his success in completing public projects. He then stated that, this considered, when the debates regarding his reelection arose, he had no doubt about the absolute necessity of Díaz's return to the presidency. He told the crowd that reelection equaled peace and peace equaled the glory of the nation's *pueblos*. Ending his address, he declared that his *pueblo*, the *potosinos*, agreed with this sentiment as they voted unanimously for the return of Díaz, something he argued was confirmed by the multitude of classes that had come to praise Díaz during the week's revelry.[30] The San Luis Potosí inauguration ceremonies, held only months after Díaz's first reelection, offered an opportunity for the ruling elite to legitimate the growing authoritarianism of the regime and its flagrant violations of the Constitution of 1857.[31] As the governor's praise indicated, the political elite were willing to sacrifice idealized democratic notions for national development, a process demonstrated most unmistakably by the railway project.[32]

El Hijo del Ahuizote, the regime's most persistent and vocal critic, recognized the ways that officials manipulated the inauguration ceremony to promote the reelection of Díaz. Writers for the weekly stated that the San Luis Potosí inauguration would be the first opportunity for the people to celebrate Díaz's metamorphosis into a "Constitutional King." In a mock report of the festivities, a journalist offered readers an account—surprisingly similar to the actual event—where Díez Gutiérrez supplicated himself in front of Díaz as he descended from the inaugural train. There Díez Gutiérrez, contemptuously referred to as Don Carlos X, recited a poem that transformed Díaz into a king and the governor into one of his vassals. Invoking the Noria Plan, Díaz's first failed revolutionary campaign based on the promise of no reelection, the poem highlighted the contradictions between the regime's discourse and its actions as he had flagrantly violated the pledge that would eventually bring him to power under the banner of Tuxtepec.[33] It also identified how officials exploited these civic ceremonies to justify violations of the Constitution of 1857, making *El Hijo del Ahuizote* a lone voice among the opposition in its critique of the government's use of pageantry. The celebration of Díaz as a patriot and nation-builder opened up opportunities for critics to attack the ways that the regime had not lived up to the promises of good government—at least as opponents defined it.

But it was not only inauguration ceremonies where the symbolic power of the railway could be harnessed. It appeared in other types of celebrations that sought to strengthen the cult of personality around Díaz. In the 1880s and 1890s, the regime felt most confident about the benefits it had secured across the nation—namely, the reduction of political turmoil, the high levels of foreign investment pouring into the nation, the boom in the export market, especially in the extractive industries, and the expansion of railroads and light industry. Elite Porfirians, during these celebrations, congratulated themselves for the progress attained and, in so doing, legitimated the rule of Díaz and the *científicos*.

Organizers repeatedly used the railway to cement the symbolic connection between Díaz and the development of the country. In 1887, the Escuela de Minas (Mining School), as well as military commanders, congressmen, and senators, arranged for a dance at the Buenavista Railway Station to commemorate the president's birthday. *El Partido Liberal*'s reporter noted that the station had been chosen to symbolize Díaz's contributions to the nation, namely, the establishment of progress and peace.[34]

Years later, the elite continued to use celebrations honoring Díaz to symbolically link the dictator to political stability and material progress. At a 1896 banquet celebrating the April 2, 1867, military victory that ended the French Intervention (along with May 5, 1862, it was one of two important battles where Díaz had played a role), a cross-section of the nation's wealthy and powerful, including many foreign representatives from banking, mining, agricultural, and railway interests, gathered to honor Díaz while dining on fine French food and drinking expensive champagne. Held in a Mexico City train yard that had been converted into a banquet hall, participants toasted the *caudillo*'s accomplishments. Organizers decorated the banquet hall to metaphorically highlight the mantra of the regime: "order and progress." At the extreme north end of the makeshift banquet hall, among the guests, stood a locomotive adorned by the flags of European and American nations. Across from the locomotive, at the south end of the hall, stood a giant statue of peace, represented by a woman holding an olive branch high in victory. Between both figures, behind the table of honor where the president sat, hung an oversized painting of Díaz, shaded by the country's flag. Organizers pushed a clear message: as the

Extremo Norte del Salón en el Banquete del 6 de Abril.

7. Artist's rendering of banquet held in honor of Porfirio Díaz at the Mexican Central Railroad's Buenavista station train yard. *El Mundo (Semanario Ilustrado)*, April 12, 1896.

nation's patriarch, Díaz represented the central figure around which peace and progress were established. Journalists for the polite society weekly, *El Mundo (Semanario Ilustrado)*, reproduced images of the event, as well as the speeches made in honor of Díaz, for their middle- and upper-class audience to further promote Díaz as the country's indispensable leader.

In particular, guest speakers praised the peace and progress that the nation enjoyed, celebrated Díaz's military achievements, and distinguished Díaz as the only man in Mexico capable of bringing together the powerful interests of agriculture, mining, banking, railways, and industry under one vision. In response, Díaz delivered a speech about the importance of commerce and industry for the country's regeneration. At the climax of his oration, he told the attendees that commerce was the heart of the social body and that rapid lines of communication represented the nation's arteries, carrying with them goods to be consumed by internal and external markets and thus breathing life into the moribund *pueblo*.[35] The loaded metaphor Díaz articulated allowed him to advance the legitimacy of his regime among both the national and foreign elite. And since Díaz had been placed between the symbols of peace and progress, his speech represented a self-congratulatory exercise that defined his presidential policies as giving life to the nation. Díaz's speech reflected the *científico* view that societies were "social organisms" and that often used biological metaphors when discussing the economy and the nation.[36]

Above all celebrations, the yearly fiestas presidenciales became sprees of self-congratulation employed to broaden the cult of personality around the president. At the 1901 celebration in Puebla, Díaz arrived on the Interoceanic Railway to a crowd of supporters. Puebla's *ayuntamiento* had the newly built Interoceanic train depot adorned with the flags of Mexico, Great Britain, and the United States placed atop its three towers. At the center of the building's outer façade hung a portrait of Díaz beneath the building's clock and above its main entrance. From there, the president toured Puebla's streets, which were decorated with fifteen hundred electric lights and three triumphal arches, the most splendid reading: "To the conqueror of yesterday, to the pacifier of today." Beneath the declaration, the initials P.D. were circled by imperial wreaths.[37] Again, organizers sought to draw symbolic links between Díaz and the railway in a manner that emphasized the connections between political stability, economic growth, and personal rule. The image offered a tour de force for a regime self-assured about the incontestability of the president at the turn of the century. It served to reinforce Díaz's new brand of liberalism that included permanent reelection, as well as a strong central government, two transformations that flew in the face of both the Constitution of 1857 and promises of the Revolution of Tuxtepec. The *científico* Francisco Bulnes had long justified the dictatorial rule of Díaz as a practical means of avoiding political chaos, comparing the president's rule to that of Caesar Augustus.[38] The use of imperial wreaths in honoring the president mirrored this kind of sentiment.

Four years later, the Society of Friends of the president celebrated his recent election with a massive parade in the nation's capital. Among the many allegorical floats displayed that day, one stood out to a reporter for *El Mundo Ilustrado* as the most original and splendid: the float representing the nation's railways. The allegorical car featured angels hovering over a locomotive with the name "Porfirio Díaz" printed on its smokestack. Of all the allegorical floats paraded that day, it was the only one to carry the name of the president.[39] Using the railway as a symbol of economic and national development during civic celebrations had become common. The 1883 Independence Day celebration's most popular float, for example, depicted a locomotive emerging from a tunnel and Lady Liberty crowning the symbol of progress.[40]

Díaz's opponents mocked the ceremonies to highlight how organizers manipulated the Fiestas Presidenciales in order to secure support for the dictator. In fact, *El Hijo del Ahuizote*, referring to them as "Las Fiestas Ferro-Presidenciales" (Presidential Railway Festivities) called attention to the government's use of the railway in these festivities as a tactic to garner support from local and state officials. In one poem, a writer for the weekly firebrand suggested that the railway's inaugural ceremonies were more about securing loyalty to Díaz than national development:

> Many of the chiefs
> Said that they were joyful:
> Good Heavens!! It is always good
> To lay down a railway
> And offer the *caudillos*
> One hundred thousand invitations, . . .
> To throw a party
> Railway-Presidential:
> [The governor] does not want
> Neither Limantour nor Baranda to go,
> It has to be Don Porfirio
> Because he's so upright and honest.[41]

The promotion of a cult of personality around Díaz was continued, and strengthened, into the late Porfiriato. The inauguration of the Tehuantepec Railway in 1907 marked an important infrastructural feat, since the completion of that inter-ocean route had been planned since 1880, only to encounter severe obstacles until the minister of finance, José Y. Limantour, handed over the contract to Weetman Pearson and his British construction company. The inauguration ceremonies for the Tehuantepec Railway took on an added significance, since the completion of that project represented both the sovereignty and prosperity of the nation. The administration, and especially Limantour, granted the contract to Pearson in an attempt to counterbalance growing U.S. control over the country's economy. Thus the Tehuantepec Railway represented an important marker to assuage the nationalist concerns among government officials, political dissidents, and popular sectors in the late Porfiriato as well as a symbol of economic prosperity as it linked the nation to markets in both the Pacific and Atlantic Oceans.[42]

While several newspapers covered the event and the president's travels to Oaxaca and Veracruz to observe the inauguration, no publication covered the event with the enthusiasm of *El Mundo Ilustrado*. Editors for the polite society magazine offered readers an array of photographs of the newly built railway, the ports at Salina Cruz and Coatzacoalcos, and the first cargo ship—the *Arizona*—to deliver goods to those ports. The reporter covered the inauguration event, including a dance in honor of Oaxaca's governor, Emilio Pimentel, where the wives of the attendants donned *tehuana* dresses (so-called traditional Oaxacan clothing). The following day, the president, along with members of his cabinet and Weetman Pearson, presided over the loading of a cargo ship at the port of Coatzacoalcos. There the president received a silver and gold key to commemorate the event before receiving a laudatory speech from Coatzacoalcos's *jefe politico* (political boss). The speech ended with the familiar and often repeated celebration of Díaz's success at fostering peace throughout the country, a fundamental prerequisite, he informed listeners, for the progress of all nations. Díaz ended the day's celebrations by attending another inauguration, this time the opening of the Coatzacoalcos Electric Company.

The inauguration of the Tehauntepec Railway also received attention in Mexico City, where El Buen Tono cigarette company released a commemorative cigarette case bearing the image of the white-haired president decked out in full military regalia.[43] As was the case in the United States, business interests took advantage of civic ceremonies to advertise their products.[44] While capitalizing on the enthusiasm cultivated by the completion of the Tehuantepec project, El Buen Tono also played on the cult of personality around Díaz, portraying him as the indispensable leader who secured peace and, as a result, material progress.

While it is difficult to gauge how the general public understood the symbolic meaning of these civic ceremonies, event organizers and government officials put forward a clear message they hoped would resonate: technological advancement, a develop-

8. Commemorative El Buen Tono cigarette pack for the inauguration of Tehuantepec Railway. *El Mundo Ilustrado*, January 27, 1907.

ment essential to material progress, was inextricably linked to Díaz as the country's patriarch, the only man capable of maintaining political stability. Not only did these events further the belief that national progress had been attained through the president's efforts as a hero in both war and peace, but its continued progress rested solely on his unwavering guidance. As the undisputed leader, Díaz provided a unifying image for the country and, in so doing, advanced the idea of *patria*, or nationhood, among Mexicans.

Nation-Building

The inauguration ceremonies allowed the ruling elite to foster, both rhetorically and symbolically, the construction of the nation. In this way, they endeavored to overcome one of the fundamental problems that had plagued its kaleidoscopic governments since Independence: the lack of social cohesion or, put another way, the lack of national unity and national identity.[45] The ruling elite sought to create a sense of a shared history through the construction of national monuments such as the statue of Cuauhtémoc and patriotic rituals such as the centennial of Mexican Independence.[46] These events served to foster a collective memory that emphasized people's shared past, present, and future. Whereas the building of statues and the commemoration of battles provided the opportunity to celebrate a common history, the railway inauguration allowed people to take pride in their nation's current progress as well as the bright future offered by the locomotive.

These festivals of progress also introduced Porfirians to different states and cities across the country and, in so doing, fostered a more intimate sense of national unity in a tangible manner.[47] Individuals could actually learn about the geography, history, and traditions of different regions as well as know that other citizens were taking part in such festivities. The press's coverage of these events played a crucial role in diffusing ideas about nationhood, especially among the literate middle and upper classes. These civic ceremonies shared specific aspects of nation-building exercises such as the singing of the national anthem, the use of flags, and, above all, the involvement of the nation's undisputed leader and unifying icon: Porfirio Díaz.[48] As has been demonstrated in the burial ceremony of Sebastián Lerdo de Tejada, when his body was carried across the country by railway, the locomotive afforded the opportunity for citizens of several states to join in honoring a national hero.[49] William Beezley, looking at the connections between popular memory and national identity, has demonstrated the importance of celebration and festivals in reinforcing a sense of nationhood on the collective imaginary. This was all the more important in a nation where low literacy rates hampered the ability of the printed word to help disseminate ideas and discussions about the nation.[50]

The railway became the vehicle that allowed people to more intimately familiarize themselves with their nation.[51] The locomotive introduced Mexico City's residents to the cities, towns, and *pueblos* that it snaked through not only by reading about these places in the press but also by visiting them for the inauguration ceremonies held in once prohibitively distant towns. For example, the 1888 railway inaugurations in San Luis Potosí and Guadalajara both received large numbers of visitors from Mexico City. In 1888, one newspaper noted that Mexico City had not celebrated the Day of the Dead (November 2) with its usual enthusiasm, since many people had traveled to San Luis Potosí for the inauguration of the National Railroad.[52] Conversely, provincial inhabitants could now more easily travel to the capital,[53] a phenomenon that led many urbanites to mock their behaviors and customs. One weekly joked about the popularity of railway inaugurations among the lower classes who, according to the author, attended not for their love of progress but for their love of free travel.[54] The railway allowed individuals to experience the diverse regions of the country, making the idea of nation more concrete. Porfirian Mexico's high illiteracy rates, then, were less important in the construction of a national identity, since individuals could experience the nation firsthand by traveling across it and thus did not necessarily have to be literate to experience a sense of *patria*.[55] By traveling to regions once difficult to reach, people could encounter fellow citizens who sang the same national anthem, shared similar customs, enjoyed similar pastimes, or faced similar hardships. At the same time, train travel could also introduce them to unknown traditions, different lifestyles, and diverse patterns of work and residency. In either case, the railway exposed individuals to a wider understanding of their nation beyond the confines of their locality.

Press coverage of railway inaugurations also sought to evoke a sense of pride. Reporters delighted in describing the beauty of the landscape when covering the inaugural run of a railway line. Writers especially focused on the ruggedness of the topography, emphasizing the engineering feats that had been accomplished in order to lay tracks across mountainous terrains. The inauguration of the San Luis Potosí–Tampico line in 1890 allowed writers to marvel at stunning panoramas. One Mexico City writer was awed by the gaping ravines and numerous waterfalls that he crossed, a scene he felt was too magical for words. He recounted how travelers sat glued to the windows contemplating the changing vegetation as the train descended into *tierra caliente* and how the landscape transformed itself from rolling plains to tropical forests. And when the train arrived in Tampico, a military band was playing the national anthem.[56] The press treated readers in Mexico City to glowing descriptions of the diverse landscapes of their country that while perhaps distant and alien to readers in the capital were nevertheless symbolically linked through the playing of the national anthem. Descriptions of the natural environment evoked pride in writers, and presumably readers, providing them with a symbol of the nation and national identity. Tourist brochures and travel literature also disseminated visions of the country's landscape and aroused national pride.[57]

In 1903 Díaz undertook several railway excursions across the nation to attend inaugurations, celebrate national holidays, and tour the provinces. In one such event, Díaz, his cabinet members, and various state governors undertook an excursion to Guanajuato, an affair that set off a statewide celebration. Leaving from Mexico City, the presidential Pullman car stopped at stations in Querétaro, Celaya, and Guanajuanto to greet scores of enthusiastic spectators who shouted *"Vivas!"* (Long Live!) and eagerly sought a glimpse of the nation's leader. In addition, a reporter noted that rural workers lined the railway between stations to pay homage to the man responsible for the expansion and exploitation of the country's riches. Indeed, the photographs provided by the journalist confirmed the fanfare, showing hundreds of *campesinos* wearing white muslin outfits and large straw sombreros following the president through the streets of Guanajuanto.[58] While middle- and upper-class readers in the capital could read about inauguration ceremonies, ordinary people in the provinces had the symbols of nation brought to them. The luxurious Pullman carried the president to Guanajuato from the capital, at once a symbol of national unity and the locus of national power in Mexico City.

In Querétaro the 1903 inauguration ceremony for a newly built trunk line of the National Railroad Company provided another opportunity for the ruling elite to symbolically link ideas of national unity and peace to the president. Pulling into Querétaro's railway station, Díaz's Pullman car carried him, his wife, Carmen Romero Rubio, and several high-ranking members of his administration, including José Y. Limantour (minister of finance), Ramón Corral (minister of the interior), and Leandro Fernández (minister of economic development). There, amid a mixed crowd sporting a range of outfits from Victorian top hats and coattails to white muslin, the presidential train passed through triumphal arches reading: "Welcome, Hero of Peace." That day Díaz would also inaugurate a newly built hospital before visiting the state's famed Hercules factory. Reporters for *El Mundo Ilustrado* noted that wherever Díaz went, throngs of people from all social classes cheered him as the "Hero of Peace."[59] The connection among railway development, political stability, and social order that was an often reiterated theme in both political discourse and popular culture clearly found expression in civic ceremonies. Linking the railway as a symbol of modernization with Díaz as a symbol of peace also represented an important aspect of the production of nationalism during the Porfiriato. In a country that had been a latecomer to industrial modernization, elite groups equated becoming a modern nation with economic development modeled on Europe and the United States.[60] The organizers of these festivities accentuated how material progress depended on the social and political stability that Díaz had established, an essential component in the construction of nationalism in economically underdeveloped countries.

The belief in the railway's ability to promote national unity could, at times, take on overtones of racial integration, albeit often framed by elite attitudes about the alleged shortcomings of Indians. The speeches delivered to the crowds attending the ceremonies emphasized how national integration through the railroad network would bring Indians into the national fold. At the inauguration of the railway linking the Federal District to Texcoco, Ignacio M. Altamirano, the country's greatest man of letters in the second half of the nineteenth century, offered a similar theme when he produced a two-part cover story of the event. In his flowery prose, he expounded on the town's Indian heritage as the ancient and splendid city of the Aztec empire and stated that today's indigenous population of that poor and moribund *pueblo* had no consciousness of its glorious past, which he identified with the great poet-king Nezahualcóyotl. The railway, he anticipated, would transform Texcoco into a city that would "forge an alliance between civilization and a prosperous future" by connecting it to other cities across the country as well as to the coast. He continued telling readers that Indians, once fearful of slavery and characterized by their misery, now demonstrated their desire to be brought into the nation. As proof he informed readers that the railway companies had hired Texcoco Indians to build the Morelos railway and that they had completed the project without delay.[61] Altamirano's prediction reflected the liberal belief in the market's capacity to reshape the values and mores of the indigenous population, just as liberals had believed in the 1860s that private property could awaken the individualist spirit among Indians through the expansion of the market and the creation of new labor opportunities.[62] By opening Texcoco to other markets both nationally and internationally, the locomotive would do the same. Altamirano's prose reflected his belief that Indians could be integrated into the nation as modern citizens, a belief that led him to support laws favoring obligatory public education across the nation and not only in the Federal District and major cities, as other *científicos* advocated.[63] For Altamirano, improved lines of communication provided a way for the government to reach once isolated Indian communities, allowing them to participate in, and not clash with, civilization.[64]

Altamirano's article reflected an idea discussed in the previous chapter, namely, that elite writers often explored the past in order to discuss the possibilities of the future.[65] In this case, the railway's regenerative potential would allow Indians to return to their former pre-conquest nobleness, offering them a future that matched their past. The celebration and pride of the country's Indian history provided liberal intellectuals with evidence that Mexico could rival European nations in terms of development and cosmopolitanism. Indeed, Vicente Riva Palacio's famed history, *México a través de los siglos*, a book reportedly born from the discussions of a group of intellectuals led by Altamirano, repeatedly noted the superiority of Indians to Europeans.[66] As the great pre-conquest empires of the Chichimeca and Aztec proved, Indians were inherently urban and hardworking, characteristics that Altamirano believed the locomotive would reawaken.

In 1888, at the inauguration of the Mexican Central trunk line to Zimapán, Carlos Pacheco, minister of economic development, called attention to the connections between the exploitation of natural resources and the locomotive. The Zimapán train stopped at local *haciendas* where crowds of ranchers and laborers greeted its arrival. At one point, Pacheco and his entourage stopped at a newly built sawmill on a *hacienda* where the group would enjoy a banquet. There, amid the noise of cheers and fireworks, James McDonald, an American in charge of the mill, helped by a group of Indian laborers, demonstrated the power of the sawmill as they used the machine to easily cut trunks of oak into cordwood length pieces. The Indian workers then carted off wood and loaded it onto the train.[67] Elite Porfirians, as Tenorio-Trillo has noted, showed ambivalence toward indigenous peoples insofar as they often celebrated the past feats of the Nahua while highlighting their perceived present-day racial inferiority,[68] inadequacies often discussed in terms of work ethic and morality.

National unity represented more than the locomotive's ability to compress time and space, bringing the country into closer communication. For some it also proved the expectation that indigenous groups could be brought into closer unity with the country's urban mestizo population. Framed by racist views about the alleged shortcomings of indigenous peoples, government officials, inauguration organizers, and the press used these civic ceremonies—much like the discussions and debates in Congress and the press in the early years of railway promotion—to stress the railway's capacity to unite the country's citizenry into one less divided between Indian and mestizo, rural and urban, or barbarous and civilized. Yet the emphasis on bringing Indians into the national fold seemed to have dissipated after 1888, perhaps a reflection of the growing influence of the *científicos* who, inspired by the work of Auguste Comte and ideas of social Darwinism, instead sought to promote immigration and race mixture as they had come to believe that the salvation of Indians rested on natural evolutionary forces.[69]

While government officials and the press portrayed the arrival of the railway as an event welcomed by all sectors of society, *corridos* demonstrate a less enthusiastic, albeit no less nationalistic, reception on the part of popular groups. *Corridos* reveal that lower-class groups interpreted economic development in a different light than the elite and, in so doing, challenged the elite's definition of progress and nationalism.[70] The songs dedicated to inaugural runs shared one specific criticism of the arrival of the train: railways were owned by U.S. companies and operated by U.S. workers. A *corrido* dedicated to the completion of the Mexican Central Railroad in 1884 in Zacatecas emphasized the so-called foreignness of the machine. Furthermore, it related to listeners that rich Americans—sometimes referred to as *güerros* (whiteys)—ridiculed Mexicans with their arrival on the locomotive:

> With a shiny ear trumpet
> at best, the passenger,
> can hear the hum
> of the foreign machine. . . .
> Aréchiga, my general,
> with the others in top hats,
> they welcomed the whiteys
> wearing pocket watches and long jackets. . . .
> They mocked us,
> the gringo salamanders,
> because we were struck dumb
> by looking at such a wondrous engine.[71]

The ballad criticized Zacatecas governor Jesús Aréchiga for catering to U.S. companies whose workers insulted Mexicans at every opportunity. The song referred to gringos as *ajoloteros*, perhaps an allusion to the pink burrowing salamanders, representing both the skin color of Americans as well as their penetration into the country. A *corrido* composed for the inauguration of the Mexican Central Railroad's arrival in Guadalajara likewise questioned the foreign ownership of the country's transportation network:

For here come the gringos,
with great satisfaction,
they come taking measurements
to raise their station. . . .
Girls of Jalisco,
the machine has arrived;
it would be better to have been brought
by the mother who bore you.[72]

The representation of the railway inauguration in popular culture evidently took on negative connotations regarding the United States' dominant presence in the project. At the same time, the arrival of the locomotive provided an opportunity for people to articulate nationalist sentiments. Composers and singers complained about the increasing U.S. presence. This conflicted with the elite's more standardized and totalizing attempts to forge a national identity, especially after the 1890s, which became increasingly narrow as it focused on promoting a more monolithic population as existed in Europe.[73] For some elite circles, the railway offered the chance to promote U.S. immigration as a way to whiten the nation.[74] These kinds of sentiments clearly clashed with popular understandings of national identity and the good of the nation.

Conspicuous Consumption

The Porfiriato introduced an era of peace and prosperity for the middle and upper classes. With it also began to emerge a society of consumers characterized by showy displays of wealth and status.[75] Polite society used the railway inauguration as a means of celebrating the material advancements of the nation as well as display the affluence they enjoyed as a result of Díaz's leadership. The press, especially illustrated weeklies, actively covered these gala events and reproduced photographic images—after 1900—to inform readers about the consumption choices of the elite. Targeted to a narrow audience, as few people could afford to imitate the country's fashionable bon ton, gaudy spectacles presented the elite with occasions to separate themselves from the common folk at a time when Mexico City's booming population had made interaction between classes all the more common.[76] The function of these events mirrored a variety of attempts by the elite to spatially, morally, and socially separate the upper and lower classes that included the construction of new neighborhoods away from working-class areas, the expansion of social spaces for the affluent, and the implementation of laws targeting the supposed immorality of lower-class groups.[77]

The 1888 inauguration of the Mexican Central Railroad line to Guadalajara provided the chance for an especially ostentatious display by the nation's plutocrats. In fact, the various events that took place between May 14 and May 18 were immediately published as a small volume by *El Diario de Jalisco*. The event began with a train of four first-class cars leaving Mexico City, carrying high-ranking politicians, foreign diplomats, and state governors. The culmination of the days' events was a buffet dinner and grand ballroom dance held at Guadalajara's prestigious Gran Teatro Degollado designed by the state's famed architect Jacobo Gálvez. There the reporter for *El Diario de Jalisco* noted that the event planners transformed an already lavish setting into a "true paradise." He gleefully described the room, commenting on the plush curtains artistically held in place by golden chains; the wall-to-wall flower decorations prepared in garlands, festoons, and bouquets; and the grand illumination of electric lights throughout the hall. The immense beauty of the ballroom led the journalist to conclude—perhaps missing the irony of his statement—that the event was a "giant dose of good taste," as no cost had been spared.[78]

But none of this compared to the open-air gallery and garden where the buffet would be served. The gallery, separated from the dance hall by three tremendous arches, accommodated a long

11.— Vestidos de viaje para señoritas jóvenes.

9. Women's railway wear. Travel attire available by mail order from Europe. *El Mundo Ilustrado*, April 28, 1903.

stretch of tables arranged with floral bouquets, candelabras, porcelain dinnerware, crystal goblets, and silverware. Further on, the garden was likewise the epitome of ostentation. In the center of the grounds stood a bronze fountain launching water into the air, a display made more fantastic by electric lights. Sand pathways diverged in all directions enclosed by an English garden. The opulence of the event led one participant to boast to reporters that the elegance surpassed even the most extravagant balls of the United States and Europe.[79] This statement revealed a belief in the country's emerging cosmopolitanism as the ostentation of the elite rivaled that of any modern society.

After dinner, the revelers prepared for a night of dancing the waltz, foxtrot, polka, and schottische, among other European dances. *El Diario de Jalisco*'s reporter described the evening gowns of more than one hundred of the aristocratic ladies who shared in the merrymaking. For instance, he described the wife of the U.S. plenipotentiary E. S. Bragg as having a pleasant and captivating beauty in her elegant black gown. Likewise, he admired Sra. Elvira Iñíguez de Cáñedo, whose dress he described as a turtledove brocade and *vert-du-mousse* velvet accentuated by her stylish pearl necklace, which was, according to the writer, worth a fortune. Ladies' attire took up one-fifth of the published account of the inauguration. The ostentatious consumption of goods and delight of leisure allowed polite society to define themselves as civilized in their tastes and activities—whether eating European foods, using fine silverware, or dancing the waltz. And, through the press's coverage of the event, the Porfirian elite could perform these values for middle- and upper-class readers. Moreover, it provided an opportunity for the elite to undertake rituals based on individualism and consumerism, an important aspect in the development of a capitalistic society.[80]

Along similar lines, when reporting on the inauguration ceremonies in San Luis Potosí, journalists took the time to detail the special railway attire, known as *cubrepolvos* (dust covers), worn by travelers. Examining the First Lady's apparel as she stepped down from the train at the station, one journalist commented on the elegance of her grey silk *cubrepolvo*.[81] The importance of proper attire for railway travel could also be found in

El Mundo Ilustrado's ladies' wear section. These dresses, available through special order from Spanish and French retailers, gave elite women the opportunity to display their wealth and status while traveling.[82]

The inauguration ceremony of the San Luis Potosí–Tampico line provided elite groups with another opportunity to flaunt their good taste, proper conduct, and refined elegance.

On the inaugural train ride, government officials — Carlos Pacheco was the highest ranking attendee — and other notables including members of Mexico City's press enjoyed the finest chilled drinks and wine, although as one reporter noted, most of the excursionists chose to refrain from alcohol. Then the travelers assembled in the Pullman dining car for an exquisite dinner. At a U-shaped table with golden candelabras and floral arrangements, the excursionists drank champagne served by an army of finely dressed waiters. After dinner, the national anthem was played before the group retired to their private cars. Arriving in Tampico, they attended a ball held at the state governor's country estate. At the entrance guests encountered a grotto accentuated by forty Venetian half-moon windows that transformed the room into a "gigantic crystal prism." Inside the grotto, an imitation English garden furthered the enchantment. From there, guests passed into the two main salons — their ceilings adorned with frescos — that were divided by a replica of a mountain range atop which the band performed. The guests, from that vantage point, could see a large fountain hurling ribbons of water into the air. The ornaments throughout the manor likewise revealed the high life of the elite. Flower arrangements, bronze statues, and stuffed wild animals adorned the various rooms of the summer retreat.[83]

While publications targeted at the elite reveled in their ostentation, magazines for a broader audience viewed these events quite differently. Less expensive humorous periodicals, for instance, used railway inaugurations to poke fun at elitism. *Las*

Novedades presented readers with a mock account where a reporter traveled with the presidential entourage to Guadalajara only to find disappointment at every turn. First, he realized that the event was much too expensive, as he could not afford a taxi, a hotel, or even food. He then attended the ball but realized that there was no one to introduce him to the beautiful women, and when the protagonist finally mustered the courage to introduce himself, he found that the young ladies had all been matched up with much wealthier gentleman. In the day's final disappointment, the hapless traveler could not afford a bite to eat, but succeeded in finding a piece of gelatin that "he ate in silence, soaking it in his bitter tears."

The following day, he attended a *soirée* where he could not afford an ice cream or a pack of cigarettes. Recognizing that the only amusement he could afford was to take a tram, he was nevertheless forced to ride in third class. He encountered his final disillusionment when the high society crowd attended a bullfight. He lamented the contradictions, stating that only in Mexico could a ceremony of progress be celebrated with an anachronistic activity such as a bullfight.[84]

Those critical of the elite's ostentatious displays of wealth repeatedly used irony to mock these ceremonies of self-congratulation.[85] Like the contradictions of attending a bullfight during a ceremony dedicated to civilization, the author also highlighted the contradictions of the social divisions between the nation's Victorian-inspired elite and the rest of the population. The author's comedic take on the events might also suggest a veiled criticism of the sycophantic subsidized press who attended the event and reported glowing accounts of the regime to readers while, as members of the middle class, they received far fewer benefits from the government's policies than the elite for whom these events were organized. *El Hijo del Ahuizote*, likewise, mocked the ostentation of the event when it produced a comic image of Victorian-styled politicians wearing suits and top hats welcomed by

El primer tren y la primera gorra.

10. The celebrations in Guadalajara. "The first train and the first freebie."
El Hijo del Ahuizote, May 20, 1888.

the state's governor, emphasizing the exclusivity and snobbery
of the festivities. The caption suggested that the elite were taking
advantage of the free food and entertainment offered by Guadalajara's organizing committee, suggesting the voracity and over-
indulgence of the elite.[86] For all the event's ostentation and pomp,
this artist highlighted the irony he viewed and depicted stingy
attendees indulging in the extravagance of the organizers.

Acts of conspicuous consumption, although sometimes mocked
in the popular press, revealed an important development in an
emerging capitalist society. These showy displays of wealth confirmed not only individual prosperity but also the nation's prosperity. It allowed the elite to demonstrate that their nation was
cosmopolitan and could match any European one in terms of
modernization and civilization. The railway inauguration provided an opportunity for elite groups to demonstrate the emergence
of a new system based on, and driven by, new values of consumerism. Government officials would require that this new system,
and by extension the regime that promoted these values, be invested with a sacredness as a means of securing legitimization.

Making the Regime Sacred

Inauguration ceremonies, often coupled with regional expositions that showcased local merchandise, allowed Mexicans to attend events that exhibited and extolled the development of national industries. Railway inaugurations in Querétaro, Guadalajara, Tampico, Veracruz, and a host of other cities organized regional expositions to coincide with the induction festivities. This is not surprising, as the arrival of the locomotive vastly increased the number of individuals from across the country who could attend, making an exposition viable. These events mirrored the rise of Europe's Universal Expositions during the nineteenth century where people traveled to view the newest commodities churned out in the industrial centers of Western Europe and the United States. Walter Benjamin interpreted these events as secular pilgrimages for commodity worship. These events were designed to entertain workers and, in so doing, emancipate them through their role as consumers.[87] In Mexico, Porfirians used the railway inauguration in the same manner. By traveling to railway ceremonies and then attending the regional expositions that often accompanied them, individuals could survey the various products of a region and, if possible, purchase them. While elite groups used inauguration ceremonies to flaunt their consumer choices and culturally separate themselves from hoi polloi, middle- and working-class groups could also participate in commodity worship. Ordinary Mexicans' participation at the same time revealed a divide in the consumer choices between the elite themselves and the rest of society. Affluent Porfirians made known their proclivity for foreign consumer products — French wines and European fashions and dances. Those ordinary people attending regional expositions explored, viewed, and purchased locally produced goods and, as such, had no choice but to develop an inclination toward national products. Thus the regional exposition created, as well as sharpened, the differences between class tastes and choices.[88]

One year before Querétaro's 1882 railway inauguration, for example, the *ayuntamiento* called on city residents to bring agricultural, mining, industrial, and artistic goods for an exposition that would take place concurrently with the event. They invited the nation's citizens to attend and view the products of local industry. The event showcased everything from locally made instruments to the newest gadgets in dentistry and medicine. The event organizers established a variety of commodity categories that could be exhibited at the exposition including works of art, modern art equipment, home accessories, textiles, foodstuffs, intellectual works for public education, mineral goods, natural resources, agricultural products, livestock, chemicals products, and machinery. The organizers boasted that these commodities represented all the necessities for the civilized individual.

The inauguration's program revealed that the event's organizers, the *ayuntamiento*, defined and promoted the ceremony and accompanying exposition as a sacred ritual. The program's introduction boldly stated that the arrival of the railway had erected an "august temple" dedicated to agriculture, mining, arts, and public education. The religious symbolism did not end there, as the introduction went on to praise the railway's redemptive qualities. It stated that in the temple of progress the enthusiastic hymns dedicated to the "sacred activity of work" could be heard, lifting that *pueblo* out of its misery.[89] The state's official newspaper, *La Sombra de Arteaga*, in a special edition published for the exposition, also used religious language and imagery when discussing the event. The reporter proclaimed that the exposition represented the triumph of science over religion. He stated that no longer would humanity be characterized by bloody crusades and cruel tribulations of faith. Instead, humanity would prosper under the banner of tolerance and the ideas made "sacred by the blood of Christ: liberty, equality, and fraternity."[90] Querétaro's leaders transformed the inauguration into a secular liturgy used to promote values of work ethic, production, and consumerism. They sought to persuade citizens to undertake pilgrimages to this so-called temple dedicated to progress.

Years later, the organizing council of the 1888 inauguration ceremony in Guadalajara also called on citizens to bring commodities for an exposition organized to correspond with the arrival of the railway.[91] The coupling of regional expositions with railroad inaugurations took place repeatedly throughout the Porfiriato. City and state leaders sought to take advantage of the railway to bring masses of consumers to their markets. The exposition thus realized the locomotive's capacity to unite distant markets and production zones with consumers across the Republic, offering, in the formulation of Walter Benjamin, a site for commodity worship.

The religious symbolism of the Querétaro railway inauguration was not an independent phenomenon. Other inductions for the locomotive used religious language to describe the benefits of railway development. The inauguration of the Mexican National Railroad in San Luis Potosí gave Jesús Ortiz, the proprietor of one of the city's largest newspapers, *El Correo de San Luis*, the opportunity to highlight the locomotive's sacred and redemptive qualities. In a special edition produced for the inauguration ceremony, Ortiz repeatedly used religious language to describe the arrival of the railway. He described the throngs of citizens arriving in San Luis Potosí as pilgrims coming to "receive the communion of progress."

Among the many poems produced for the special edition, "Ayer y hoy" (Yesterday and today) juxtaposed the anachronistic practice of building churches and convents with the modern practice of building railways and factories:

> Yesterday churches and convents were erected. Along the streets of San Luis Potosí strolled armies of monks, and their most beautiful daughters were cloistered nuns. The catechism of Father Ripalda was all the instruction the people received.

Today we build railways and raise factories: along the streets
popular demonstrations; men and women, singing hymns to progress and progressive men that have been lifted from ignorance, that
have been yanked from their abject state, educating and instruct-
ing them.[92]

The poet plainly stated that modern technologies had now
replaced the cathedral as the key to people's salvation. Rather
than blindly obey the Church, individuals would be lifted from
their wretchedness not by God but through positivist education
and work.

The railway inauguration provided a modern secular liturgy used to promote the values of the regime as well as to make
sacred Porfirian understandings of social order and function.
Above all aspects of the inauguration ceremony, the civic procession harkened back to the religious festivals of the colonial
era and, in so doing, provided national and local leaders with a
potent tool in inculcating new values of work ethic, social order,
and progress they hoped to make sacred. Like its religious colonial counterpart, the festivals of progress paraded the success
of the government to make onlookers feel optimistic about future prosperity and, in so doing, garner support for local, state,
and national leaders.[93] The civic procession was typically composed of various local groups—for example, foreign colonies,
professional associations, and military groups—who marched
through the city's main streets and visited important buildings
and sites. The processions undertaken during inaugural festivities highlighted elite notions about urban space and social order as well as the connections between the two.

The procession routes chosen revealed attempts to imbue city
space with a sense of sacredness.[94] In Querétaro, for example,
after the arrival of the inaugural train, the state governor led a
procession—sometimes referred to as Manifestación Patrióti-
ca (Patriotic Assembly)—from the railway station to the Al-

ameda.⁹⁵ Parading to the railway station and Alameda represented a common practice of inaugurations, as it underscored the connection between the state (represented by the Alameda) and material progress (represented by the railway station). The National Railroad's inauguration procession in San Luis Potosí followed a similar route from train depot to Alameda.

For the inauguration ceremony in San Luis Potosí, the event organizers made the civic procession one of the highlights of the week's merriment. After the arrival of the presidential train, organizers kicked off the inauguration with a civic procession of representatives of the city's neighborhoods divided into four groups, each led by a band. The group, which was reportedly more than 10,000 strong, paraded down the principal streets. The following day's festivities, likewise, began with a civic procession. But this time the procession was composed of San Luis Potosí's various educational institutions, again divided into groups and led by bands. One group of eleven schoolgirls carried with them a large portrait of President Díaz.⁹⁶

The choice of procession participants—city neighborhoods and educational institutions—suggests that event organizers sought to emphasize the involvement of an educated citizenry in the pageant. The symbolic meaning of that choice represented an attempt by liberals to replace Catholic ceremonies that stressed religious dogma and individuals' subjugation before God. Instead, the planners extolled the importance of citizenship—represented by the neighborhood organizations—and rational, enlightened, and progressive thought—represented by the educational institutions. Yet, at the same time, the centrality of Díaz's portrait in the procession indicates that organizers also wanted to place emphasis on the state as the new focal point of Mexicans' lives. As Mona Ozouf has demonstrated, the French revolutionaries came to rely on religious imagery and symbols when organizing festivities to impart Republican virtues.⁹⁷ In Mexico, government officials likewise borrowed from religious ceremony as it represented a constant part of most people's lives.

A final procession took place later that day made up of the city's foreign colonies and commercial, industrial, and scientific associations. The procession was divided into groups, each led by a band, like the two previous marches. Nevertheless, one difference did stand out: each section was also led by one of the town's foreign colonies (Spanish, German, Italian, American, French, and English). The first section, for instance, was led by a military band followed by representatives of the Spanish colony, the association of tailors, students from the schools of primary education, and shawl makers.[98] Again, the symbolic arrangement of the parade reflected the values aspired to by the Porfirian regime, stressing the importance of industry as well as the value of foreign participation and guidance in commercial, industrial, and scientific development. The emphasis on foreign colonies and educational institutions is especially noteworthy considering the positivist belief that education and foreign colonization offered a solution to the social question.[99] It was through education and foreign colonization, they maintained, that progress would be realized. The civic procession put positivist values on display.

Conclusion

Railway inaugurations, as well as other civic festivities where the locomotive played a central role, represented elite attempts to forge a liberal, capitalistic, and secular form of ceremony. Government officials at the national, state, and local levels all used the railway ceremony to symbolically link Porfirio Díaz to the peace and progress that Mexicans believed had come to define their country. In this way, government officials and organizers employed the railway ceremony as a festival of progress that worked to legitimate his rule. The paeans dedicated to the train's arrival and the inaugural celebrations that symbolically highlighted the locomotive's potential to transform the country and its citizenry demonstrate the magical qualities that people imputed upon it. Inaugurations also helped shape nationalist ideas throughout the country, as those individuals who traveled to these festivals, or those who merely read about them in the press, realized the broader nation that they shared with their fellow countrymen. These civic ceremonies symbolically demonstrated the values that the regime hoped to promote among its citizenry, namely, hierarchy, social order, work ethic, and industry as well as so-called civilized behaviors more generally. This, in turn, allowed elite Porfirians to separate themselves culturally from the rest of the population while simultaneously providing a model for social organization.[100] Officials turned the railway inauguration into pageants that played on older colonial and religious rituals — for example, the use of the procession and the pilgrimage — in order to emphasize the sacredness of these values among the people. Yet at the same time, these events also demonstrated the impermanent character of symbols as various social groups often manipulated the meaning of inaugurations to highlight the snobbery of the elite or question their brand of nationalism.[101] Moments of technological crisis such as train wrecks, the focus of the following chapter, offered opponents a powerful symbol with which to challenge the regime's policies and dampened the popular enthusiasm for railway development displayed in ceremony.

FOUR

The Price of Progress

Popular Perceptions of the Railroad Accident

> The pilgrims travel
> On our railways,
> They experience frights in thousands
> And are hauled like baggage;
> The driver is a savage,
> The trains smell . . . not like flowers,
> (dirty, old . . . a horror!)
> And accidents
> Are now so common
> That travel causes terror. . . .
> And when the company kills,
> It says: "I wash my hands";
> And if someone charges a penny
> Asking for compensation,
> the gringos scream: "No way!"
> and here they respond: "Bravo!"
>
> *El Diablito Rojo,* May 11, 1908

The often devastating consequences of railway accidents altered the relationship between Mexicans and the Porfirian government and its brand of modernization. This chapter explores a popular perception that train wrecks had become all too common, leading various sectors of society to grow disenchanted with the government's program of order and progress. It was not that opposition groups disagreed about the country's need to exploit technological advancements, but they disagreed about the government's methods. A belief that the government catered to foreign companies who did little to protect travelers galled the general public. Newspapers that targeted middle- and working-class audiences articulated a growing disillusionment with the utopian promises of modernity and technological progress so often expressed by the ruling elite. Since illiteracy rates were high, this chapter also examines the tradition of *corridos*, as well as illustrations printed in the penny press and opposition newspapers, in order to gauge understandings of what the railway, and modernization more generally, meant to "popular" groups.[1] Penny presses, it has been argued, were written for working-class audiences, while satiric opposition newspapers have been defined as having a "middle-class" character.[2] Yet critical publications identified as middle class used well-known images that reached a wider audience, especially those that appeared repeatedly in penny presses such as Tio Samuel (Uncle Sam), El Pueblo (the people), and La Republica (the republic). Lithographic and woodcut images represented, especially in their roughness compared with the images produced in elite publications, a medium of counter-discursive illustration.[3] As such, these images published in the penny press and satiric newspapers were necessarily of opposition, protest, and critique. Political ideas articulated in the press also could be circulated to illiterate individuals through public readings at social gatherings as well as through popular culture such as ballads and cornerstone parodies.[4] *Corridos*, likewise, revealed the opinions, values, and norms of the often poor, illiterate people who sang these songs, leaving behind documents about their beliefs and feelings.[5]

Train wrecks were reported weekly. While the majority of accidents did not necessarily claim lives, journalists nevertheless used these sensational stories to fill up the *gacetilla* columns

Table 1. Injury rates of major European railways in 1897
(for every 10 people injured on the Mexican Central)

Mexican Central	10.0
Germany	0.5
France	1.0
England	1.8
Belgium	1.1

Source: *Dr. Gloner v. F. C. Central, Indemnización de Daños, Dolores Físicos y Morales: Apuntes de Alegato Al Sr. Juez de lo Civil, Lic. Angel Zavalza por el Lic. José Diego Fernández* (Mexico: Imprenta de "Le Courrier du Mexique et de L'Europe," 1899), 48.

(short news stories usually located at the back of newspapers). Indeed, the vivid descriptions of trains roaring off the tracks and dragging behind them the mangled ruins of iron and wood never failed to find space in newspapers. As much as the railroad represented the pinnacle of modern, sophisticated societies, a symbol indicative of economic and social advancements, accidents became moments where people's apprehensions toward modernity, industrialization, and technological change found intimate expression. And while industrial accidents represented a tragic reality that modern societies faced, in Mexico it spurred an antiforeign backlash, especially against the nation's mainly American owned and operated railways, making it a unique case study.

Although one study produced by the Secretaría de Comunicaciones y Obras Públicas (Ministry of Communications and Public Works — SCOP) during the Porfiriato did suggest that the country's main rail line, the Mexican Central, had a much higher injury rate than its European counterparts, train wrecks nevertheless affected only a small portion of the population.

The studies of accident rates, as well as the rates of injuries and deaths, produced for the SCOP reveal that when wrecks did occur, it was railway employees and bystanders who were most often the victims, not passengers.[6]

Table 2. Injuries and deaths on the Mexican Central and National Railroads in 1897

		Mexican Central	National
Killed	Travelers	1	0
	Employees	40	11
	Bystanders	37	9
	Total	78	20
Injured	Travelers	19	4
	Employees	179	30
	Bystanders	58	13
	Total	256	47
	Total killed and injured	334	67

Source: Dr. Gloner v. F. C. Central, Indemnización de Daños, Dolores Físicos y Morales: Apuntes de Alegato Al Sr. Juez de lo Civil, Lic. Angel Zavalza por el Lic. José Diego Fernández (Mexico: Imprenta de "Le Courrier du Mexique et de L'Europe," 1899), 101.

But the constant—and often brutally graphic—reporting made the train wreck command more of the public's attention and imagination. Wrecks often occurred close to the towns, villages, fields, and farms where people worked and lived. Thus people from all sectors of Porfirian society, in one way or another, encountered the destructive consequences of modern travel. Since many victims seemed to be doing routine activities when killed—traveling to work, walking along the tracks, taking a weekend excursion, or making a religious pilgrimage—the train wreck introduced an unprecedented form of carnage and chaos into everyday life.

Train travel was modern insofar as it allowed people to experience mechanized movement, but it also embodied various characteristics of modern life: technical sophistication, mobility, urbanization, and industrialization. In addition, the railway journey transformed humans into living cargo conveyed by technological forces completely out of their control. Thus the railway accident's arbitrary and abrupt nature, which seemed to disregard the victim's class or status, made the accident itself a symbol of democracy. In most accidents, passengers in some cars might not experience any turbulence whatsoever, only to realize that cars behind them had jumped off the tracks. While this understanding about the meaning of train wrecks might have been prevalent among late nineteenth-century passengers, it was not completely accurate.[7] Those individuals traveling in the cramped quarters of the third-class compartment often bore the worst injuries, a reality often repeated in the lyrics of *corridos* and lines of the penny presses. Adding to the sense of arbitrariness, railway accidents were most often caused by minor oversights such as a rotten track, a missing bolt, a badly timed signal, an obstruction in the train's path, or an engineer miscalculating the speed of the locomotive. Under these circumstances, the possibility of experiencing a wreck, for some travelers, offered the possibility of adventure and provided occasions for them to demonstrate their willingness to take risks. The travel writer for *El Cronista* told readers that the "imminent risk" of derailment allowed passengers to undertake feats of danger comparable to modern explorers such as David Livingston and Henry Stanley.[8] Like the accident's egalitarian nature, the willingness to take risks also represented a modern sensibility.[9]

From the early years of Porfirian railway development, newspapers, weeklies, and special interest journals demonstrated a sense of allure and anxiety when reporting on accidents. A survey of newspaper reports regarding accidents reveals a changing view of the railroad over the thirty-five-year dictatorship. During the railway building boom that took place between 1880 and 1884, news reports on the crashes and derailments of locomotives tended to view them as a small price to pay for the rewards of modernization.

Newspapers, both government-subsidized and independent, reported accidents but rarely placed blame on any group in particular, a tendency that would become less common during the final years of the Porfiriato. At first, the press gave companies the benefit of the doubt more often than not. Reporters instead blamed the provisional equipment and structures used as temporary measures to sell tickets for travel, or to move agricultural and mining products, before the railway lines had been completed. Heavy rains and the country's mountainous topography were frequently used to explain accidents. Reporting on an accident that took place on May 22, 1883, where a cargo train of the Mexican Central derailed off a provisional bridge that had been weakened by torrential rainfall, *El Cronista* told readers not to worry because iron bridges would soon be erected and that the company had employees inspecting the tracks until they were built. Another report on June 17 stressed the caution used by train engineers when operating their locomotives, a necessity resulting from the poor quality of the provisional bridges that could not stand up to the heavy rains experienced in Morelos. Even a horrific accident on the newly inaugurated Morelos railway, an accident that the foreign traveler William Henry Bishop claimed took five hundred lives, received little attention in the press. Bishop blamed heavy rains and the provisional equipment and concluded that the event had served as a valuable lesson for the nation's railway builders.[10]

El Monitor Republicano, in contrast, criticized the railway companies for their failure to properly inspect the tracks, but nevertheless offered a tempered assessment of their perceived shortcomings, a position that would change drastically over the years. On August 12, 1882, when reporting an accident near the station of Lechería, Mexico, the correspondent criticized the minister of development for not holding the Mexican Central accountable for its failure to properly inspect the tracks. He noted that the Mexican Central was far too important a line to be repeatedly experiencing derailments. The writer lamented that neither the government nor the company nor its employees ever accepted responsibility, finding this an unacceptable precedent to be established. On August 1, a writer for *El Monitor Republicano* explained that there had been little public outcry over the frequency of railway accidents despite the fact that they had become daily occurrences. He suggested that it was the popularity of railroad development, demonstrated by the enthusiasm of people who attended the various Mexican Central inaugurations, which helped balance people's anger. Nevertheless, the reporter again blamed a lack of track and apparatus inspection as well as the ambivalence of railway employees regarding passengers' safety. *El Monitor Republicano* began demanding that accident victims be compensated for their injuries by the railway companies. Indeed, the issue of people's rights to compensation would become an often debated topic in the press and the courts.

Railway accidents increased throughout the Porfiriato as the nation's transportation network expanded and more people used trains regularly. And, between the 1880s and 1900s, Porfirians began to view accidents as becoming more common, more deadly, and more destructive. The destructive force of wrecks led to public outcry regarding the government's relation to the foreign companies that owned much of the nation's railroad network and the American workers who manned the machinery. The Mexican Central and Interoceanic companies, in particular, were targeted by the press as especially negligent in their upkeep of tracks and their passenger service.[11] Critiques of the government and its railway policies represented one of the most common condemnations in the press of Díaz's regime. At the same time, when periodicals supportive of Díaz discussed the growing problem of train wrecks, they explained the dreadful condition of rolling stock and equipment as a result of the poor profits that foreign railway companies regularly reported to their shareholders.[12] Condemnations against railroad companies reached their most ardent expression after an Interoceanic wreck near the town of Temamatla, the worst during the Porfiriato.

Temamatla

On the morning of February 28, 1895, a train prepared to pull out of the Interoceanic station at Amecameca, Mexico, carrying 1,200 passengers, mainly sightseers, to Mexico City. Many were pilgrims who had come to visit the Shrine of Sacromonte during Ash Wednesday. The locomotive, consisting of eleven cars, was so crowded that many travelers had climbed onto the roof in search of a makeshift seat. As the train screeched out of the station just after 11 a.m., a crowd of family, friends, and onlookers waved good-bye. Less than an hour into the journey, as the train roared toward a sharp curve at a point known as Piedras Blancas, between the towns of Temamatla and Tenango, five third-class cars jumped off the track and collided, leaving three of them in pieces. The crash killed dozens who had been riding on top of cars. Others frantically tried to save themselves by jumping from the roofs and running boards and out the car windows. One sensationalized report claimed that the screams of the horrified victims could be heard as far as Coatepec, a town over twenty kilometers away.[13] The cars then flipped twice across the man-made embankments that paralleled the tracks, tossing out passengers and leaving a trail of bodies, limbs, and entrails. The first-class and second-class passengers had felt a strong jolt before the train came to an abrupt stop, but many had no idea what had happened. They left their cars and encountered the gruesome scene outside.

In the ensuing chaos, the train's engineer, James Nuffer, fled, perhaps afraid of being arrested by Mexican authorities or being the target of public retribution. Indeed, *El Monitor Republicano* reported that uninjured passengers and townspeople immediately searched for the engineer with guns in hand.[14] Nuffer eventually reached the United States, aided by fellow railway men who gave him safe passage.[15]

The Interoceanic managers did not receive word of the wreck until three hours later, when they dispatched another train with police and medics. Meanwhile, on hearing about the accident, President Díaz dispatched the Military Medical Corps to tend to the victims and transport them to the San Lucas Hospital. That night, the auxiliary train pulled into San Lázaro Station in Mexico City carrying passengers, cadavers, and body parts. A massive crowd received the train at San Lázaro and waited anxiously to learn whether or not their loved ones had survived. In the immediate aftermath, 104 people died and 86 were injured, the majority of whom were third-class travelers. In the following days, several more succumbed.[16]

Newspapers printed a plethora of stories about the victims and the hardships they faced. Reporters told readers about passengers who had lost limbs or been severely crippled, about passengers who had seen individuals torn to pieces or who had to help authorities recover strewn body parts, and about passengers who had lost family members. One seven-year-old girl, Otilia Herrera, had lost her parents and three brothers. Her plight was so heartbreaking that Pedro Rincón Gallardo, the Federal District's governor, offered to adopt the hapless youngster.[17] The often sensationalized reports provoked a powerful public backlash against the railway companies, which were accused of gross negligence and of showing indifference toward their passengers. Making matters worse, newspapers reported that the American engineer had been a well-known drunk and had received several warnings about driving too fast.[18] One newspaper went so far as to contend that Nuffer and his entire crew were inebriated for the trip.[19]

The Temamatla incident gave rise to a great deal of public sympathy for the victims. Many newspapers, private organizations, mutual aid societies, and individuals donated money to the injured and families of the dead. Indeed, several newspapers ran articles requesting public donations for the survivors. El Congreso Obrero, a workers' organization, opened a fund for the victims, calling on mutual aid societies and factory workers to donate.[20] Lawyers offered to represent victims free of charge in seeking compensation from the Interoceanic Railway Company.[21] Mexico City's *ayuntamiento* also sought to help by organizing a philanthropic benefit concert, although, in the end, they were unable to secure a venue.[22]

The horrors produced by the accident at Temamatla — the worst wreck in terms of civilian deaths experienced during the Porfiriato — were remembered for years to come. Even the word "Temamatla" became synonymous with accidents. *El Universal*, for example, when discussing the poor state of the Interoceanic Railway, told readers that it feared another Temamatla.[23] *El Tiempo* expressed concern that another Temamatla would take place as a result of the poor state of the nation's tracks.[24] Three years after the event, *El Hijo del Ahuizote* used the term *temamatlazo* as a noun meaning "train wreck."[25] Even twelve years later, the workers' weekly *El Diablito Bromista*, in a humorous poem about life and love in the streets, joked about a woman who dressed so flamboyantly that she was louder than the trains of Temamatla.[26]

The episode found expression in popular culture as well as print culture. "El corrido del descarrilamiento de Temamatla" gave a detailed account of the mutilation of victims and the destruction of families. The ballad suggested that the accident was the fault of the company and the American engineer, rearticulating public perceptions regarding the causes of derailments. Finally, the *corrido* emphasized that it was the poor, third-class passengers who bore the brunt of it when those cars were destroyed:

> Listen up, gentlemen, to this sad story
> that I bring in mind,
> of what recently took place in Temamatla
> with the derailment. . . .
> Thursday 28 of the month of February
> in the year ninety-five,

everyone in Ameca went to the station
with great joy. . . .
Three cars of third class were left
completely in pieces,
and wherever one looked they saw
heads, legs, and arms.[27]

Temamatla incited a public uproar about two crucial issues
that would continue to be debated in the press until the final
years of Díaz's presidency: accident victims' right to compensation from railway companies and the foreign ownership and operation of the nation's transportation network. The debates demonstrated a changing public opinion about the benefits and costs
of railroad development and, in turn, about the nature of Porfirian modernization. It was not only for the most vocal opposition of Díaz's regime that Temamatla would become a powerful
symbol to question the government's relationship with foreign
companies. The middle-class press—which included Catholic,
independent, and pro-government organs—and the working-
class penny presses articulated these antiforeign sentiments most
vociferously.[28]

The response provided by the executives at the Interoceanic
Company only served to aggravate the public further. The company, in the following weeks, reported through its lawyers that it
would not pay compensation, infuriating many members of the
press. Several lawyers representing the victims stated to reporters from *El Siglo Diez y Nueve*, Francisco Bulnes's sometimes
critical daily, that the Interoceanic board of directors refused to
pay, even though the company had admitted responsibility for
the derailment.[29]

In the months and years following Temamatla, newspapers of
various political leanings engaged in a discussion about the responsibility of railway companies regarding accidents. *El Noticioso* pleaded with the victims' lawyers not to allow the Interoce-

anic to get away with murder. One reporter maintained that the company must be held responsible or accidents like Temamatla would become more common. They cited an accident twelve years earlier where a train had plunged into a ravine as a result of a poorly constructed bridge. In that case the railway company had managed to avoid paying any compensation whatsoever to the victims. Arguing that Temamatla had resulted because the railway companies felt no pressing need to invest in the safety of passengers, the reporter maintained that the company must be held both legally and financially responsible.[30] Even *El Partido Liberal*, a pro-Díaz and government subsidized publication, demanded that the Interoceanic pay compensation.[31]

The independent middle-class newspaper *Gil Blas*, directed by Francisco Montes de Oca, reported the most detailed accounts of the first district judge's investigation into the causes of the wreck. The newspaper took on a fervently nationalist tone. Over several days of coverage, it reported that the judge had interviewed many of the company's employees, both Mexican and American. *Gil Blas* noted the major discrepancies between the testimony of employees and the conclusions of the judge and those statements provided by the railway company's director, who was referred to only as Sr. Jackson. The judge told reporters that the employees confirmed that the train's engineer, James Nuffer, had been going excessively fast. Yet Jackson's testimony contradicted those accounts, maintaining that no one was at fault and that the driver had not, in fact, driven at too high a speed. *Gil Blas* also reported that Jackson seemed to be protecting Nuffer as he repeatedly denied that he knew how the engineer had found safe passage to San Antonio, Texas.

The judge concluded that Nuffer lacked the proper skills as an engineer and had not taken all precautions, and he confirmed what employees and passengers testified about the speed of the train—testimony corroborated by the Mexican stoker who had accompanied Nuffer on the ill-fated trip. *Gil Blas* also reported interviews it had undertaken with the victims' families. In those accounts, macabre stories emerged, accusing the railway company of body snatching. It reported that twenty corpses had gone missing from the scene of the crash and that Interoceanic employees had buried the bodies before families could recover them. It connected this accusation to the company's general disdain for Mexicans as demonstrated by their poor treatment of native workers, who were paid considerably less than U.S. employees. Going further, it accused Jackson of acting like a "sultan" who treated employees like "dogs."[32] For *Gil Blas* the Temamatla wreck inspired an anti-U.S. attitude toward the failures of the foreign owned railway, connecting the transportation system's lack of safety to other serious grievances that provoked nationalist outrage.

The Catholic press, which perhaps felt a stronger link to the accident since the majority of victims had been third-class passengers heading back to Mexico City after a pilgrimage to the Shrine of Sacromonte, called on President Díaz to step in and resolve the matter. *El Tiempo*, also directed by Montes de Oca, charged that railway companies used the slow nature of the legal system to stall judicial proceedings until victims either could not afford to continue or became alienated by the process.[33]

In the end, the nation's courts would have to decide whether or not the Interoceanic Railway Company would be held liable and, as a result, pay compensation. Fifty-two people, representing twenty dead relatives from the Temamatla wreck, declared they planned to sue for compensation. These individuals, too poor to hire personal attorneys, worked with Lic. Agustín Verdugo, who offered to represent the victims free of charge.[34] The Interoceanic executives and lawyers did their utmost to stall any court proceedings. It took six months alone for the Federal District's Supreme Court judges to decide that the Temamatla victims had the right to sue.[35]

The slow judicial process reflected the lack of any specific laws relating to financial compensation. While the Law of December 16, 1881, stated that companies could be fined up to 500 pesos for accidents caused by the imprudence of their employees, issues regarding financial compensation were dealt with on a case-by-case basis.[36] After reporting on the group seeking compensation, *El Partido Liberal* reminded readers on May 2, 1895, that a precedent had been established when a child's family successfully sued a railway company for the loss of a finger in an accident. Nevertheless, in the following months and years, the press reported few compensation cases, and those individuals who did receive compensation were mainly prominent members of society and foreigners. Five years later, a short article in *El Chisme* noted that fourteen victims finally settled with the Interoceanic for 314,000 pesos.[37] The group represented a fraction of those injured, suggesting that the lawyer quit the case and that few victims had the financial resources to undertake a long court battle of this kind.

At least at first, most sectors of the government-subsidized press defended the railway companies and their decision not to pay compensation. The illustrated weekly *El Mundo (Semanario Ilustrado)*, run by *científicos* Rafael Reyes Spíndola and Luis Urbina and targeting an elite audience, defended the railway company and further maintained that the government had no responsibility to seek financial compensation on behalf of the citizenry. The reporter stated on March 17, 1895, that while European nations might have laws that allowed the government to intervene in such matters, there were none in Mexico. He explained to readers that railroad companies such as the Interoceanic did not have the money to pay large settlements to the victims, and if forced to pay compensation, it would further retard the construction and upkeep of the transportation network. He admitted that if the companies were found to be negligent in causing the accident, then the compensation payments would be completely justified. Nevertheless, he lamented such a development, as it would drain the coffers of the railway companies, while simultaneously recognizing that it would teach those companies a valuable lesson.

In the same edition, Claudio Frillo's "*Crónica*," which offered readers fictional dialogues about current events, attempted to inject the tragic events with a bit of humor. He provided readers with a dialogue between a lawyer desperately seeking Temamatla victims to represent and individuals who had suffered various personal injuries or disabilities. The lawyer, hoping to find a "fat profit," chased down a hunchbacked man, asking him if he had been a victim of Temamatla, only to end up insulting the man, who had no idea of what the lawyer was getting at. Frillo then went on to ask whether or not a scar was enough proof of being a Temamatla victim and whether or not some individual might sue for his mother's death, although she died of typhus and not Temamatla.

For some members of the elite press, legal cases seeking financial compensation for personal injury or the loss of loved ones represented a dangerous precedent that undermined national progress. Since the majority of the people injured were poor, writers for the elite press suggested that they would attempt to take advantage of the legal system to make some ready cash. As an example, the author warned readers of a case of a worker who had killed his own daughter and sent the certificate of her death to the minister of finance in an attempt to swindle the government out a month's salary.[38] His shrill assessment made clear the classist prejudice of the elite press. Articulating beliefs often held by the well-to-do, those poor and working-class passengers who had suffered injury in the wreck would take advantage of the legal system as a means to enjoy idleness.[39]

Six months later, writers for *El Mundo (Semanario Ilustrado)*, although not completely changing their opinion about the matter, nevertheless offered a rare critique of the Díaz regime. In an article looking at the work of Francisco Mena, the appoin-

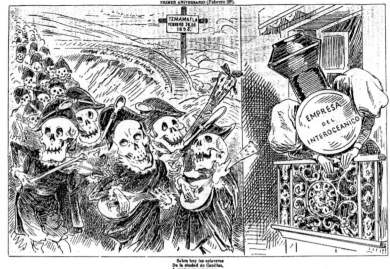

11. Temamatla: The first anniversary. *El Hijo del Ahuizote*, March 1, 1896.

tee to the newly created Ministry of Communications and Public Works, the author lambasted Mena for pandering to foreign interests while, at the same time, promising to come down hard on the railway companies for the poor state of their service. In addition, the journalist blamed the government for the pitiable condition of the railways, since foreign companies had not made enough profit to maintain the nation's transportation network safely. The companies, as a result, treated the government and people of Mexico like vassals powerless to stop abuses (not maintaining the transportation network in a safe condition) that led to catastrophes like the Temamatla wreck. In a rare, blunt critique of the government, the author described both the railway network and national politics as trapped in feudal times.[40]

For the most fervent sectors of the oppositional press, Temamatla provided a potent and often utilized symbol with which to attack the policies of the regime. *El Hijo del Ahuizote* employed the horrors of Temamatla as a coalescing image that allowed challengers to equate it with a number of other grievances against the Díaz administration. Invoking train wrecks allowed the writers to criticize the growing détente between church and state, the use of draconian laws such as *la ley fuga*—a practice used by rural police of shooting prisoners in the back on the bogus excuse of attempted escape—and the commanding presence of foreigners who dominated national industries.

On the first anniversary of Temamatla, *El Hijo del Ahuizote* printed an image of its victims rising from the dead to serenade the Interoceanic Railway Company—represented by a damsel leaning over her balcony—near the infamous curve of Piedras Blancas where the accident occurred.

The image and accompanying poem offered a scornfully sarcastic take on modernity, emphasizing the destructive nature, especially the human toll, of Porfirian progress:

> Today the Skulls come out
> From the city of leg bones [*Canillas*],
> To sing songs of
> Your glorious wonders.[41]

Considering the usual nationalist critiques offered by the publication, it also suggested a willingness by the government and its supporters to accept the indiscretions of foreign railway interests who seemed to have little concern for public safety.

The following year, the same publication offered readers an image that used Temamatla to lampoon the well-known coziness between the government and the church. The image, which adorned the cover of that week's issue, showed Puebla's Bishop Perfecto Amézquita y Gutiérrez and Oaxacan Archbishop Eulogio Gillow about to bless the doomed Interoceanic train, with the president immediately behind them carrying a cauldron of holy water. The blessing of newly inaugurated railway lines, as well as those lines that had experienced wrecks such as the Interoceanic, was repeatedly used by *El Hijo del Ahuizote* to assail the government and the Church. When asked why he blessed the machine, the archbishop replied that it had proved to be a better killer than Díaz's infamous sword, La Matona (the bully/the killer), and that it exorcised the condemned James Nuffer, represented as a devil arising from the locomotive's smokestack.[42]

The satirical image implied that while the national government had failed to protect the safety of citizens through laws and policymaking, it instead relied on superstitious rituals to protect people from the dangers of railway travel. The image clearly targeted Gillow's predilection for the profane as he had fashioned himself a railway promoter since the early years of the Porfirian railway boom, being awarded a concession in 1878.[43] Here, the tragedy of Temamatla united three themes that were the crux of many of the anti-Díaz assessments: the regime's violent attack on individual liberties, its continued failure to seek accountability for foreigners' misdeeds, and the Church's unabashed return to public life. The comic illustration might also have been attempting to trivialize Gillow's 300 peso donation to the Temamatla victims.[44]

Another issue offered readers "Un Refuerzo á Temamatla" (A reinforcement to Temamatla) where Francisco Mena, the minister of communications and public works, handed over a large pistol labeled "The Suspension of Guarantees" to a Yankee, half-man and half-train, at the "Killings Station." The slogan on the gun referred to the suspension of constitutional guarantees, a law promulgated under Benito Juárez and periodically reinforced throughout the Porfiriato and used against train robbers or individuals found tampering with railway equipment. Again, *El Hijo del Ahuizote*'s publishers drew a connection between the perception that Porfirian policymakers not only failed to safeguard the interests of their citizens but also gave foreign railway companies protections that undermined the liberal guarantees of citizenship outlined in the Constitution of 1857.[45] In the context of the Temamatla episode, this highlighted the irony of gov-

El Hijo de
El Ahuizote

MÉXICO PARA LOS MEXICANOS.

Semanario de oposición feroz é intransigente con todo lo malo.
Fundador, Director y Propietario DANIEL CABRERA.
DIRECCIÓN: Calle de Cocheras núm. 15.— Apartado 141.

UN RESPONSO EN TEMAMATLA
Ó LA BENDICIÓN DEL INTEROCEÁNICO EN PUEBLA.

GILLOW.—¿Y por qué bendecimos este animal, compañero?
AMÉZQUITA.—Porque ha salido más matón que la Matona y
que el mismo Leopardo Márquez; y además para que se le sal-
ga Nuffer el condenado.

12. A response to Temamatla, or the blessing of the Interoceanic in Puebla.
El Hijo del Ahuizote, December 12, 1897.

161

ernment railway policies, namely, that government officials used violence against their own people found tampering with railway materials in an attempt to keep them safe from the injury and death that might be experienced as a result of train wrecks.

Even periodicals aimed at middle- and upper-class readers that were ardently supportive of Díaz used the terrible memories of the Temamatla wreck to offer veiled critiques of Porfirian modernization. In the January and February 1897 issues of *El Mundo (Semanario Ilustrado)*, a weekly segment of mock travel literature appeared for readers' amusement. Titled "El Dante en México," the fictional travel account told the adventures of a news reporter traveling across Mexico by railway and steamship, only to eventually end up in Hell. The reporter encountered a series of misfortunes throughout his travels, misfortunes that pointed out some of the alleged problems of the Porfiriato. The correspondent fell off a train that went too fast (a common criticism of railway companies), encountered rude Americans selling overpriced goods (a common complaint about the increased U.S. presence in the nation), and witnessed the torture of journalists critical of the government (a common condemnation of Díaz's crackdown on the free press).

Yet nothing prepared the reporter for the horrors he experienced when he arrived in Hell. There he boarded the Interoceanic (or the "terror railway," as he told readers), where passengers bought tickets in order to commit suicide in a prompt and timely fashion. And, as promised, the Interoceanic derailed, sending the passengers plummeting to a horrific death, although *El Mundo(Semanario Ilustrado)*'s faithful reporter managed to escape the wreck. Then, after being tossed from the train, the reporter stood up and observed that the Temamatla victims were being ferried across a lake of fire on the steamship *Donato Guerra*—an allusion to one of the steamships used for presidential travel—powered by the mythical Charon. A lost soul informed the reporter that the victims were forever to wait on the steamship, unable to cross the lake, until the Interoceanic Railway Company agreed to pay compensation.[46] The dangers of railway travel, demonstrated most evidently in Temamatla, even opened the door for some occasional attacks on the Díaz government by the subsidized press.

Although railway accidents had always been reported in the press because they provided a titillating topic for readers, after 1895 the railway accident emerged as a theme used by writers, artists, and social commentators to question the values and beliefs that underpinned Porfirian rule. Even for the publications most loyal to the government, railway accidents, and especially the infamous Temamatla wreck, were employed to discuss the negative aspects of the government's modernizing policies. The poor condition of the nation's railways and the dangers that this posed travelers became an often repeated topic.

In the wake of Temamatla, many sectors of the press began to argue that the government should play a greater role in the operation and regulation of the country's transportation system. *El Tiempo*, for example, maintained that the government needed to be more active in regulating the railways in order to lower the extremely high accident rate. It argued that the government did not have stringent enough laws to hold companies accountable for accidents and that France, Great Britain, and the United States all had laws to hold companies liable for negligence.[47] *El Popular* agreed with this argument and contended that officials needed to take more action to ensure that companies maintained the safety of their tracks and rolling stock.[48] In addition to these critiques, the press generally argued that foreign companies had little concern for safety and that they saved money at the expense of travelers' security. The 1899 Railway Law did not resolve these matters, leaving the issue of compensation vague. Article 176 maintained that railway companies would fall under the nation's legal jurisdiction in cases where negligence by employees or poor conditions of rolling stock were to blame for accidents.[49] The Railway Law failed to set conditions for the indemnification of passengers and bystanders injured or killed in train wrecks.

The refusal of foreign owned transportation companies to compensate accident victims heightened the public's animosity. Two lawsuits—one by a Mexican and another by a foreigner—grabbed headlines in the 1890s. Wealthy foreigners appeared to have a greater likelihood of receiving compensation from railway companies, although this was not necessarily the reality. These cases further promoted the perception that citizens did not have the same recourse to justice as foreigners, something that increasingly offended newspapers that targeted middle- and working-class audiences.

Joaquín Cardoso and the Interoceanic Railway Company

The popular opinion that railway companies would not compensate Mexican victims of wrecks received reinforcement in the case of Joaquín Cardoso and his lawsuit against the Interoceanic Railway Company. On February 28, 1892, Cardoso was traveling from Jalapa, Veracruz to Mexico City when the locomotive of his train collided with a freight train. The driver had confused the signals that warned him to stop. Near Lagunilla, the freight train barreled into the first-class train where Cardoso rode, sending it rolling off the tracks and tossing the passengers against the walls of the car and into one another. No one was killed, but several passengers, including Cardoso, were injured. After several hours, an auxiliary train arrived to take them to Puebla for medical attention. Cardoso suffered severe lesions to his face and body, a fractured jaw, and broken teeth. Five months after the wreck, he had a stroke, which paralyzed the right side of his body.[50] His medical examiners blamed the attack on nervous trauma endured during the accident. Unable to work, Cardoso left his job as the manager of La Bella Jardinera, a small textile factory that produced the white muslin clothing worn by rural workers, and sued the Interoceanic Railway for the cost of his medical bills, lost wages, and what his lawyer referred to as the "deformity" that resulted from his cerebral hemorrhage. In total, Cardoso sued for 69,535 pesos, the largest individual indemnification suit against a railroad company on record.[51]

The lawsuit became a long, drawn-out court battle as the Interoceanic's lawyers stalled whenever possible in an attempt to break Cardoso's conviction. The defense provided the court with an extensive rebuttal to the plaintiff's arguments, questioning the testimony of his witnesses and the expertise of his doctors. At first, the Interoceanic offered Cardoso 2,000 pesos in compensation while clearly asserting it had no legal obligation to do so.[52] The defense targeted Cardoso's position and earnings to undermine his compensation claim. He contended that his paralysis had left him unable to work and thus he sued the company for the wages, 140 pesos per month, he would have received if he had continued working. The defense maintained that Cardoso had not provided enough proof of his earnings, only submitting the testimony of customers and not the company. Nevertheless, years later the Interoceanic offered Cardoso a settlement that would give him a pension of 75 pesos per month, an offer Cardoso flatly rejected.[53] The Interoceanic's lawyers emphasized the lack of technical expertise of Cardoso's witnesses, as well as their provinciality, to challenge their testimony.

Two passengers on Cardoso's train testified on his behalf. One said he had seen the cargo train coming toward their car at full speed (á todo vapor), and the other maintained that he saw the cargo train coming at too fast a velocity (a una velocidad demasiado rápida) before hitting the car that he shared with Cardoso. The defense then questioned the technical expertise of the two witnesses, alleging that neither had the knowledge to support their claims and asking how the court could trust their amateur assessments of the train's speed. They submitted testimony from the train's engineer, who insisted he had lowered his speed when he observed another train on the same track and that he had blown his whistle in a failed attempt to avoid a disaster.

They then turned their attention to Cardoso's medical claim, especially his declaration that he suffered a stroke as a result of the trauma experienced during the wreck. Cardoso's medical examiners concluded that his cerebral hemorrhage, suffered five months after the wreck, had resulted from "cerebral shock" (*conmoción cerebral*) that he sustained in the accident. The diagnosis of psychological trauma caused by industrial wrecks, just emerging as a medico-legal condition in the United States and Europe, had not yet received much attention in Mexico.[54] Indeed, the Interoceanic's lawyers seized upon the lack of studies to sustain such arguments and alleged that his medical diagnosis was the product of the "fecundity of imagination."[55]

The defense questioned the testimony of the seven medical examiners, arguing that they did not meet the medical credentials outlined in law. Beyond highlighting the five months between the accident and the hemorrhage as a period where Cardoso might have sustained another injury causing his paralysis, the defense lawyers cited the Reform era legal expert Don Blas José Gutiérrez's *Código de la Reforma*. In it, Gutiérrez maintained that the testimony of physicians used in court should meet certain universal requirements. The defense, in particular, called attention to a passage that stated that medical experts from small towns could not be trusted as their knowledge, education, and expertise were insufficient to form accurate assessments of injury. It was up to judges, Gutiérrez wrote, to use discretion in accepting the so-called expertise of small-town medics.[56] Thus, since Cardoso's medical exams had taken place in Puebla and not Mexico City, the defense sought to undermine the credibility of the doctors through their provinciality. As we have seen, urbanites often portrayed provincials as lacking the sophisticated forms of knowledge needed to grasp the complexities of the modern world. In this case, the sophisticated technology of the railway that had caused an injury with a cutting-edge diagnosis—shock—could not be accurately assessed by provincials.

No record exists of whether or not Cardoso succeeded in his lawsuit. Three years after the incident, the Temamatla wreck brought the issue of compensation back to the national headlines, leading one newspaper to revisit Cardoso's case. In a short article, the journalist lamented that three years after the accident Cardoso had not received any compensation whatsoever. The case had been suspended for ten months in an attempt to see if some sort of compromise could be reached between the parties, leading the journalist to conclude that the promise of compensation for the victims of Temamatla looked bleak as the company had succeeded in not paying Cardoso a peso. The reporter bemoaned that Cardoso's case revealed the immense power of the Interoceanic, the tenacity with which it defended its wealth, and the complicity of the government that permitted its abuses.[57]

Years later, another compensation case grabbed headlines. This time a powerful foreigner stood at the center of the legal battle, and as a result, the case would undertake a markedly different trajectory, at least in its discussion in the press.

Dr. Próspero Gloner and the Mexican Central

On May 16, 1897, Dr. Próspero Gloner, a representative of Bleichröeder of Berlin, an important German banking house, accompanied a fellow banker, Walter Hermmann, on a train traveling from Mexico City to New York, where Hermmann would board a steamship to Europe. In the middle of the night, outside the town of León, one of the wheels of a third-class carriage fell apart, sending the train off the line. The jolt also pulled Dr. Gloner's first-class Pullman sleeping car from the track. The wreck killed five and injured eighteen, most of whom were third-class passengers. Dr. Gloner received a few minor injuries, including a three-centimeter gash on his head.[58]

Dr. Gloner contacted the Mexican Central Railroad Company and asked for financial compensation for his injury as well as for damage to his property. The company responded that it would only compensate Dr. Gloner for the value of his train ticket. Livid at the railway executives' flippant attitude, Gloner sued the Mexican Central, entering into a three-year court battle. Gloner's lawsuit revealed important aspects regarding public opinion about the relationship between the Díaz regime and foreigners as well as public opinion about the country's foreign owned railways.

Gloner's lawyer, José Diego Fernández, provided the court with a plethora of evidence proving the poor state of the Mexican Central's tracks and equipment. Fernández submitted more than one hundred newspaper articles, from 1897 and 1898 alone, from both the independent and government subsidized press, discussing the poor state of the Mexican Central's rolling stock. In fact, he demonstrated that in 1897 alone, Mexican Central accidents had caused 78 deaths and 278 injuries (see tables 4.1 and 4.2). He also gave the court dozens of reports from the official inspector of the Mexican Central, all of which described the railroad's deplorable state, including rotten tracks, broken ties and rails, run-down locomotives with faulty wheels, and dilapidated bridges and embankments. Inspectors had filed some of these reports less than three weeks before Gloner's train wreck. To make matters worse for the Mexican Central, official reports submitted to the courts also contained numerous allegations of U.S. engineers driving too fast and driving under the influence of alcohol.[59]

Then Fernández interrogated three engineers who worked for the Mexican Central. The lawyer managed to have all three employees verify the negative reports regarding the state of the track and equipment as well as to admit that the Mexican Central's negligence had caused these problems. Indeed, the employees all agreed that not only had the state of the tracks been appalling, but that the engineers often drove too fast.[60] The prosecutor, having convincingly established the Mexican Central's neglect of the railway, turned his attention to the issue of financial compensation.

Since civil laws did not have specific regulations dealing with financial compensation for victims of railway accidents, Fernández used a roundabout way to show the company's responsibility. He cited Articles 33 and 34 of the SCOP's *Reglamentos general de ferrocarriles* (General regulations for the railways), published in 1894, which stipulated that all railway companies must keep their lines in safe condition. He then cited Article 2,512 of the Civil Code, which maintained that railway companies were responsible for any accidents caused by employee negligence, meaning that they were legally responsible for paying a fine, not necessarily compensating victims. Finally, he argued that the Mexican Central had been willing to compensate Gloner 450 pesos for the price of two train tickets (Dr. Gloner and Mr. Hermmann) and, in so doing, had already admitted fault for the wreck.[61]

The final component of Fernández's argument centered on convincing the court that financial compensation for physical and mental injuries (*dolores morales*) represented the only way that civilized nations dealt with such incidents. Fernández provided the court with dozens of European examples where railway victims had received monetary recompense for their injuries. He fell back upon the well-known discourse that emphasized cosmopolitanism and progress, arguing that all civilized nations had passed laws making railway companies accountable to accident victims. He placed into evidence several newspaper reports that argued in favor of holding the railway companies financially responsible and that cited European examples for support. One article submitted to the judge told readers that the country's courts must follow the model of England, France, and the United States, all of whom had promulgated laws dealing with the issue of compensation for accident victims.[62] This statement carried all the more weight considering that Dr. Gloner represented a powerful German banking house with intimate ties to finance minister José Yves Limantour and the government more generally.

While the issue of compensation for physical damage appeared reasonable enough, having companies pay for mental distress had not been addressed before. In fact, European nations, although having several studies dealing with the psychological effects of train wrecks, had few cases adjudicated surrounding the issue. In the mid- and late nineteenth century, medico-legal conclusions about psychological trauma emerged as a result of the mental anguish and distress experienced by railway travelers who had suffered accidents. The first reports of mental shock, trauma, fright, and terror appeared thirty years earlier than Freud's studies on hysteria and half a century earlier than the medical fields' recognition of psycho-neurosis, also known as shell shock, after World War I.[63]

The matter of *dolores morales*, while not receiving a lot of attention in the regular press, did receive notice in Mexico City's English-language newspaper, the *Two Republics*. It noted that medics had undertaken an examination of Dr. Gloner to discover the extent of his mental injuries and that legal experts eagerly awaited the diagnosis, as mental injury represented a novel proposition.[64] Fernández submitted a score of accident cases from the United States and Europe that showed legal precedents regarding compensation for so-called moral injuries. The term, not having a strict definition, encapsulated a series of conditions that could not be described as physical injury. The examples provided by the plaintiff's lawyer defined moral injuries as physical distress, nervous trauma, and possible future suffering by accident victims.[65] The diagnosis represented a new concept in medico-legal circles and, as a result, led to ambiguous definitions of what actually constituted moral damages.

Concurrently, between the 1860s and 1890s, European courts first dealt with the issues of moral injuries and mental trauma caused by train wrecks, a condition that at first was known as "railway spine," when discussing the side effects of physical shock. Eventually, by the 1880s, psychopathological shock would be referred to as "traumatic neurosis."[66] With this model, the court looked to European precedents when deciding the verdict of Gloner's case. Fernández further argued that Gloner's moral injuries worsened because the accident took place during his holiday, which he had planned for mental relaxation. Like the Cardoso case examined earlier, Gloner's lawyer emphasized the psychological effects over the physical as the linchpin of the case. This was especially important because Gloner's physical injuries appeared to be quite minor. And, in the end, Gloner sued for 30,000 pesos in compensation to cover the cost of his medical bills, clothing that had been damaged, and a pair of eyeglasses that had been lost. How he calculated the sum of 30,000 pesos remained unclear. The prosecuting attorney provided a list of the medical bills, train tickets, and lost clothing and eyewear. It amounted to less than 1,000 pesos,[67] suggesting that Gloner's lawyer believed that the moral injuries sustained by the German banker should receive a greater amount of compensation.

For some who followed Dr. Gloner's case in the press, it might have offered tangible proof of national development along modern, cosmopolitan guidelines. Not only did the court system adjudicate a cutting-edge case that paralleled legal proceedings in Europe and the United States, but the court also acknowledged that Gloner had indeed suffered some kind of mental trauma—a new diagnosis just becoming understood by the medico-legal professions at the time. Compensating Gloner would assure foreigners that Mexico was indeed a safe place for them to travel, and it would place Mexico among progressive nations that compensated injured travelers. The Gloner episode provided an opportunity for medical and legal professionals to promote the image of their nation abroad and show foreign nationals that they would be protected.

For others, Dr. Gloner's case may have revealed something much different. The issue of financial compensation, whether for physical or mental injuries, appeared among nationalist circles as further evidence of the government's catering to foreigners. To validate this sentiment, Minister of Finance José Y. Limantour submitted a statement to the court on behalf of Dr. Gloner. In it, Limantour confirmed Gloner's valuable service to the nation, a statement used by Gloner's attorney in an attempt to prove the value of his work, work he could not do as a result of the "moral injuries" he suffered, when evaluating the amount of financial compensation due.[68]

Limantour's support for Gloner would have been especially offensive to the nationalist press, who often accused the government of failing to defend the safety of its citizens. Railway companies rarely compensated accident victims. Most victims rode in the overcrowded third-class compartments with a much greater risk of sustaining significant injuries. These passengers could never afford to engage railway companies in long court battles. *El Hijo del Ahuizote* highlighted this situation when it produced a parodied presidential address to Congress. In it, Díaz told his fellow politicians that foreigners asked for financial compensation on a daily basis and that they forced the government to pay for the slightest injury on a finger or toe.[69] Even weeklies that rarely expressed antiforeign attitudes conveyed their disdain for the indemnification of foreigners. *El Progreso Latino* published a four-line poem that carped about how only wealthy foreigners received compensation from the nation's railway companies, after a French traveler successfully sued the Interoceanic railway. The poem suggested that individuals only succeeded in receiving compensation when they hired high-priced lawyers and had the financial resources to engage in extensive court battles:

Well if they want
their just compensation in cash,
they must first earn
a law degree . . . and hush [until they do so]![70]

A comparison of the Cardoso and Gloner cases provides valuable insights. In Cardoso's case, the Interoceanic's lawyers undermined the credibility of his witnesses and medical experts based on their provinciality. They scoffed at Cardoso's claim that a cerebral hemorrhage had occurred as a result of the accident. Gloner's lawyers, in contrast, emphasized his European identity to seek compensation for a new medical condition—*dolores morales*—that had no precedent in Mexican courts. It was his very cosmopolitanism that allowed such an argument to be made as Gloner and his lawyer's (and, for that matter, Limantour's) urban sensibilities could indeed accurately assess such a cutting-edge diagnosis. Statements by the press regarding the ability of foreigners to seek financial compensation, while Mexicans could not because they lacked the needed resources, reveals a public understanding that foreigners had more recourse to justice than Mexicans. This sentiment was most vociferously expressed against foreign railway employees.

Yet, in the end, Gloner's case revealed the considerable gap that existed between the common belief that the courts gave foreigners preferential treatment in providing injury compensation and how the court, in this instance, actually adjudicated the matter. On May 31, 1900, three years after the outset of the lawsuit, a short letter from Gloner's lawyer reached Limantour's desk. In the letter Lic. Fernández regretted to inform the finance minister that the judge "failed" to award Dr. Gloner any indemnification for "*dolores físicas y morales.*"[71] No newspapers reported this verdict. While it is unknown how the court reached its decision—whether it reflected a judge's nationalist sentiments or a strict reading of legal codes (there were, after all, no laws outlining just compensation for *dolores físicas y morales*)—the verdict makes clear an irony in the press's spleen against the government and the courts. In this case, the perception that officials protected foreigners did not match the reality of the Gloner case, as neither his nationality, his high-priced lawyers, nor his high-ranking friends swayed the court's ultimate judgment. The press's decision to not publicize the verdict perhaps suggests that they preferred to cater to readers' nationalist sentiments, promoting a perception—a perception that could be more powerful than reality in generating public animosity toward the government—that the legal system favored foreigners.

Animosity toward foreigners, in the context of railway development, reached a fever pitch, especially toward U.S. engineers and conductors whom Mexicans viewed as reckless and indifferent to their safety. As with the widespread belief that foreigners received more support from the national government than ordinary citizens, U.S. railway employees were also seen as having protections not afforded to the country's native population. These matters were connected to two other common grievances articulated in the press and popular venues: U.S. employees' poor treatment of Mexican workers and passengers and the higher wages paid to Americans.

Foreign Railroad Employees

The Temamatla wreck and the issue of financial compensation for accident victims intensified public scrutiny of the ownership and operation of the nation's railways. The apparent lack of concern among U.S. engineers for the safety of Mexican travelers proved especially offensive. Temamatla's James Nuffer represented the epitome of this problem. Both local officials and the press placed the blame for the wreck squarely on his shoulders: he had been accused of being drunk and going too fast when the accident occurred. Both these allegations were commonly made against foreign engineers.

While placing the blame on foreign, especially U.S., employees found expression in popular culture, it also became an issue of contention between foreign companies, local authorities, and the national government. In several railway accidents, as well as cases where trains hit pedestrians, local officials placed U.S. engineers under arrest for criminal negligence. One high-profile case included the arrest of a Mexican Railway engineer, Edward Turner, an American, whom authorities arrested after a train wreck near Orizaba, Veracruz. Authorities claimed that Turner, as well as his fellow engineer Angus McKay, had been criminally negligent in an accident that left three Mexicans dead. Turner languished in jail for ten months before becoming ill, being taken to a hospital, and then dying. This caused an international incident. Turner's family claimed he had received cruel treatment by local authorities, even suggesting he had died at the hands of Veracruz's local authorities. Nevertheless, no hard proof existed that Veracruz officials had acted inappropriately, so Turner's family instead sought indemnification for his lengthy detainment without being charged or brought to trial.[72] Authorities eventually released McKay on bond, despite his sentence of fifteen months imprisonment for criminal negligence. After his release, he told reporters that Turner had not been treated poorly by his jailers, but confirmed he had become sick from the squalid conditions of the prison.[73] One Mexico City newspaper speculated that Turner had died of alcoholism, asserting that there had been several complaints against him for operating locomotives while under the influence.[74] The exaggerated claim reiterated a common characterization of American railway drivers as reckless and inebriated. Turner's family, with support from the U.S. government, sought $20,000 in financial compensation from the Mexican authorities.[75]

The incident set off a public debate in the press between Spanish-language newspapers and their English counterparts. Government subsidized newspapers, especially *El Universal*, characterized the U.S. press as alarmist and argued that they portrayed Mexicans as a savage and backward people. Moreover, they pointed out the incongruity in the United States' position, telling readers that the orphans and widows produced by the frequent train wrecks rarely received compensation from foreign companies. And yet Americans often sought financial compensation from the national government for even the most minor incidents.[76] A wide range of periodicals agreed, including the long-running and increasingly antigovernment newspaper *La Patria* and the short-lived humorous illustrated weekly *El Chisme*. Both expressed disdain for Turner's family, as well as the American colony newspaper, the *Two Republics,* which had lambasted Mexican officials for wrongfully placing the engineer under arrest, equating their attempt to be awarded indemnification to blackmail.[77]

After railway accidents, including those cases where pedestrians had been hit by locomotives, U.S. engineers and conductors often fled the scene, fearing arrest. Indeed, local authorities frequently placed U.S. employees under arrest for the killing of passengers and pedestrians even in cases where little or no evidence existed of their negligence. In one case, the U.S. secretary of state, Elihu Root, intervened on behalf of U.S. railway workers employed by the Sonora Railway Company. The workers protested that Mexican authorities were regularly arresting U.S. workers for accidents for which they had no fault. The secretary of state's petition cited three cases in particular, all of which took place between 1904 and 1906, where U.S. citizens had been wrongly arrested. In one case, police detained a U.S. engineer for hitting an intoxicated old man walking along the tracks. He spent thirty-five days in a small, adobe cell before being set free after paying a bond of 350 pesos.[78]

The arrest of U.S. train engineers became a repeated occurrence during the Porfiriato and reached a climax during its final years. Even in wrecks where it was clear that U.S. engineers

had little or no fault, local authorities nevertheless apprehend-
ed them, causing awkwardness, if not tension, between the U.S.
and Mexican governments. While the Mexican government did
not necessarily approve of the arrests, local officials regularly
took matters into their own hands, demonstrating a deep sense
of suspicion toward U.S. railway employees. Mirroring these
sentiments, the opposition newspaper *Regeneración*, edited by
the Flores Magón brothers, in a rare laudatory article about the
regime, applauded the new, tougher laws introduced for drivers who were found drinking alcohol, going too fast, or fleeing
the scene of an accident. The new laws, for example, carried a
sentence of three to eleven months in prison for engineers who
fled accident scenes even if no passenger was injured.[79] Ironically train engineers most often suffered the worst injuries. Local
judges and police forces, nevertheless, found those individuals
culpable, at times arresting severely injured employees. In the
final years of the Porfiriato, the resentment toward U.S. railway
companies revealed a strong sense of nationalist outrage articulated most evidently during the Mexican Revolution.[80]

By 1906, the growing hostility toward foreign railroad employees gave way to an emerging movement that pushed for
transportation lines to be operated by Mexican workers. The
newly formed Gran Liga Mexicana de Empleados de Ferrocarril (League of Mexican Railway Employees) petitioned the national government and both nationally and foreign owned railway companies to begin hiring Mexicans. The league argued
that native workers, by not being hired by foreign companies,
had suffered the injustice of not having the opportunity to make
a decent wage. They also asserted that those companies that did
hire Mexicans showed them no respect and paid them less than
their U.S. counterparts.[81] In its treatise to the national government, a document that dealt primarily with workers' issues and
the formation of a railway union, the league stated that one important benefit of having such an organization would be that

it could take care of Mexican workers who had been injured in accidents, something that foreign companies failed to do.[82]

With the 1908 nationalization of the railways, La Gran Liga found an opportunity to push its agenda. This opportunity would emerge over the issue of safety and new regulations that sought to make wrecks less frequent. The rise in labor disputes and strikes carried out by railway workers, especially between 1890 and 1908, has been well studied in Rodney Anderson's seminal work.[83] Yet one important labor dispute has received little attention. It involved the striking not of Mexican workers but of American employees after the 1908 consolidation of the railway system. The episode would further reveal the emerging radical nationalism on the part of the working and middle classes. In 1909, the newly created Ferrocarriles Nacionales de México (National Railways of Mexico — N R M) implemented the *vía libre* system, also known as the "block" system, a practice already used in the United States, where train dispatchers between two stations would communicate with each other in order to report whether or not the line was clear. If so, the train would be allowed to pass on that "block." The change in systems fueled a debate between the newly created National Railways and its U.S. employees.[84] The dispatchers maintained that the new system, while working well on small trunk lines, would be too taxing on the larger and more complicated national lines.

On July 17, 1909, U.S. dispatchers working in Mexico, in an act of defiance against the new regulations, refused to acknowledge the *vía libre* system and called a strike. In solidarity, U.S. engineers and machinists refused to allow any trains to roll that day, saying they would maintain this position until both groups resolved the matter. The dispatchers had hoped to paralyze the transportation network, forcing the government to revert to the old system. The dispatchers, reassured that the railways could not operate without their expertise, boldly told reporters that no trains would roll until the government conceded to their demands.[85]

The NRM immediately went to work getting Mexican workers to fill the positions of the absent U.S. employees.[86] In response, U.S. engineers and machinists stated that they would not take orders from inexperienced dispatchers, citing the safety of travelers and employees as their chief concern. U.S. tourists, as a result of the dispute, began filling up trains heading to the border in an attempt to avoid getting stuck in Mexico. But the following day, despite the U.S. dispatchers' claims, the nation's railway networks operated without any delays or derailments whatsoever. In this way, the NRM broke the ranks of the U.S. engineers and machinists, most of whom went back to work and followed the instructions of Mexican dispatchers.[87]

Days later, the press reported that three hundred new Mexican workers were prepared to take over the jobs of conductors and machinists that opened as a result of the employees' refusal to cooperate with new railway safety regulations.[88] The highly nationalistic middle-class periodical *Gil Blas* reported with satisfaction that the U.S. engineers and conductors who had struck in solidarity with the U.S. dispatchers were forced to repentantly ask for their jobs back while the "U.S. dispatchers were dispatched and told to go to . . . hell (*á la porra*)."[89] Native railway workers most often protested the low wages offered by foreign companies, their poor treatment at the hands of employers, and the lack of skilled positions available to Mexicans.[90] On the other hand, the press targeted railway accidents and the perception of American disregard toward people's safety in their charges against these companies. The struggle over the implementation of the *vía libre* system and dismissal of the U.S. dispatchers united those two perspectives into a broad bloc of opposition against the foreign run railways.

In response to the growing view that the nation needed Mexicans to operate the transportation system, Minister of Finance Limantour opened a school at the Buenavista Railway Station in Mexico City to train stokers (who fueled the boiler engines) and brakemen. The school would be operated by members of the Hidalgo and Northeastern Railway Company, the only Mexican owned and operated line. This important measure fell short of the hopes of La Gran Liga, which wanted to see a vocational school for engineers and machinists.[91] Nevertheless, the measure demonstrated one of the earliest steps toward mitigating popular sentiments that viewed the Díaz government as pandering to foreign interests. Indeed, the press reported these events with a great deal of pride and nationalistic fervor. Even Limantour boasted that the 1908 nationalization would allow workers to undertake railway services and operations in Spanish, a policy he viewed as commonsensical.[92] Limantour's comments reveal that he had fallen in line with an outlook expressed years earlier by the press, coming to recognize that the employees of a Spanish country's transportation system should operate their day-to-day business in Spanish. In this regard, the issue of public safety was also intimately connected. La Gran Liga's lobbying for the introduction of the safer *vía libre* system linked three other issues that had long been criticized in the press and in popular venues such as the penny press: the country's poor record of transportation safety, the failure of U.S. employees to learn Spanish, and the poor treatment of native workers by American bosses.

La Gran Liga's grievances were reflected in the sentiments of the penny press. These working-class organs repeatedly pointed out the abuses of the U.S. railway companies and demonstrated a sharp disdain for American employees. *El Pinche*, for instance, compared U.S. railway and tram drivers to "devils" because of the dangers they posed to passengers.[93] Throughout 1905, *El Chile Piquín* regularly criticized the tyranny of American bosses who underpaid native workers and who often took away work hours from Mexicans without notice. It noted that although it most often did not support workers on strike, the Mexican employees had no choice because of the U.S. companies' terrible and abusive treatment.[94] *El Ahuizotito* likewise complained that the nation's railways demonstrated the clearest example of the foreign domination of the economy and how Yankees stole jobs from Mexicans.[95] U.S. companies and their employees also drew the ire of the writers for *El Diablito Bromista*, who reported numerous abuses such as Mexican Central bosses taking bribes in exchange for giving native people jobs.[96] Writers for that press also called for the Mexicanization of the railway system as a means of stopping the poor treatment of Mexican workers that was becoming worse despite the companies' promises to clamp down on such abuses.[97] One week later it lamented that U.S. companies preferred to hire American workers despite the fact that Mexicans were equally qualified.[98] Indeed, as late as 1909, 68 percent of the engineers and 86 percent of the conductors were foreigners while native workers filled most of the unskilled positions such as brakemen and boilermakers.[99]

This popular view, repeatedly articulated in the middle- and working-class press, has received little attention from scholars. Indeed, historians' examinations of the 1908 nationalization of railways have ignored that popular attitude toward foreign owned railway companies, an attitude shaped, in part, by the frequency of train wrecks and the belief that foreign companies lacked concern for the welfare of Mexicans. The middle- and working-class press connected these two issues to other serious grievances they held toward the foreign owned railway companies such as the low pay and few job opportunities available to native workers. Scholars have correctly explained the nationalization as an attempt by the Porfirian administration, especially Limantour, to prevent a foreign company from creating a monopoly.[100]

Porfirian policymakers likewise demonstrated increasing concern about the nation's economic sovereignty, especially in regards to U.S. dominance in transportation and mining, albeit for significantly different reasons. The administration, starting around 1900, began attempting to lessen U.S. economic control by attracting new capital from Europe and creating a more balanced field of foreign investment. Porfirian officials began to promote more European competition, challenge U.S. monopoly capitalism through antitrust campaigns, offer new contracts in infrastructure development and oil production to British companies, and, most notably, assume government control of the railway network.[101]

In 1902, Limantour began to purchase and nationalize the country's major foreign owned railway networks as a result of rate wars and a recent spate of unnecessary and costly trunk line construction by the Mexican and National companies. These actions, according to Limantour, wasted much needed capital and did little to integrate vast regions of the country, which undermined national interests.[102] In 1903, Limantour began purchasing the controlling interests in major railway stocks, concluding in the formation of the National Railways of Mexico in 1908. Significantly, as John Hart points out, the government nationalized a majority of American owned lines while not absorbing any British railways.[103] The NRM, by 1910, controlled two-thirds of the nation's network. And as noted earlier, with the 1908 nationalization the government also planned to establish fifteen schools to train Mexican railway workers and to make Spanish the official language of railway service.[104] In this regard, nationalization not only tackled issues of economic sovereignty but addressed the concerns long expressed about the experience of travel that often emphasized the annoyances and aggravation of dealing with U.S. workers and the English language.

Alan Knight and Paul Garner, have argued that the nationalization of the country's railway system represented a modest example of economic nationalism.[105] Arturo Grunstein has maintained that Limantour sought to eliminate the negative competition between the nation's largest railway companies and to facilitate the reorganization of capital that would allow the government to maintain and expand the rail network. Grunstein observed that despite the nationalist rhetoric used during the 1908 nationalization, as well as government fears about the possibility of a foreign monopoly owning the nation's lines, Limantour viewed the protection of foreign capital as the first priority of the administration. Thus, for Grunstein, nationalism had little to do with the government's decision making.[106]

In the later years of the Porfiriato, an upsurge in nationalist sentiment, especially in regard to the U.S. presence in Mexico, erupted and articulated itself in both popular venues and official discourse and policies. While newspapers and songs highlighted the frustrating quotidian experiences of the lower and middle classes — such as rude, careless, and highly paid (at least in comparison with native employees) Yankee workers[107] — changes in elite policymaking regarding the ways that the regime undertook railway development in the early Porfiriato likewise revealed nationalist concerns. These discourses dovetailed at the issue of American workers and the need to have the national system operate in Spanish. In this regard the scholarship on the 1908 nationalization, focusing on its economic and political aspects, has downplayed the social dimensions of that project.

How much of a role public opinion played in the nationalization proves difficult to determine. Nevertheless, the consolidation of the railways and the shift toward employing native workers — the latter a development that first emerged due to the issue of new safety regulations — received popular approval.[108] The episodes examined here reveal a strong nationalist fervor among various sectors of society articulated in official policymaking as well as among middle-class publications and the penny presses. As John Hart claims, Limantour's decision to nationalize the transportation system, while not undertaken solely out of patriotic motivations, responded to growing nationalist concerns among the people,[109] a phenomenon demonstrated most clearly in public enthusiasm for the replacement of U.S. dispatchers by Mexicans as well as the growing belief that railway travel would become safer as a result.[110]

Popular Views of the Railroad Accident

The interconnecting issues of train wrecks, the perception of the government's support of foreign over Mexican accident victims, and anti-Americanism coalesced, at times humorously and at times bitterly, into a critique of the Porfirian regime. During the early years of the Porfiriato, lighthearted publications targeted railway accidents as a topic with which to poke fun at the hazards of modern life. These flippant analyses revealed an anxiety about the social and technological changes that people experienced. At the same time, the more virulently anti-Díaz press used railway accidents to raise awareness about the values of the government's brand of modernization and its relationship with foreign, especially U.S., firms. Indeed, in the 1890s, changing attitudes about technological development, national progress, and the Porfirian regime surfaced and revealed a critical shift in people's understandings of the utopian potential of the railway. Songs, stories, and social commentaries offered new ideas that challenged the increasingly precarious consensus achieved by the government and its supporters about the strategy and efficacy of the transportation program.

El Rasca Tripas was a musical and literary weekly that printed humorous caricatures and that offered readers poems poking fun at the dangers of modern travel. The magazine put forward some of the earliest critiques of the railway at a time when most newspapers lauded the progress and civilization represented by transportation development. In one article, the author depicted the Mexican Central's service as chaotic and disorganized, demonstrated by its regular derailments. He went on to chide government officials and railway owners, stating that they couldn't care less about their passengers. A short poem then suggested that the government cared more about commercial development than about social dangers (that is, derailments):

> And what . . . what are we going to do
> With these social ills [train wrecks],
> Which have, for these evils,
> Been turned a deaf ear![111]

In another, the author carped that although the company had inaugurated the Mexican Central line to León, the public had little interest in riding the train only to risk their lives.[112]

From 1895 onward, it became more common for popular journals to use humor to highlight the feelings of fear and disillusionment about national progress. *El Mundo Cómico* offered readers a variety of cartoons about the fears of experiencing a train wreck. The issue of compensation for accident victims, especially the popular perception that railroad companies rarely took responsibility for accidents, was lampooned by the magazine's caricaturists. For example, in one such illustration, a passenger confronts a train conductor, asking him, if he dies in a wreck, will the company hold *him* accountable.[113]

The working-class weekly *El Diablito Rojo* reflected this sentiment, although tackling the matter from a different angle, when it published a cartoon that depicted foreigners stating: "We enjoy the privileges of the laws and legal codes, and you greasers get the penalties."[114] Weeks later, another penny press made a similar point when it reported that a U.S. pickpocket had robbed a fellow Mexican traveler, only to be robbed by a Mexican when he arrived at the Buenavista Station. The writer wondered whether the U.S. "tramp" would demand compensation from the government.[115]

The carelessness of train employees was likewise a target for *El Cómico*'s lampooning eye. The image showed a passenger train that crushed a man and two railway employees fighting over who was at fault.[116]

13. Those journeys! "And tell me, conductor: If the train derails and I get killed . . . will I not be held responsible?" *El Mundo Cómico*, December 12, 1897.

The image played to public opinion that often viewed the cause of accidents as the fault of drivers and conductors, who were usually Americans. If the public did not blame railway employees, they directed the brunt of their criticism at the poor state of the country's railways. Along these lines, a writer for *El Cómico* produced a column that fused social commentary with biting humor that poked fun at the almost daily occurrence of

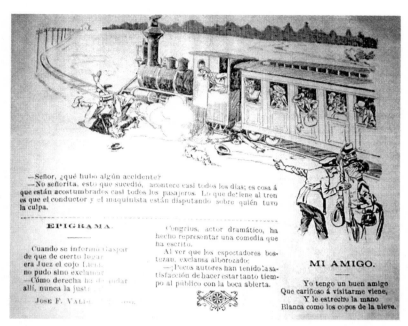

—Señor, ¿qué hubo algún accidente?
—No señorita, esto que sucedió, acontece casi todos los días; es cosa á que están acostumbrados casi todos los pasajeros. Lo que detiene al tren es que el conductor y el maquinista están disputando sobre quién tuvo la culpa.

EPIGRAMA.

Cuando se informó Gaspar
de que de cierto lugar
era Juez el cojo Lucas,
no pudo sino exclamar
—Cómo derecha ha de andar
allí, nunca la justicia.

JOSÉ F. VALLE

Congrius, actor dramático, ha hecho representar una comedia que ha escrito.
Al ver que los espectadores bostezan, exclama alborozado:
—¡Pocos autores han tenido la satisfacción de hacer estar tanto tiempo al público con la boca abierta.

MI AMIGO.

Yo tengo un buen amigo
Que cariñoso á visitarme viene,
Y le estrecho la mano
Blanca como los copos de la nieve.

14. "Sir, was there an accident?" "No, miss, what happened here happens almost every day; it's something that almost all the passengers are accustomed to. What's delaying the train is that the conductor and the engineer are fighting over who was at fault." *El Cómico*, August 20, 1899.

accidents. He sardonically told readers that the excellent construction and operation of the railways had given the railroad an outstanding reputation. The author then lamented that, unfortunately, it was a reputation only held by doctors working in hospitals who had been given ample opportunities to perfect the craft of amputation. He concluded his column by telling readers that the locomotive would prove to be a greater killer than the bubonic plague.[117] The author's dark humor offered a powerful, yet cheeky, analysis of the terrible conditions affecting the railway network, a view shared by almost all sectors of the Porfirian press.

While finding humor in train wrecks might seem strange, humorous critiques of the regime allowed some sectors of the press to avoid the censorship that affected newspaper reporters who made harsher attacks.[118] The oppositional press, especially *El Hijo del Ahuizote*, repeatedly used the frequency of train wrecks to highlight the problems of development and the contradictions it viewed as inherent in the regime's ideology. Along these lines, the first issue printed in 1894 ominously celebrated the New Year with a cover image of a train wreck, representing the greatest national problems of 1893. In the image, the artist labeled each of the demolished railway cars with the main problems that he and his cohorts viewed as racking the nation: the devaluation of silver, epidemics, public misery, and national debt.[119]

The railway, for the editors and writers of *El Hijo del Ahuizote*, became a metonym representing the entirety of social, political, and economic ills they believed faced the nation.

Newspapers such as *El Hijo del Ahuizote* associated the railway with the "human hecatombs" that it produced.[120] They furthermore viewed the frequency of railway accidents as most often the fault of U.S. workers. The opposition press framed their examinations of train wrecks in intensely nationalistic rhetoric, arguing that it was the fault of foreign companies that failed to repair the tracks and locomotives. They understood the railway companies' shortcomings as the result of a lack of concern for the safety of travelers, a belief that often aroused intense anti-Americanism in the press.

El Alacrán, a weekly that offered readers political satire, printed an image titled "Las delicias del Valle" (The valley's delights) that mocked the regular derailments on the Valle Railway.[121] The image showed a human hecatomb caused by a train wreck where the Grim Reaper sat on the derailed locomotive. In the foreground Uncle Sam and Díaz strolled hand in hand, unperturbed.[122] The illustrated weekly *El Correo de México* opined that while all civilized nations valued life, the same could not be said for Mexico, as the Valle Railway wreck demonstrated. The government, it alleged, had not held companies legally accountable for their poor safety record or their irregular main-

El Hijo del Ahuizote

Número 404

Precios.—Un mes en la Capital, 50 centavos. En los Estados, 75 centavos. En
el extranjero, un peso. Números suel-
tos: en la capital, 12 cts.; en los Estados
18 centavos; en el Extranjero, 25 cents.

SEMANARIO POLÍTICO, DE OPOSICIÓN FEROZ
É INTRANSIGENTE CON TODO LO MALO.

DIRECTOR Y PROPIETARIO, DANIEL CABRERA.

Direcciones:—Apartado Postal número
421.—Administración é Imprenta: Calle
Primera de la Pila Seca número 318.
Para todo asunto dirigirse al Director
y propietario.

TOMO IX.　　　CIUDAD DE MEXICO, DOMINGO 21 DE ENERO DE 1894.　　　AÑO NOVENO.

1893--1894.

Dos años en parangón:
Uno incierto y bonachón,
Otro en el pasado hundido
Habiéndonos producido
De desastres un millón.

15. 1893–94. *El Hijo del Ahuizote*, January 21, 1894.

tenance of the tracks. It further argued that officials needed to seek indemnification on behalf of Mexican travelers from the companies that mocked the government's sweetheart contracts it offered to foreign interests.[123] Antigovernment newspapers insinuated that the Díaz government failed to hold companies accountable for wrecks, and they characterized the Díaz administration as an accomplice to the murder of its own citizenry.

This idea found further confirmation in the fact that the Hidalgo and Northeastern Railway Company, the only entirely Mexican owned and operated railroad, had never suffered an accident, a feat that no other railway company could claim.[124] In one image, the Justicia Federal (Federal Justice) interrogates the major railways, depicted in human form. Both the Mexican Central and the Interoceanic, the two most often chastised because of their notoriously poor safety record, sit accused of causing too many deadly crashes, to which the trains reply, "*Mi non tende*,"[125] a joke mocking the poor Spanish of U.S. conductors so often criticized by writers in the press (the statement represented the Anglophone version of "*yo no entiendo*," I do not understand). Nevertheless, the Federal Justice sets free both trains, one for a lack of evidence and the other for the lack of clearly defined laws with which to charge the culprit. In sharp contrast, the Hidalgo railway, brought before the justice for not having killed any civilians, replies, "Sir, since I am from this land, I respect its people." Despite its positive track record, the justice promptly sends the Hidalgo railway to jail.[126] Again, the major voices of opposition during the Porfiriato latched onto the belief that the government protected the murderous activities of foreign companies at the expense of the nation's people and homegrown industries. Critiques of the government's railway policy paralleled the criticisms made by both the independent press, such as *El Monitor Republicano*, and the subsidized press, such as *El Universal*, all of which had sought to draw public attention to the country's poor record of transportation safety as a patriotic concern.

Those newspapers that voiced a strong nationalist viewpoint had a powerful symbol in the foreign owned railway. Along with mining, outside interests, especially those from the United States, dominated the country's railroads.[127] Nationalist newspapers used the railway to promote the idea of developing Mexican owned industries. The repeated use of the railway to critique the Díaz government's pandering to U.S. companies suggested that it was an effective tool and that readers identified with the problems of economic and political sovereignty. This kind of nationalist rhetoric would prove to be compelling, convincing many to take up arms in 1910.[128]

While popular understandings of the railway accident most often found expression beyond the printed word, one penny press used railway accidents to highlight the attitudes of the Porfirian regime, especially those that affected the working class. *Don Cucufate's* cover donned an image of dismembered bodies with a poem that sardonically heralded the everyday horrors faced by the poor, joking that derailments, along with the closing of *pulquerias* (popular drinking establishments), were ways to educate the poor:

> Twenty-five crushed
> A bunch of suicides,
> Every other pigheaded person
> Divided by the knife.
> Pulqueria closures
> Derailment at the curve.
> That is how you teach the mob,
> With gossip and junk.[129]

The poem contrasted government concerns about the working class's morality and drinking habits with its indifference to their safety on the railway, drawing attention to what the poet felt were the misguided priorities of the elite.

The railway accident also surfaced in the tradition of the *cor-*

rido. Songwriters made three wrecks the subjects of ballads that lamented similar themes as those outlined in the press. Public opinion about the irresponsibility of foreign railway employees represented a common condemnation in the press and in popular expressions such as the *corrido.* Indeed, the "Corrido del descarrilamiento de Temamatla" placed the blame of the accident on its foreign driver; something it suggested was, in general, the main problem of the railway system:

> The locomotive pulled ten cars
> Number fifty-four,
> And its engineer was a foreigner,
> The cause of so much grief.[130]

Other *corridos* about train wrecks placed the blame on engineers who, as the ballad "El terrible choque y descarrilamiento del tren numero 2 con El Paso" (The terrible crash and derailment of train number 2 with El Paso) suggested, failed to listen to orders, again reiterating the theme of the recklessness of foreign drivers:

> The order was given
> he didn't want to obey it,
> it was to wait
> on another train in Santa Maria.[131]

One *corrido* went so far as to name the drivers directly and blame them for a 1904 Zacatecas railway wreck. In the ballad, two U.S. railroad employees, referred to as Lee and Moore, were blamed:

> The engineer Lee
> was taken to jail guilty
> and despite being a whitey
> it will be difficult to save himself.
> The conductor Mr. Moore
> finds himself in hot water,

> and it will not be easy, they assure,
> for the poor mister to save himself.[132]

At the time of the accident, the passengers of the doomed train pleaded with the driver to slow down. The accident prompted a virulent anti-Americanism in the Zacatecan press that led one reporter to conclude that Lee had been overcome by rage, a common occurrence among his people, who were "worse than savages" in their lack of humanitarian sentiment.[133]

But no *corrido* lambasted the American owned railways more than one published in the popular penny press *El Diablito Rojo*. Mexico's famed printmaker, José Guadalupe Posada, provided an image to accompany the song.[134] "El camino de ultratumba" (The track from beyond the grave) showed a train flying off the tracks, tossing religious pilgrims left and right, with the devil and a Yankee looking on and laughing. Above them all sat President Díaz on a throne untroubled by the disaster before him. The song went beyond blaming U.S. employees for train wrecks, as it also attacked those foreign firms for failing to properly compensate the victims, a phenomenon that became an especially contentious point after the Temamatla accident:

> When the company kills,
> it says: "I wash my hands,"
> and if someone charges a penny,
> asking for compensation,
> the gringos scream: "No way!"
> and here they respond: "Bravo!"[135]

Working-class penny presses often bemoaned the government's preference for U.S. capital over Mexican interests. In this case, *El Diablito Rojo* focused its ire not only on the administration's failure to support citizens seeking compensation for injuries and deaths but also on its defense of those companies' intransigence. This sentiment reflected an array of attacks made by working-

16. José Guadalupe Posada's "Camino de Ultratumba" (The track from beyond the grave). *El Diablito Rojo*, May 11, 1908.

class periodicals against the ruling elite's lack of patriotism.[136]

Together, the view of railway accidents in the popular press and in popular culture, especially the *corrido* and illustrations, demonstrated a widely held belief about the carelessness of foreign employees and the government's acceptance of their oversights. Expressions of animosity toward foreigners, revealed in the actions taken by local judges against railway conductors and engineers who often placed them under arrest for criminal negligence after a wreck, mirrored these sentiments. Even in cases where American railway employees proved not at fault, local officials—as the Sonoran case shows—nevertheless imprisoned them, sometimes for long periods and in squalid conditions. The actions of local officials reflected the growing popular sentiment about the impropriety and intolerance of U.S. companies and their employees toward Mexicans, represented in its most violent form: the train wreck.

As the public outrage over railway companies and their poor track record of safety shows, a pervasive radical sense of nationalism emerged during the Porfiriato. Historians of the Revolution have emphasized the role of national indignation against foreigners as one of the chief reasons for the popular rebellion. In particular, these scholars have highlighted the Cananea strike (1906) and the Río Blanco strike (1907) as crucial moments in the mobilization of workers against the Porfirian regime.[137] Rodney Anderson has asserted that the foreign ownership of railway lines and the poor treatment of railroad workers detailed by the press played an important role in fomenting nationalist sentiment and pushing individuals toward revolution.[138] An examination of railway accidents, and the perception that foreign companies cared little for the lives of Mexicans, reveals a long-standing and percolating antiforeign attitude. Indeed, the frequency of train wrecks—reported in the press, heard in ballads, and illustrated in popular art—underscored a sense of social injustice. Newspapers such as *El Hijo del Ahuizote* had a circulation of 24,000,[139] but the anti-American feelings espoused in *corridos* and artwork such as Posada's broadsheets reached a far wider audience. In this context, arguments that reject anti-Americanism as an important factor in the foment leading to revolution must be reconsidered.[140]

Conclusion

Together, the case of Temamatla, the Cardoso and Gloner lawsuits, and the increasing animosity toward foreign railway companies and their foreign employees all coalesced in the social imaginary, finding expression in poetry, songs, artwork, and press coverage. During the early years of railway development, the accident appeared as a negative consequence of a society moving toward modernity. The regularity of train wrecks and the view that the national government catered to the demands of foreigners while ignoring the plight of Mexicans convinced many sectors of Porfirian society that the price of progress had been too high. The railway accident helped undermine the fetishization of progress that many individuals had held toward the locomotive's utopian potential. The visceral reactions that people experienced as a result of railway accidents—whether reading graphic descriptions of wrecks or experiencing wrecks firsthand—exposed the human toll that underpinned the civilizing and modernizing mission.

The inauguration ceremonies explored in the previous chapter demonstrated that the ruling elite used these events to promote a sense of national identity for a country of villages and isolated rural areas. Inauguration ceremonies also promoted national identity by allowing city dwellers and provincials to visit regions of the country once prohibitively far away and by making the nation a more tangible concept. This chapter's examination of the social and cultural reactions to the perception that railway accidents resulted from the foreign ownership and operation of the transportation system shows yet another level of national identity, one built on a widespread belief that the fruits of progress and modernization should be enjoyed by Mexicans. In their attacks against the outside interests that controlled the railways, these sources reveal a popular (middle- and working-class) counter-nationalism that—at times blatantly, at times implicitly—defined the ruling elite's transportation policy as unpatriotic. Yet ironically, at the very same time that public opinion had coalesced around this belief, high-ranking members of the government such as Limantour likewise came to view foreign control of the railway as jeopardizing national sovereignty and economic development, an understanding that underpinned the 1908 nationalization.

After 1900, popular sentiment toward foreign railway companies turned sour, a phenomenon demonstrated not only in popular culture and the press but also in the actions of local officials and workers against foreign railway employees. Indeed, opposition and popular newspapers exploited the iconic power of the railway to highlight the growing animosity toward the government's modernization program. These cultural productions revealed a symbolic "war of position" that worked to undermine the government's legitimacy in civil society and to put forward an alternative understanding of what constituted just and fair policymaking. It was not that the middle and working classes shunned modernization per se but that they disagreed about how the Porfirian government had navigated through it. This is the topic to which we next turn.

La Loco-Matona

The Railroad in the Popular and Opposition Press

Hurling a groan from his chest
The monster roared forward,
And the body of the child was torn apart
Into pieces beneath the wheels.
And upon the inert body,
The train that swiftly retreated,
Left behind black plumes
As a death shroud.
Venus, seized by terror,
Fell upon her child
And, seeing his remains, unleashed
A harrowing scream.
And with the weight of pain upon her,
She cried out with profound sorrow:
There is no longer love in this world,
Because progress has killed it!

Gil Blas Cómico, October 26, 1896

While the railroad served as a symbol that government officials and supporters used to help legitimize Díaz's rule, opposition groups also used it to question, if not challenge, the regime's policies. The government's nation-building project of railway development, while fostering economic growth, foreign investment, and national integration, nevertheless incited a great deal of acrimony. The government's success at promoting the railway as a symbol of establishing order and progress proved to be a double-edged sword. The perceived failures of railroad development—what many believed to be the government's crowning achievement—not only served to question policymaking but also emerged as a common theme in the art, literature, and social commentaries in the popular and opposition press.[1] This chapter argues that the disillusionment about the efficacy of the railway, and the regime's economic, political, and social policies more generally, were also reflected in cultural venues such as popular art and literature that portrayed a darker, nefarious view of modernity and the consequences of technological progress. Opposition intellectuals shaped a counter-hegemonic discourse that underscored the contradictions inherent in the government's modernization program as well as in modernization itself. These expressions of disillusionment bridged the political and cultural realms seeking to reach people's hearts as much as their minds. In so doing, they offered people the opportunity to reconsider the so-called universal truths that defined the railway as the harbinger of national unity, prosperity, and civilization.

In contrast to the elite publications that made the railway a symbol of order, progress, and civilization (see chapter 2), publications targeting a broader audience tended to highlight the negative aspects of the locomotive's impact on daily life. Stories, poems, and broadsheet artwork instead focused on disorder, death, and tales of romance gone awry. They emphasized chaos and confusion as the consequences of modern life. They reflected the divergence between the elite's quotidian experiences with the railway and those of the middle and lower classes. They also made known a dual understanding of modernization that stressed the positive and negative impact of the locomotive on people's daily lives.

Likewise, orthodox liberal and working-class publications exploited the railway's iconic power to challenge government policies. They used it as a tool to attack not only government decisions related to transportation development but also a wide range of issues not directly related to railroad expansion. Writers and artists drew on the railway's symbolic power to challenge issues such as reelection, violations to the Constitution of 1857, foreign domination of the economy, the return of the Church into public life, and the growing authoritarianism of the regime. The opposition and penny presses—from serious newspapers such as El *Monitor Republicano* and *El Diario del Hogar* to sardonically humorous periodicals such as *El Hijo del Ahuizote* to the penny publications such as *El Diablito Rojo* and *El Chisme*—often employed the same discursive techniques as Díaz supporters during the early years of railroad development. The language of movement, energy, patriotism, civilization, and political stability was appropriated by challengers who wanted to undermine Díaz's political credibility. More than any other group, Daniel Cabrera and Ricardo, Enrique, and Jesús Flores Magón, men whose intellectual works represented the most articulate national opposition prior to the 1910 Revolution,[2] repeatedly used the locomotive to represent all aspects of Porfirian policymaking they viewed as detrimental to the nation.

Gil Blas Cómico and *El Hijo del Ahuizote* represented independent organs that opposed Díaz's program of authoritarian modernization. Both used humor, satire, and art to undertake political attacks against the regime. *Gil Blas Cómico* was a middle-class weekly costing five cents. Its founder, Francisco Montes de Oca, also the onetime managing editor of the long-running Catholic newspaper *El Tiempo*, demonstrated his opposition credentials with his repeated attacks on the government and by his imprisonments in the country's infamous Belén jail.[3] His weekly provided its audience with an array of readings from social commentary to amusing fiction. It offered poetry and stories, many of which featured the locomotive. While it only published for two years (1895–97), the daily it supplemented, *Gil*

Blas, ran for twenty-two years after it was launched in 1892. Its short lifespan might have resulted from the unfair competition of the more financially stable literary weeklies directed by Rafael Reyes Spíndola that were subsidized by the government. *Gil Blas Cómico* represents a valuable source as it covered a broad array of tastes, appealing to liberals and Catholics alike. Its contributors included Heriberto Frías, author of *Tomochic*, and the prolific author Antonio de P. Moreno as well as the famed illustrator José Guadalupe Posada. The country's leading Catholic intellectual, Trinidad Sánchez Santos, likewise wrote for the newspaper, publishing several conservative opinion pieces.[4] It also distinguished itself as one of the few periodicals that accepted and published materials submitted by the public.[5]

El Hijo del Ahuizote, edited by Daniel Cabrera and, then, the Flores Magón brothers and cousins Juan and Manuel Sarabia, established itself as the most irritating gadfly on the Porfirian windowsill. It represented the earliest clear opposition to the Porfirian government and the publication where several founding members of the Partido Liberal Mexicano (PLM) first cut their teeth as political dissidents.[6] It claimed a substantial circulation of 24,000.[7] In an era when most periodicals were ephemeral, *El Hijo del Ahuizote* survived from 1885 until 1903, a testament to its popularity. Furthermore, it did not go out of print for lack of readers but instead as a result of government persecution, a reaction that revealed government fears about the periodical's constant critiques and its wide readership. While Cabrera's newspaper clearly targeted the middle-class opposition dismayed by the regime's policies, it also took up the cause of workers and peasants. In this regard, *El Hijo del Ahuizote* could reach a far broader audience than the literate middle class as its centerfold images offered clear, didactic critiques of the government's authoritarian modernization.[8] While newspapers do not offer a complete representation of its readers' beliefs and ideals, the success and long life of Cabrera's weekly demonstrates that they identified with its subject matter and shared its concerns. With the wide array of competing periodicals, most of which failed to survive nearly as long as *El Hijo del Ahuizote*, Cabrera's subject matter and blistering critiques must have appealed to its audience; otherwise, his publication would have surely folded years earlier.

Disorder and Death

Railway poems and stories printed in the popular and opposition press emphasized considerably different themes than their more expensive, polite society counterparts. While elite publications did stress some negative consequences of modern life represented in locomotive travel, such as the fear of strangers or the increased risk for women in the public sphere, less expensive presses that targeted a broader readership provided tales about railway travel that highlighted confusion and chaos as part and parcel of modern life. *Gil Blas Cómico*, which clearly targeted middle-class audiences, stands out from other literary periodicals as it rarely published tales or poetry that represented the railway as a positive presence in the world, suggesting that its contributors—whether professional or amateur authors—used popular culture to question modernization and the capacity of new technologies to create order and promote civilization. These discourses presented a starkly different view of the locomotive than those offered by liberal politicians and intellectuals during the early Porfiriato or by bon ton periodicals such as *El Mundo Ilustrado* or *La Revista Moderna*. By characterizing the railway as a force of destruction and disorder, *Gil Blas Cómico*—as well as other independent and humorous periodicals such as *El Alacrán*, *El Chisme*, and *El Diablito Bromista*—rejected the conviction that it would regenerate and revitalize society.

In *Gil Blas Cómico*'s writings, modern marvels represented the increased complication of life and not time-saving tools made to ease people's lives. One such story, "El primer volido" (The first time away) told the tale of a young man who desperately wanted to travel outside Mexico City and, as the author put it, break free from his cage and fly. In a fortuitous bit of luck, he encountered Roberto, an old school chum, who invited him to his hometown, San Juan Teotihuacán, to celebrate the municipal president's birthday. Roberto told him that he could catch a train in the morning, arrive in San Juan, eat with his family, visit the pyramids, and then spend the day dancing before boarding a train back home in the evening. The narrator, excited about his upcoming journey, ordered a special travel outfit made by his tailor, purchased a new suitcase, as well as a travel flask with cognac, an ensemble so lavish he believed it was fit for a trip to Paris.

The day of the festivities, the narrator arrived at the Buenavista station and boarded a first-class train. As the train pulled out of the station, he chatted up an old woman who was also headed to San Juan. He told her that he planned to breakfast with his friend's family. Surprised, she explained that they would not arrive until the afternoon, much too late for breakfast. The narrator assured her that they would arrive soon. By noon, the narrator had not yet arrived in San Juan, and the old woman sat smiling, assured in her knowledge of the train schedule. As his stomach began to rumble, and there was no site of San Juan, the narrator began to curse Roberto for providing him with such poor information. Late in the afternoon the train pulled into San Juan, but Roberto had not shown up to meet his guest. The furious narrator decided to at least visit the pyramids alone. So he asked the old woman to please give him directions. Confused by the question, the old woman asked to what pyramids he referred. The narrator, about to explode from rage, exclaimed that he obviously meant the famed pyramids of Teotihuacán, to which she replied that she supposed they were in San Juan Teotihuacán, explaining that he had taken the train to San Juan del Río.[9] As this story suggested, modern travel might actually complicate life rather than offer convenience, a possibility that undermined assumptions about progress and the role of technology in society. Literature printed in middle- and upper-class periodicals often touted how railroad travel demanded a certain level of sophisticated expertise to make known the values and behaviors essential to urban life—for example, punctuality and knowledge of a train's schedule and routes. Yet here the author acknowledged the demands of the modern world while, at the same time, crafting a tale that revealed a frustration toward these newfound complexities.

The confusion spurred by railway travel depicted by writers also found expression in a tale about escapades in the train car itself, a story that emphasized the annoyances posed by strangers forced to ride in close quarters. In "En el interior de un coche del Ferrocarril Nacional Mexicano" (Inside a Mexican National Railroad car) various travel companions pestered the narrator. A widow in his compartment showed him the different pets she had brought on her trip, something the narrator could not care less about. First she showed him her Chihuahua puppy, which, to his irritation, nestled itself against his legs. Then she pulled out a parrot and insisted that he ask it questions so that it could respond. The annoyed traveler reluctantly obliged. Finally she took a sparrow out of a cage and allowed it to fly around the compartment. While the woman slept with her menagerie running loose, the author lost patience and grabbed all three animals and slammed them on the floor, creating an even more chaotic scene with the dog yelping, the parrot attacking the sleeping woman, and the sparrow flying out a window. The woman awoke to the frenzied action and began to hurl insults at the narrator.

Once she calmed down, the two traveled in complete silence to the next station, where a pair of Americans joined their compartment. While the train was stopped at the station, the Americans purchased some *aguardiente* (an alcoholic beverage) through the window of the train car. Unaccustomed to the strong flavor, they spat out their drinks, soaking both the *aguardiente* vendor and the older woman. The furious woman picked up her Chihuahua and flung it at the Americans. But the Americans were quick, ducked, and the dog flew out the same window that the sparrow had used to make its escape, striking a bystander outside. The woman, inconsolable and hysterical at the loss of yet another pet, demanded that the Americans compensate her financially for her dog, all the while the narrator laughed to himself. Then, while the woman sobbed into her hands, the narrator took advantage of her distraction to grab the parrot by the neck and toss it out the window. When the woman recognized that the last of her beloved animals was missing, she told all three of them to go to hell, leading the narrator to find another compartment to avoid further hostilities. At the next station, the narrator could see the two Americans outside buying *atole* (cornmeal drink) from a vendor. As one gulped down the hot liquid, he burnt his mouth and began screaming and jumping around like a madman.[10] And, with that peculiar scene, the story ended.

This story, like the one before it, characterized train travel in a way that highlighted disorder, confusion, and exasperation, experiences that flew in the face of more idealized representations of the railway as a symbol of order and civilization. In fact, the story discussed above perhaps offered readers a portrayal of railway travel that most people could identify with, even first-class passengers. Surely people who had ridden the railway could identify with the sentiment of being annoyed by fellow passengers or finding themselves in uncomfortable situations as a result of the compartment's close quarters. Like the tales published in elite periodicals, it also emphasized the importance of proper behavior and etiquette in the public realm. The story then made a veiled reference to the issue of compensation. The Americans ignored the woman's plea for financial compensation for her lost dog, while the narrator, perhaps realizing the futility of such a demand, laughed to himself.

Disorder and chaos most often found expression in stories about train wrecks. Especially in the years following the infamous Temamatla accident, authors characterized the Interoceanic Railway as the sum of all fears for passengers. Various periodicals joked about the Interoceanic. In *Gil Blas Cómico*, a short story about a man taking a trip to Veracruz began with the protagonist considering whether or not to receive his last rites before boarding the train.[11] The penny press, *El Chisme*, told readers that before traveling across the country, passengers should prepare their last will and testament.[12] Similarly *El Hijo del Ahuizote* advised that all passengers must follow six steps when preparing for a trip: bring a priest to confess at every curve; bring a doctor; write a will before boarding; hand out an obituary; write a suicide note; and prepay for a burial.[13] One story about a honeymooning couple headed to see the Shrine of Sacromonte in Amecameca, Mexico, offered an incredibly pessimistic view of modern travel. The tale, fraught with disaster for the newlyweds, involved three derailments, a fight on board between the engineer and disgruntled passengers, and the bride being seriously injured, all leading the groom to conclude that he would never travel on the Interoceanic again.[14]

El Alacrán, a ten-cent weekly that offered middle-class readers biting political and social commentary, used a mock account of Interoceanic Railway travel to highlight the failures of the regime. In a running travel chronicle called "De viaje" (On tour), produced in verse, the author ridiculed the elite travel narratives made popular among polite society by weeklies such as *El Mundo Ilustrado*. It recounted the travels of tourists headed to Veracruz. In the poem, the group encountered many annoyances, including rude Yankees who put their feet on the seats and only spoke English in the car. The tourists arrived in Veracruz to filthy streets, illegal gambling, and a sense that the city's inhabitants disliked the government:

> Arriving in Veracruz. Intense heat, . . .
> And although this train moves fast
> We arrived in Veracruz to no light.
> On the train there were many Yankees; almost all
> The travelers are Yankees
> Becoming so, by various ways,
> A lot of feet and few passengers.
> The Yankees' feet placed
> On the backs of seats,
> All of them swaying back and forth
> With the train's constant movements,
> In Yankee-land there are such manners.
> Everywhere we go
> We see a great unity of views;
> The eternal ideal
> In the port city is to speak ill of the government.[15]

By highlighting anti-American sentiments and the failures of government policy in regards to hygiene and policing, the poet took aim at social policies most often celebrated by the middle class.

The fear of traveling on the Interoceanic was also described in "Un día en el campo" (A day in the country), a short story about a man, desperate to get out of the city, who decided to take a train to the countryside. Although worried that he must take the "Interfernal" railway (a play on the name Interoceanico that combined it with "infernal"), he hailed a coach to take him to the station. But the driver, confused about the destination, took him to the Buenavista Railway Station, where the Mexican Central, not the Interoceanic, departed. While there, the coach was hit by a streetcar and the protagonist had to scramble to find another coach to take him to the correct station. But the new coach driver, rushing to the station and going too fast, hit a streetcar track, sending the wheels of the coach flying off. Fortuitously for the main character, he managed to arrive ten minutes before the train pulled out of the station. As he prepared to board, he spotted a sign reading "Cuidado con los Rateros" (beware of thieves). At that very moment, an individual pushed the narrator and stole his wallet with his train ticket. The protagonist was forced to postpone his trip.[16] The emphasis on crime and poor policing, again, demonstrates middle-class concerns about the failures of the government to properly secure social order, a policy that supporters commonly regarded as one of the regime's successes.

In another tale featuring the dreaded Interoceanic Railway, also titled "Día en el campo," a man told readers his first experience with locomotive travel. Before his parents' death, he had promised to take care of the family home after they passed away. His parents had stressed to him the importance of a sedentary life where he would responsibly handle the family business. For many years he had kept his promise, but eventually the desire to leave the city and breathe the country air had become too great, and the narrator decided to visit the Sierra Nevada. He decided to take the Interoceanic, although he feared the company's poor safety record. After arriving at two stations safe and sound, disaster struck as his train crashed into another locomotive, sending him out the window. Injured, he searched for a town to find medical attention. Two hours later, he came upon a small village where he spent the night. In the morning he realized that he was in a picturesque and majestic part of the country, although the villagers soon explained that it was governed by a tyrant. The narrator spent several days in the village recovering and making friends with the villagers. The day he planned to go back to the city, September 16, the villagers invited him to celebrate the Independence Day festivities, leading him to have one of the most entertaining nights of his life, a night marked by dancing, singing, and revelry. In the early morning hours, as the crowd of celebrants dissipated, the town master (*Amo*) had them arrested in an attempt to extort money from them. The narrator was likewise arrested and forced to pay before being set free. The story ends with the protagonist telling his readers that never again will he leave his small home in the city.[17]

Not only does this story highlight danger as a central aspect of railway travel, especially on the Interoceanic, but the author also posed a contradiction between the locomotive as a symbol of freedom, movement, and modernity with a portrayal of an antediluvian countryside characterized by the arbitrary authority that continued to exist outside the city. Yet the story suggested a reverence for a simpler, sedentary life demonstrated by the parents' warning not to leave town and by the kindness and joie de vivre of the villagers. Tales printed in *Gil Blas Cómico* that highlighted the railway as an agent of disorder represented the cultural expression of the nationalist critiques that the weekly's political counterpart—*Gil Blas*—leveled against the foreign owned Interoceanic Company and its safety record. Moreover, middle-class periodicals used cultural works to home in on a number of issues that concerned their readership about the failures of Porfirian rule. Hygiene, policing, corruption, tyranny, and foreigner domination of the economy were all topics that could be addressed through the genre of travel literature. The locomotive, often representing order, progress, equality, and freedom to the middle class, provided a powerful icon with which to undertake a series of policy critiques not related to railway development per se.

A novelette published in *Gil Blas Cómico* in five weekly installments connected the themes of love and death with disorder in a story where the railway again played a central role. "Percances de un peregrino Guadalupano" (The mishaps of a Guadalupe pilgrim) involved Don Serapión Seramiento de Parra, his sister, Doña Cleofas, and their servant, Antonio. The siblings, heirs to a fortune, lived in Chihuahua and spent their days in religious worship. The story began with Don Serapión about to embark on a railway journey to Mexico City to attend the crowning of the Virgin of Guadalupe. Doña Cleofas, wanting to attend the monumental event, implored her brother to take her. He refused, telling her that he "feared another Temamatla." The following day, he boarded a train to the country's capital.

Don Serapión's reservations proved to be well founded, as Yaqui Indians attacked and derailed his train, taking him prisoner. Back in Chihuahua, Doña Cleofas, accompanied by Antonio, had decided to catch a train to the capital despite her brother's warning. In the excitement of preparing for her travels, Doña Cleofas forgot that she had promised another servant, Atenógenes, that she would meet him that morning at a nearby ranch, and so she stood him up. Doña Cleofas and Antonio set out on a long walk in the desert heat toward Chihuahua City's train station where they prepared to board a Mexican Central train. At the station, Antonio opened the suitcase that held the tickets, and he made a problematic discovery: he had grabbed the wrong luggage, finding only dirty laundry that belonged to Doña Cleofas's brother.

Meanwhile, the Yaqui Indians decided to make a meal out of Don Serapión and marched him across the desert to their leader. Preparing to become a martyr to his faith, Don Serapión nevertheless prayed to the Virgin of Guadalupe to rescue him. The thought of being eaten by "savages," coupled with the extreme heat and exhaustion, began to drive him insane, and he collapsed on the ground, screaming the name of his sister, Cleofas. His Indian captor, in response, pulled out a knife and plunged it through his heart.

The melodrama continued the following week, leaving eager readers in suspense. The story continued with the Yaquis, who had disrobed Don Serapión and laid him on a pile of dead bodies he would surely join. While Yaqui Indians danced around his naked body, others prepared the fire where he would be cooked. As they began to lift him over the fire, gunshots rang out in the night, killing several Indians. The surviving Yaquis fled. Federal troops fighting the Indians had arrived and found the body of Don Serapión. The soldiers prepared a makeshift grave—only to realize that his heart still beat. They rushed him to the nearest city for medical attention. There Don Serapión laid in a coma for fifty days before awakening. Once recovered, he set out to return home, but despite the requests of military aides who agreed to return with him, he refused to ever ride a train again. So Don Serapión set off on horseback. Two days into the journey, he began to scream that he had been tricked, convincing himself that his horse was actually a locomotive in disguise. Don Serapión left the horse on the road and continued by foot, convincing everyone that he had lost his mind.

The story then shifted back to Doña Cleofas. She and Antonio commenced the long walk back home from the station, as they had no money or tickets with which to travel. Once home, days and days passed without any word from her brother. Then her neighbor arrived with terrible news she had read in the daily: Don Serapión had been eaten by cannibals. Doña Cleofas, after hearing the news, became seriously ill, teetering on the brink of death for five days. Antonio, a faithful servant, cared for her with supreme dedication. Once she recovered, Doña Cleofas told Antonio an important secret. She confessed that Don Serapión and she were not siblings but married. As she told Antonio, this was not the most shocking secret. She explained to the baffled servant that Don Serapión was actually the prince of China, Fi-Kan Chu-Pipí, and that she was Picu-Karo-Fan, daughter of the Sultan of the Tartars. She told Antonio that they had fallen in love, but since their fathers warred over a disputed territory, their love was forbidden. Together they fled, traveling half the globe, in an effort to find anonymity. She then offered Antonio a shocking proposition. Since Antonio was a loyal and handsome man, and since it would be immodest for a widow and young man to live together, she proposed that they marry. Days later, Antonio agreed. Rumors and gossip passed through the community about the scandalous wedding, but after a few days everyone forgot about Don Serapión. One day, as the newlywed couple lay in bed, Doña Cleofas heard a knock at the door. Opening it, Doña Cleofas thought she was staring at a ghost. There stood her first husband. She collapsed into his arms, babbling incoherent words about the ghost of Don Serapión.

But the story did not end there. In the final installment, Doña Cleofas, overcome by the vision of her late husband before her, dropped dead. As Antonio saw his wife gasp her last breath, he too succumbed to death, overcome by guilt and grief. Don Serapión, seeing the two dead bodies at his feet, began shouting: "The Apaches! The Apaches!" He likewise met his maker, falling on the body of Doña Cleofas. The story took its final odd turn when Atenógenes — the servant that Doña Cleofas left waiting at the ranch at the start of the story — reentered the narrative. The author told readers that Atenógenes, a man madly in love with Doña Cleofas, had never forgiven her for leaving him stranded. To make matters worse, after waiting hours for her, he saw her walking with Antonio toward that railway station. Overcome by his jealousy, made only more intense after his mistress's marriage to Antonio, Atenógenes plotted his revenge. Hearing the screams and commotion caused by Don Serapión's return, Atenógenes rushed to the scene to find three people dead and concluded that they had taken his revenge for him. He relieved the newlywed couple of their gold rings, looted the house, and headed to the train station. There he found a police officer and informed him that a terrible crime had taken place. As the officer hurried to the scene, Atenógenes boarded the locomotive.[18]

While the tale's overt racism made it an exception from the others discussed thus far, the subject matter played within broader discourses articulated in a variety of liberal, working-class, and Catholic newspapers that characterized Yaqui and Mayan Indians as obstacles to modernization and that ridiculed the perceived cultural differences of the Chinese. Yet it shared more similarities than not with the other narratives. This melodrama emphasized the confusion that characterized the modern era. Indeed, the world's growing interconnectedness that resulted from new transportation technologies represented one of the central aspects that furthered confusion in this story. The locomotive played a central role in causing disorder and death. Writers juxtaposed modernity—above all, the increased speed of communication and movement—with aspects of their society that they viewed as backward or uncivilized: the arbitrary authority exercised in the countryside, the dangers of train travel, or the "savage" Indians who attacked the locomotive. In all these examples, forces beyond the reach of modern technology undermined the civilizing capacity of the locomotive. In "Día en el campo," the train's derailment brought about the protagonist's tribulations, causing him to fall victim to the capricious power of the town boss. Likewise, in the novelette, Don Serapión's coma, stemming from the Yaqui's attack on the train and his subsequent refusal to ride the locomotive back to his home in Chihuahua, caused his wife to remarry and throw their world into flux. While these writings might appear as lighthearted distractions, they offered readers exaggerated accounts about aspects of railway travel that they could nevertheless understand: losing tickets, missing a train, boarding the wrong locomotive, or even experiencing a derailment. These all represented features of modern travel that were not as forgiving as older methods of travel that required less punctuality, expertise, or technical sophistication. Writers for the opposition presses examined here, as all these fictional accounts reveal, repeatedly used railway travel to emphasize themes of chaos and danger, a phenomenon, in some cases, similar to their elite counterparts. Yet

Gil Blas Cómico was distinct insofar as its subject matter overwhelmingly highlighted the negative aspects of modern travel and life more generally.

Death, along with disorder, became one of the most common themes articulated by *Gil Blas Cómico* writers on the subject of the iron horse. Since train wrecks had captured people's imagination, especially after Temamatla, the belief that railway travel risked life and limb gained prominence. Writers reflected this newfound anxiety by concentrating on the locomotive's destructive capacities and at times equated it with death itself. The emphasis on death not only found expression in narratives concerning derailments or accidents but also emerged in writings about everything from the loss of love to the nostalgia for simpler times. Railway travel proved to be a powerful and familiar symbol — familiar insofar as new transportation technologies affected people's lives at all levels of society — used to engage a plethora of different issues.

Like the periodicals targeting the country's bon ton, the train's function of taking groups of people to the same destination reminded many writers of death as a universal reality that everyone faced. One poem about a terminally ill man preparing for death was titled "Tren Expreso" (The express train), the name of the capital's tramways. The poet used the streetcar as a metaphor for death:

> My letter, that is joyous, searches for you,
> And will give you an account of my memory,
> I am that ghost, for loving you,
> Vowed to be alive by your side one day.
> When he delivers this letter to your ear
> The echo of my love and my pain,
> The body in which my spirit has lived
> Will be sleeping under some flowers. . . .
> But perhaps up there we will see each other,

After this fleeting existence,
When the two of us, like the train, reach
The last station of our lives. . . .
Goodbye, goodbye! As I deliriously speak,
I don't know how to say what I want to say!
The only thing I know of myself is that I'm crying,
That I'm suffering, that I loved you, and that I'm dying![19]

The connections between love, death, and the railway emerged as a popular topic in *Gil Blas Cómico*. A poem submitted from Puebla, "En la estación" (In the station), lamented the capacity of modern technology to create distance between lovers. It recounted the story of a young man who, while eagerly waiting to see his sweetheart return from Paris, dreams of her death:

Fifteen years ago . . . the adolescent girl
Was carried away by merciless fate. . . .
She went to Paris . . . fatal melancholy
Accompanied me while she was away.
She arrives today . . . joyful and impatient
I await her . . . what commotion?
Ah! . . . the train whistles . . . it approaches . . . and my Maria?
Eureka! . . . here she comes . . . she sees me smiling . . .
My girlfriend arrived sick; in love
I passionately embraced her . . . she looked at me uncertain . . .
She placed a frozen kiss on my mouth;
Uttered a cry of pain and . . . fell dead:
We were set in motion . . . I lie! I woke up frightened,
Embracing the bar of the door.[20]

While the locomotive had the capacity to compress time and space, it also fostered a perception that the speed of mechanized motion created greater distance between people. This poet envisioned that distance as a void where the unknown could have grievous consequences.

Another poem, one imported from France, lamented that progress had destroyed love, suggesting the cold, indifferent nature of modernity. In "Ya no hay amor" (There is no longer love), the poet told a story of Venus and Love taking a stroll unaware that they were walking along train tracks. Love, portrayed as an innocent child, ran along the tracks getting further and further away from Venus. Then Venus heard the monstrous roar of the locomotive approaching, and she called out to Love, but it was too late. The machine had crushed the child and continued to march on, unmolested, spewing black smoke into the air. The poet concluded by telling readers that Love no longer existed, as it had been killed by progress.[21]

The image provided a haunting metaphor of progress relentlessly driving forward, indifferent to the devastation it might cause. *Gil Blas Cómico*, in the two years it was published, provided readers with literature that celebrated a bucolic past that longed for simplicity and a sense of social harmony. The evils of the modern world were explored through a nostalgic view of the past that while imperfect nevertheless appeared more innocent and moral. In this case, the poem revealed the same concerns shared by Catholics such as the intellectual Trinidad Sánchez Santos, who criticized developmentalist liberalism as too materialistic and individualistic, qualities that undermined social cohesion.[22] The poem suggested that progress had undermined the collective well-being represented by Love. Here the author chose a romantic metaphor, but the message could be projected onto a variety of issues: the loss of life, the loss of people's land, or the loss of political freedoms. The negative assertions about the railway in this poem reflected sentiments expressed in the political critiques of the Porfirian regime. The perception that Díaz and the *científicos* had promulgated draconian laws and policies as a means of securing material progress matched well with the attitudes expressed by opposition groups, especially *El Hijo del Ahuizote*, *El Ahuizote Jacobino*, and *Regen-*

eración. These newspapers constantly attacked decrees such as the *ley fuga* and the 1884 Land Law implemented to protect and promote economic development as devastating to the people's livelihood. Furthermore, these same periodicals often looked to the past—for example, the presidency of Benito Juárez—as an idealized time when the country adhered to the Constitution of 1857.[23]

Another *Gil Blas Cómico* narrative that drew connections between love, death, and the railway offered readers a suspenseful story about love gone awry. "Un drama por celos" (A tragedy as a result of jealousy) centered on Pedro, a fifty-year-old railway employee whose loyal service and work ethic had secured him the job as a tunnel guard. Near the tunnel, he built a small home for himself and his wife, Rosa. She was a tall, dark-skinned beauty of thirty-five years whom travelers admired as they went by on the train or when they bought goods from her at the nearby station. Pedro and Rosa's jobs required waving a white flag at the locomotive's engineer if the tunnel was clear or a red one if the tunnel was obstructed. The tale's drama centered on Rosa, who did not recognize the extreme love and devotion that Pedro showed her. Pedro had always considered himself inferior to Rosa because of her beauty, and she took advantage of this, repeatedly making a cuckold of her husband. Pedro nevertheless accepted his wife's infidelities and continued to show her affection. The story took a darker turn when one day Pedro heard noises coming from the tunnel. Investigating the commotion, he caught a glimpse of his wife with a man from a nearby village. No longer able to control his anger at his wife's flagrant challenges to his honor, he prepared to confront the pair of illicit lovers. At that moment, he heard the whistle of an approaching train. He scrambled to get the red flag to warn the train's engineer that people were inside the tunnel, but then, with a "diabolic smile," he grabbed the white flag and gave the train free pass. The train roared through the tunnel and Pedro could hear screams of distress and, then, only silence. The train came out the other side spewing a cloud of black smoke.[24]

In this story the locomotive appears as an agent of retribution in a tragedy it helped spur. It not only became the tool with which a betrayed husband exacted revenge on his cheating wife, but it also was the object that brought her into contact with other men. While the drama might not have fed into people's apprehensions about government policies, it nevertheless reminded readers about the destructive potential of modern technology. The story could also have played on men's fears about the changing roles of women who became more present in the public sphere. In this case, Rosa sold goods at the station and assisted her husband with his duties as tunnel guard. The writer used the growing presence of women in public to highlight the perceived breakdown of the family structure, a theme likewise articulated in the elite press.

The era of progress, as argued by Claudio Lomnitz, introduced the "massification of death" that resulted from the capacity of new technologies to mechanize killing through, for example, railway wrecks. It also fostered a perception that the accelerated pace of modern life hurried people toward death.[25] Literary themes played on the idea of death to represent a world of endless flux where forces beyond people's control pushed them forward into the unknown, a phenomenon that was not always understood as progress in a positive sense. The various works that associated modernity, symbolized by the railroad, with death demonstrated a new self-consciousness about the turbulent, ephemeral nature of the times. Writers translated this anxiety into tales about family, love, and life, all of which no longer appeared as familiar, constant, or controlled.

While periodicals targeted to middle- and upper-class audiences at times demonstrated concerns about the changes spurred by modernization, *Gil Blas Cómico* was unique insofar as its literature consistently represented the locomotive as a symbol of death and disorder. In part this reflected a general and growing disillusionment with the failures of modern technology to improve people's lives. It also revealed that the directors, editors, and writers of *Gil Blas Cómico* shared a nostalgic view of a past that had been lost as a result of modernization. Stories and poems often emphasized the violence, confusion, and complexity that resulted from technological change. In these negative portrayals, the authors appeared to yearn for a more innocent past identified with childhood, home, and hierarchy.[26] This literature, above all, stressed the dangers of the increased mobility offered by industrial travel, coveting the isolation and sedentary life that characterized the past to which society could not return.

The Railroad and the Critique of Economic Policy
While the short-lived *Gil Blas Cómico* offered readers poems, tales, and anecdotes about railway travel, the majority of popular and opposition newspapers preferred to use the locomotive to criticize government policies. In 1885, Daniel Cabrera's *El Hijo del Ahuizote* embarked on an unyielding crusade against Díaz and his administration. Its writers' relentless critiques—both satirical and serious—landed Cabrera in Mexico City's notorious Belén jail several times. In 1902, due to ill health resulting from his stints in prison, Cabrera handed over control of the newspaper to the Flores Magón brothers and then to the cousins Juan and Manuel Sarabia, who continued to publish the periodical until the following year, when Díaz had them arrested as well as their staff, closing down the fiery periodical for the final time.[27] Among the many aspects of Porfirian economic development that the newspaper condemned, the railway program served as one of the most often criticized aspect of policymaking. Railroad expansion cut across almost every other issue that concerned radical liberals: political centralization, suspended rights, land expropriation, foreign domination, and agricultural, mining, and industrial policy.

Since railway development played a central role in invigorating economic activities and provided faster transportation of goods and resources to ports, underpinning the export economy, opponents of the government regularly targeted it in their critiques of trading, agricultural, and industrial legislation. The high subsidies offered by the government to foreign companies to undertake railway building, a policy decision that substantially increased national debt through the negotiation of foreign loans and the release of domestic bonds,[28] came to represent an especially troublesome development to writers for *El Hijo del Ahuizote.*

In an article discussing the country's financial woes and foreign debt as a result of the railroad, *El Hijo del Ahuizote* printed an article titled "Liquidación de Tuxtepec" (Liquidation of Tuxtepec), emphasizing its importance with a parenthetical note above the heading that read, "Seriously." In it, Cabrera told readers that the government had offered too many compromises to foreign railway companies through subsidies and amortization payments, claiming that this policy would lead to a national financial crisis. He asserted that the people could not support the unbearable weight of debt placed on their shoulders and that the republic would develop too slowly and unevenly as a result. Cabrera linked this problem to the Revolution of Tuxtepec, telling readers it was the despotism of Díaz that allowed for the implementation of misguided economic policies.[29]

The war of words waged by *El Hijo del Ahuizote* represented one dimension of its critique, but its war of images reached a far wider audience.[30] The images used by the newspaper, illustrations made at first by Cabrera and then by Jesús Martínez Corrión, repeatedly showed Tio Samuel (Uncle Sam) riding a locomotive and threatening the nation's well-being. The weekly's mysterious artist Fígaro—actually Cabrera himself—illustrated a Yankee locomotive characterized by a bull riding along tracks labeled "contracts," about to trample an infant representing the

17. Attitudes for the future: The cattle of Uncle Sam. At the expense of the *pueblo*. *El Hijo del Ahuizote*, December 23, 1887.

country's nascent industrial sector. An individual representing the people (*el pueblo*) and a woman representing the Republic stood alongside the infant in a fruitless attempt to stop the raging machine.[31] The image made a clear point: the government had supported U.S. interests over the good of the people, the Republic, and, in so doing, had also impeded the development of the nation's own industrial sector. *El Hijo del Ahuizote* and other orthodox and radical liberal organs put forward a different vision of economic and political policy. They promoted more nationalist policies where the country could develop its own native industries, demonstrating an early example of economic nationalism.

The completion of the San Luis Potosí–Tampico line in 1890, while celebrated by federal and state governments, irritated *El Hijo del Ahuizote*'s contributors, who protested against the large government subsidies offered to complete the line as well as the high freight rates that they viewed as undermining any hope of promoting national industry. For the inauguration of the line, the cover of *El Hijo del Ahuizote* donned its fanged namesake mascot greeting the inaugural train with a poem that juxtaposed the country's hopes and happiness toward the new railway with what its editors understood to be overly generous subsidies to the railway companies:

> The swift locomotive
> That arrives at the heroic port.
> It unites those brotherly pueblos,
> And I too scream: Long Live!
> And applaud with my soul and hands.
> By force of subsidies
> And fat contributions,
> Tampico and San Luis end up
> In close [but hard-up] relations
> With the rest of the country.[32]

Months after, they printed an illustration showing a character representing the country's commerce forced off the top of the San Luis-Tampico train by a menacing snake labeled "tariffs." Jumping off the train, the frightened man recognized he would land on a cluster of powder kegs identified as merchandise and freight.[33] The image offered a condemnation of the Mexican National's increased tariffs, which, according to the editors of *El Hijo del Ahuizote*, undermined the flow of local products and the development of local markets.

Years later, the belief that railway policies stymied national economic development continued to draw the ire of Daniel Cabrera and his coworkers. In response to raised freight rates by the Mexican and Interoceanic lines in 1900, *El Hijo del Ahuizote* produced an illustration that showed the minister of communication and public works, Francisco Mena, on a locomotive labeled "freight hikes" chasing down a bride and groom, identified as commerce and industry, who frantically scurried from the train.[34] This sentiment was by no means solely that of oppo-

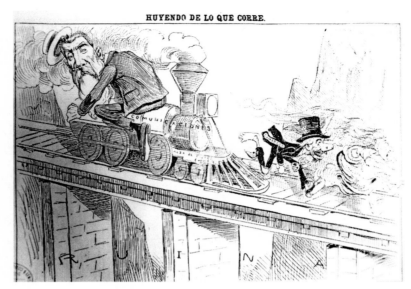

18. Fleeing from what runs: Taken instants after the last railway disaster.
El Hijo del Ahuizote, June 10, 1900.

sition groups. Between 1892 and 1899 the Mexican Chamber of
Commerce made repeated protests about increased cargo rates
as high as 100 percent for third-class freight.[35] Cabrera and his
staff never offered readers probing economic analysis or complex
formulas regarding freight rates like the newspapers *El Monitor
Republicano*, *La Industria Nacional*, or *Semana Mercantil*; instead, they simply pointed out that the government offered foreign companies huge subsidies paid for with foreign loans. In
this way, *El Hijo del Ahuizote* could reach a much greater audience by not alienating lay readers with long-winded economic
analyses or mathematical equations. The simplified assessments
of government economic policy could be easily reproduced in
images that resonated among the country's large illiterate population.[36] These images also provided common people the opportunity to take part in discussions about economic and political policies from which they were excluded. Railway policies
favored by the Díaz administration provided fodder to question
the export-based model of economic growth and allowed them

to advocate for nationalist policies that favored homegrown industry and less dependence on foreign capital.[37]

Opponents of the regime, then, understood the government's program of railway development as centered on expanding the export economy at the expense of developing national industry. In so doing, the government had failed to defend national interests in their transportation policy.[38] Recent studies have attributed more agency to Porfirian officials in their policy decisions, arguing against studies that emphasized the government's weakness in relation to foreign owned companies. Furthermore, they have challenged traditional conclusions and maintain that transportation infrastructure allowed for the development of internal markets.[39] Yet as the cultural works examined here clearly show, opponents of the regime did not view railway development in this way. While these recent studies have offered a needed tempered assessment of the Porfiriato, the regime's fiercest critics understood foreign domination of the economy and the inability to promote national industry as the central failure of Porfirian transportation and economic policy. Even Francisco Madero, who harbored little animosity toward U.S. business interests' role in Mexico, had been angered by the administration's licensing to large U.S. companies whose price-lowering trade practices had undermined his families' agricultural profits, especially in the cotton industry.[40] Criticisms regarding national sovereignty, above all, reflected the ideas espoused by the early PLM that feared a transition from economic to formal imperialism,[41] a concern most clearly expressed in *El Hijo del Ahuizote*'s slogan, "*México para los Mexicanos*" (Mexico for the Mexicans).

The Railroad and Foreigners

The opposition and popular press considered the increased presence of foreigners as inextricably linked to Porfirian economic policy. Railway development not only irritated opponents of the regime insofar as it fostered foreign, especially U.S., domination of the economy; it also offended their sensibilities regarding cultural values such as manners and morality as demonstrated by the press's regular complaints regarding the behavior of foreign workers, either in terms of their impolite actions or their disdain toward Mexicans. The government's transportation policy cultivated a strong nationalist sentiment among the opposition press throughout the entire Porfiriato, beginning from the earliest railway concessions handed out by Díaz in his first term.

Between 1880 and 1884, during the presidencies of Díaz and Manuel González, a cross-section of the press feared that railway concessions to U.S. companies would allow for a military invasion. Prominent members of Congress had showed trepidation about the possibility of a U.S. attack, or at least U.S. economic supremacy over the nation, contending that the government should promote the construction of a railway linking the Pacific and Atlantic coasts before completing a railway to the northern border. Indeed, even long-time political supporters such as Ireneo Paz, who supported the Revolution of Tuxtepec and whose son Arturo headed the "Circle of Friends of General Porfirio Díaz,"[42] demonstrated unease toward the president's railway strategy. His periodical *El Padre Cobos*, in 1880, depicted a powder keg—branded "railroad business"—on the verge of exploding with politicians and businessmen scrambling for safety.[43] Likewise, in 1882, the humorous periodical *El Rasca Tripas*, by no means an opposition newspaper, questioned the patriotism of President González and accused him of making himself rich from corrupt contracts offered to U.S. companies.[44] They predicted that the completion of a railway to the northern border would allow their northern neighbors to enter the country with guns in hand.[45]

Despite early fears that linking the United States and Mexico with railway lines would facilitate a military invasion, this sentiment dissipated while fear of U.S. economic control of the country increased. The heavy investment in railway projects by U.S. interests denoted a particularly troublesome phenomenon for the opposition press. These reservations were justified, as one-third of foreign investment went to railway development and of that 42 percent came from U.S. companies.[46] Critiques regarding U.S. domination of the railway system shifted to concerns about an economic takeover of the country as well as a fear that U.S. immigration would allow for a slower, less violent conquest. In one edition, *El Hijo del Ahuizote* displayed its xenophobia, complaining that the railway had allowed Yankee and other foreign colonies to pour into the country. In an illustration, they showed a train crammed with gigantic feet—a common caricature portraying U.S. citizens—arriving in Mexico.[47] Cabrera blamed the perceived dangers of a growing U.S. presence on Díaz and the Tuxtepec Revolution that brought him to the presidential chair. Since, in his first term in office, Díaz succeeded in finalizing contracts with two U.S. companies that would connect the two nations, an accomplishment lauded by supporters, Cabrera's sardonic "Dictionary of the Tuxtepec Language" defined the word "railroad" as a "Trojan Horse, replete with Yankees."[48]

In 1903, the final year *El Hijo del Ahuizote* was published, before authorities arrested the Flores Magón brothers and destroyed their printing presses, its editors rang in the New Year by offering readers a state of the union address. In it, they acknowledged the economic and material advancements made under Díaz but questioned whom those changes benefited. They confirmed that the people, entering into 1903, would see the countryside crisscrossed by railroads, the rivers by steamboats, and the air clouded with dense columns of smoke rising from workshops and factories, heralding activity and work. Yet they reminded readers that the product of that work would not be for the people; rather, it would replenish the coffers of a few elite and line the pockets of foreigners.[49] They continued to make known their fears of foreign exploitation the following year in the periodical's short-lived successor, *El Ahuizote Jacobino*, also founded by Cabrera, when they attacked the proposed Pan-American railway that, theoretically, would link Alaska to Argentina. Cabrera made known his fear of the United States' imperial ambitions in the Americas with an image of Uncle Sam straddling the continent and holding a locomotive spewing smoke. Its plume read, "100,000,000 in gold."[50]

While U.S. economic domination clearly distressed Cabrera and the Flores Magón brothers, the increased presence of Yankee workers and their attitudes toward Mexicans also offended their nationalism. Opponents who criticized the U.S. command of the railway industry focused their indignation on railway employees whom they characterized as rude, careless, or malicious. Much of this attitude resulted from the frequency of railway accidents that all sectors of the press—even pro-Díaz and subsidized periodicals—blamed on foreign companies and their American workforce. The press attacked all levels of railway employees from ticket agents to conductors and engineers.

The opposition and popular press regularly printed accounts of rude employees at train stations across the country. Of all the railway companies, the Mexican Central received the most criticism for its ticket agents. *El Nieto del Ahuizote*—a one-penny daily that supplemented *El Hijo del Ahuizote*—admonished the Mexican Central for its employees' poor conduct. They reported that at the Celaya station a family arrived to buy tickets and board a train, but the ticket agent ignored their requests, choosing instead to sleep at his post. Then, when awoken, he bombarded them with insults, forcing the family to buy their tickets from the conductor.[51] Likewise, *El Chisme*—another penny afternoon daily—directed by Montes de Oca and replete with Mexico City gossip, provided regular accounts of disrespectful and dishonest U.S. employees. For example, it lambasted the Mexican Central for hiring a rude U.S. worker that whenever possible demonstrated his aversion to Mexicans, insulting and beating native employees under his command.[52] They again reported the misconduct of a Yankee ticket agent who refused to make change for second- and third-class passengers and allegedly kept the extra money.[53] Months later, they bemoaned another American who refused to allow a family to board a train with a small basket of fruit, allegedly taking it for himself.[54] When possible, *El Chisme* writers printed accounts of Mexican railway workers who demonstrated respect or concern for their countrymen. In one case, an old man boarding an Interoceanic train in Mexico City was caught with one leg on the train and the other on the platform as the train screeched out of the station. A Mexican employee, risking his own life, pulled the man from the train, saving him from serious injury.[55]

El Hijo del Ahuizote had a running joke, sometimes accompanied by a caricature of a portly U.S. train engineer or conductor, about the poor Spanish spoken by railway employees. In one issue, it displayed a train called *"La mi non tende"* (satirized poor Spanish meaning "I don't understand") with an American conductor hanging on for dear life as his train barreled down a winding track at 100 kilometers per hour. A poem accompanied the illustration that told readers that the railways, while paid for by Mexicans, killed as a result of their reckless U.S. engineers. The poem highlighted the apparent contradictions of the regime that sought to civilize the people yet allowed the railway system to be operated by savage Yankees who constantly put passengers in peril.[56] In a mock presidential address to Congress, Díaz boasted that the country had secured 80,000 kilometers of track operated by highly paid Yankees who did not know a word of Spanish and treated Mexicans terribly.[57]

In the final years of the Porfiriato, two other notable penny presses — *El Diablito Bromista* and *El Diablito Rojo* — kept up the attacks against the railway companies' foreign employees. They especially targeted the poor treatment of workers, publishing accounts of bosses who refused to hire or fairly pay Mexi-

19. La mi non tende. *El Hijo del Ahuizote*, March 17, 1895.

cans and of conductors who insulted or abused native passengers.[58] In one case, *El Diablito Bromista* reported that a U.S. conductor had attempted to kick off a passenger for having been five cents short of his fare. When other Mexicans passengers offered to pay the difference, the Yankee conductor refused, instead taking the man's blanket as payment.[59] As with the *corridos* about train wrecks examined in the previous chapter, the penny press's nationalist outrage against the American owned and operated lines revealed a popular counter-nationalism to the ruling elite's that stressed cosmopolitanism and that was inspired by foreigners. By attacking the government for selling out the nation to outside interests, a decision that made the lives of the poor more precarious (due to accidents) and economically insecure (due to the favoring of foreign employees), popular sectors by extension vilified the government as unpatriotic.[60]

The cultural divide between Americans and Mexicans—whether expressed in language or manners—likewise emerged as a common theme in the popular press and popular music. *El Diablito Rojo*, which printed the illustrations of the famed and influential graphic artist José Guadalupe Posada, published *cor-*

ridos critical of U.S. behavior in Mexico. One such *corrido*, "Golondrinas . . . Ferrocarriles" (Swallows . . . Railways) used the lyrics to condemn Americans as rude and insolent visitors and as thieves who stole the country's wealth. The song put forward an eerily prophetic prediction—as the Revolution would erupt only months later—that they would leave and never return, stating that Americans would return home and never eat Mexican food again:

> The herds of gringos
> Will emigrate once again from
> Yankee-land
> And will again come to Mexico
> So rude and insolent.
> For those converted into masters
> That want to rule on the trains,
> Those that suckled at two teats
> They . . . will not return!
> They will again sing Yankee Doodle
> They will sell tobacco by the sack full;
> But they will never again
> Eat tortillas and beans.[61]

As these examples demonstrate, the opposition's commentaries about railway development revealed a deep hostility toward American control of the country's transportation system.[62] Emphasis on the role of anti-Americanism in the outbreak of the Revolution represents one principal strand of its historiography. These studies have emphasized issues of economic and political domination as an important factor that led people to support a revolution aimed at securing national liberation, especially among the working and middle classes.[63] Yet the press's condemnation also resulted from people's quotidian experiences in mundane encounters such as buying train tickets, riding in passenger cars, or working alongside disrespectful foreigners. These encounters encouraged strong reactions by ordinary individuals that the penny presses reflected.

The Railroad and Securing Social Order

Before significant railway development could be achieved, the Díaz administration needed to establish internal political and social stability. Díaz succeeded in ending the endemic political volatility that had characterized the country since Independence through the rotations of military commanders and state governors, and promoted social order through the use of local police forces, *rurales* (rural police), and the military.[64] These various strategies allowed for decades of unprecedented peace, a period that gave confidence to foreign companies to invest in the country's agricultural, mining, and transportation sectors. Nevertheless, in the case of railway development, opponents of the government viewed the sometimes draconian methods of securing social order as an unacceptable sacrifice to make for material advancement. Indeed, political gadflies such as *El Hijo del Ahuizote* repeatedly used words and images to underscore the heavy social and political costs for securing "order and progress." They offered commentaries that accentuated the contradictions of the regime and, in so doing, undermined the characterization of the so-called *pax porfiriana*, emphasizing government-sponsored violence as the prerequisite for social peace. As much as the elite understood railway development as a marker of civilization, opposition journals stressed the barbarity of government policies related to modernization.

Above all, the suspension of guarantees enshrined in the Constitution of 1857, first implemented by Benito Juárez, but fully exploited by Díaz, used against lawbreakers—from train robbers to persons caught tampering with railway materials—received harsh criticism from the regime's opponents. The suspension of liberal guarantees found its most ruthless expression in the infamous *ley fuga*, a practice used by the *rurales* of shooting prisoners in the back on the bogus excuse that they were attempting to escape. The opposition press regularly represented the *ley fuga* as a cornerstone of the government's railway program. *El Hijo del Ahuizote* chided Mexico City's pro-government newspapers for their support of the suspension of guarantees, and its most violent articulation, the *ley fuga*, used against bandits who held up trains. It commented that President Manuel González had made millions in corrupt contracts and thus had robbed more from the nation than any bandit. Indeed, the press often criticized Manual González for the corruption of his administration. In his overseeing of railway concessions, handed out at a remarkable rate during his time in office, González was well known for acquiring land along planned railway routes.[65] The article concluded by questioning why some bandits received the death penalty and others, like the onetime president, did not.[66]

That same year *El Nieto del Ahuizote* attacked the U.S. newspaper *Railway Age* for its support of the suspension of guarantees when it applauded the arrest and execution of an individual who derailed a train. It grumbled sarcastically that the U.S. government should implement such legal practices, considering their fondness for the policy in Mexico, something it predicted would lead to the downfall of its economic activity and progress.[67] *El Hijo del Ahuizote*, days later, printed a sinister image illustrating the suspension of guarantees and the *ley fuga*. It showed Díaz as an engineer, his locomotive reading "Tuxtepec," hauling behind it wagons heaped with skulls and bones. The exterior of the trains read: "The bones of bandits or the accused. Suspensions, escape (*fuga*), and company. Sent to history in the name of the pretext given for moral and public order."[68] The image offered a scornful picture that depicted the use of the *ley fuga* as a despotic tactic employed by the government to ensure, by whatever means, material progress. The program of authoritarian modernization, together with opponents' under-

20. A freight train—with history as its destination, outside of all rights and police authority. *El Hijo del Ahuizote*, November 21, 1886.

standing that it benefited the economic exploitation of the country, provided a two-pronged critique of railway policy. It simultaneously stressed that foreign control of the economy not only jeopardized sovereignty, both economic and political, but also jeopardized the safety of ordinary citizens by suspending rights guaranteed in the Constitution.

Cabrera and his staff relished every opportunity to highlight the contradictions it viewed in government policy and rhetoric, especially in regard to its self-glorification about the social order it had established. The government's claims that it had eradicated banditry provided fertile ground for criticism as *El Hijo del Ahuizote* subverted that assertion by characterizing foreign interests as plunderers. They often pointed out the irony that while the government sought to protect the country from train assaults and robbery, U.S. companies extracted money and resources by exploiting the government's low tariff and subsidy policies. In one commentary, they noted acerbically that while the railway company and the government could guarantee safety

El Hijo del Ahuizote

NÚMERO 355

SEMANARIO POLÍTICO, DE OPOSICIÓN FEROZ
É INTRANSIGENTE CON TODO LO MALO.

DIRECTOR Y PROPIETARIO, DANIEL CABRERA.

TOMO VII.   Ciudad de México, Domingo 13 de Noviembre de 1892.   AÑO SÉPTIMO.

UN OBSEQUIO A LA MATONA.

(Inauguraciones de los ferrocarriles de Oaxaca y de Durango.)

Doña Matona la egregia
De Tuxtepec esperanza
Con esta mejora regia
Perfecciona la estrategia
Que demanda la Ordenanza.

21. A gift to the Matona. *El Hijo del Ahuizote*, November 13, 1892.

235

from bandits, they also guaranteed thieves at every station, the comfort of a sardine can, and a derailment every twenty minutes.[69] They used this issue of banditry to likewise lampoon the government's obsession with making the country safe for investment. After a 1902 train robbery in the Laguna region, one illustration ridiculed the Chihuahua and Durango police forces, showing them as drooling dolts mistakenly keeping a look out in the wrong direction. Behind them, an Express train roared by replete with laughing Yankees carrying bags of money.[70]

One final symbolic link made by *El Hijo del Ahuizote* between railway development and the regime's heavy-handed tactics at maintaining social order coalesced in the image of Díaz's infamous sword, La Matona (the bully/the killer). Cabrera and his staff regularly employed it to accentuate the violence that underpinned order. They expressed this connection on the front cover of an issue that questioned the regime's celebrations of the inauguration ceremonies held for the Durango and Oaxaca railways, the International and the Mexican Southern, respectively. It showed Díaz offering two tiny trains, labeled Durango and Oaxaca, to a woman representing the embodiment of La Matona standing at her windowsill. Below the image, a short poem expressed how government violence enshrined in law buttressed the social order that had allowed for railway expansion:

> Mrs. Killer the illustrious
> The hope of Tuxtepec
> With this regal improvement
> Perfects the strategy
> That the order requires.[71]

Alluding to the high accident rates of the foreign owned railways, Cabrera and his cohort referred to the locomotive as the *loco-matona* (the crazy killer, also a play on the name of Díaz's sword). One illustration juxtaposed the enthusiasm people felt toward railway travel with the carnage it could cause. It warned

22. The great loco-matona (crazy killer). What it receives. What it delivers.
El Hijo del Ahuizote, March 10, 1895.

readers with a split image: on one side a jubilant group of travelers cheer the arrival of the train, on the other side the train delivers a pile of skulls and bones.[72]

Again, *El Hijo del Ahuizote* offered readers effective, yet
jocular, criticism of the regime, a strategy that allowed them
to reach a wider audience without the more highbrow, alienating style of newspapers such as *El Monitor Republicano* or *El
Diario del Hogar*. While these newspapers were no less relentless in their critiques, they could not foster the same popular
appeal as a heavily illustrated publication such as *El Hijo del
Ahuizote*. These commentaries and illustrations allowed challengers to highlight the discrepancies between the national image that the government wanted to portray and the realities that
opponents believed the people endured. These criticisms demonstrate that the same symbols and rhetoric—in this case, the
themes of railway development and social order—that the regime highlighted in an effort to legitimate its power were, at the
same time, turned on their head. Opponents could latch onto

the same symbolic and rhetorical themes, reversing their meaning and, in so doing, attempting to question the government's policies of authoritarian modernization. The policies the regime used to promote civilization became barbarous, and their policies of progress spurred regression. As Tenorio-Trillo has demonstrated, the government's celebration of the success of its policymaking provided fodder for *El Hijo del Ahuizote* to shoot holes through its discourse of progress, making known the ironies and failures in their program.[73]

The Railroad and the Church

El Hijo del Ahuizote railed against what it viewed as growing détente between the national government and the Church as well as the Church's increasing role in the public sphere. Although the Church played a small role in promoting transportation development, Cabrera and his followers invoked the railway's image when assessing the relationship between the government and the Church. While it was perhaps the least common way that *El Hijo del Ahuizote* used the railway to condemn the Díaz regime, it reveals the ubiquitous power of the railroad as a symbol in attacking government policy. In particular, they targeted Archbishop Eulogio Gillow's success as a railway promoter because he had secured an important concession between Santa Cruz and Panzacola during Díaz's first term in office.[74]

Cabrera and his staff ridiculed the practice of the blessing of railroads undertaken at events such as the 1892 inauguration of the Durango-Oaxaca railway, an event the president attended. As Oaxaca's governor, Gregorio Chávez, laid the last spike, the writer sneered that after almost nineteen centuries the Church was desperate to find its role in the modern world and demonstrate that it too could progress. To do so, he charged that they had attempted to infuse a ceremony of progress with religious ritual. The author continued using the episode to accuse Díaz of exploiting the Church, and especially the Oaxacan diocese, to undermine the sovereignty of the states and further his control over the country. The article ended with a mock prayer offering glory to Díaz and peace to the Republic.[75]

The event provided a perfect opportunity to highlight the reconciliation between Díaz and the Church, a development that angered radical liberals such as Cabrera and the Flores Magón brothers. The participation of the Oaxacan diocese in the event further confirmed this sentiment as it had been its Archbishop Gillow—the first foreign born archbishop, a native of England—who played a central role in the easing of tensions between church and state during the Porfiriato. Indeed, Gillow, a good friend of Díaz, had convinced the president to have his marriage to Carmen Romero Rubio performed by the Archbishop of Mexico City, Pelagio Antonio de Labastida y Dávalos, a watershed moment in the reconciliation process.[76]

In 1899, *El Hijo del Ahuizote* provided readers with an illustration condemning the Vatican's emissary to Mexico, Nicolás Averardi. In the image Averardi was shown riding a train, piled high with bags of money labeled "alms to Rome," from the Mexico City Cathedral to the Vatican, where Pope Leo XIII awaited his donations. The image referred to the departure of the emissary after three years, an event the newspaper depicted as a thief running off with his loot.[77] While the Church and the government's shifting stance toward the role of religion in society had little, or nothing, to do with railway policies, the image nevertheless suggested a complicity on the part of the Díaz administration in aiding what liberals viewed as a Concordat between the national government and the Vatican. Here Cabrera used the railway, so often exploited symbolically by the Díaz regime to highlight their successes in national development, to represent the government's complicity and reconciliation with the Church, a development that angered the orthodox liberal press as a regression from the policies enshrined in the 1857 Constitution.

The Railroad and Representations of the Government

The government and its boosters had utilized the railway to symbolically and rhetorically underscore their accomplishments, especially in regards to economic development. Demonstrated by its use in public rituals—for example the inauguration ceremonies discussed in chapter 3—it provided the ruling elite with a powerful icon of the achievement in implementing "order and progress." Yet the symbolic force of the railway also allowed opponents to draw on it as a representation of the government, the perceived failures of its policies, and the violations of the Constitution of 1857. Indeed, in 1885, *El Hijo del Ahuizote* provided an illustration, "El Tren del Progreso" (The train of progress), of Díaz atop a train car, accompanied by members of Congress, veering off a track branded "the upright constitution" that led toward national prosperity. Instead, Díaz and his supporters proceeded toward the curve labeled "arbitrary power" and risked falling into the depths of hell below them. Accompanying the image, a poem suggested that the president's reelection marched the country toward a political catastrophe: dictatorship.[78]

Mexico City's opposition press often used the railway as a symbolic device in its attacks against Díaz's perpetual reelection. In their efforts to highlight the duplicity of the regime, newspapers such as *El Hijo del Ahuizote* repeatedly referred to the Revolution of Tuxtepec that brought Díaz to the presidential chair when it ousted Sebastián Lerdo de Tejada, a revolutionary plan based on the political promises of no reelection and local autonomy. In 1887 and 1888, when Díaz sought and secured his first consecutive reelection, Cabrera and his staff linked his political victory to his achievements in the realm of railroad expansion. In 1887, the same year that Congress approved a constitutional amendment to allow Díaz to seek his third four-year term in office, *El Hijo del Ahuizote* lampooned the fraudulent electoral process in an illustration titled "Political Races." The image showed Díaz carried by a train representing "reelection"

23. Political races—laughing at those of the donkey and sack. The locomotive is better, making a path of iron. *El Hijo del Ahuizote*, September
18, 1887.

on a track labeled "congress" past Manuel González and Justo
Benítez—two former presidential candidates—who each rode
donkeys. In the foreground, an individual representing the people
struggled to become free from a sack that enveloped the hapless
victim.[79] Likewise, a year before his fourth reelection, Cabrera
and his staff depicted the shift toward dictatorship in the image of a train carrying bags of tax revenue and with cars labeled
"generals, friends, and statutes," a reference to Díaz's reliance
on *camarilla* politics.[80] The train, belching out a plume of black
smoke, headed directly toward a tunnel labeled "dictatorship."[81]

The following year *El Hijo del Ahuizote* again equated railway development with Díaz's shedding of the ideals of Tuxtepec. One editorial told readers that Díaz had reached reelection
in the same manner that representatives reached Congress: by
express train. It sardonically commented that while the president claimed that the country would reach prosperity through
the railway, only politicians had enriched themselves through

corrupt contracts.[82] Through the symbolic use of the railroad, newspapers that sought to challenge the Díaz administration not only were able to contest his economic policies but also could use railroad development to underscore the growing authoritarianism of the regime. Writers for *El Hijo del Ahuizote* identified the government's success at railroad expansion as the basis of their ability to manipulate, or outright ignore, the Constitution of 1857 with little opposition.

El Hijo del Ahuizote also made use of the symbolic potential of the railway to offer readers an optimistic message about challenging the regime and its violations of the Constitution. For example, in response to the pro-government press's common characterization of Díaz as "el Necesario" (the indispensable one), a practice begun in 1892, Cabrera and his staff presented readers with an illustration of a locomotive that they named "*necesarismo*" (indispensable-ism) carrying Díaz's infamous sword, La Matona, derailed and plunged off a cliff by a group of anti-reelectionist students and workers.[83] The image provides another example of the ubiquitous nature of the railway as a symbol of the regime itself as its development marked what many identified as Díaz's greatest success, at once representing social order and economic progress. Yet, as such, it could also be manipulated to signify the government's iniquities. In this case, the journal's artist employed it to denote the regime's relentless march toward dictatorship, a plan it depicted protestors derailing.

Cabrera and the Flores Magón brothers also repeatedly used the symbol of the railroad to emphasize the social injustice that intensified during the Porfiriato. They frequently employed the same rhetorical strategies as policymakers and the pro-Díaz press, emphasizing energy, movement, civilization, order, and progress as national qualities that government policies had failed to promote. The anti-Díaz press often criticized the gains that Mexico had received as a result of the administration's social, political, and economic policies. They questioned who really

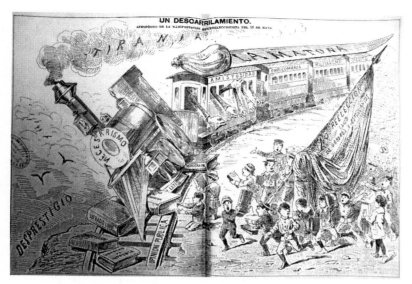

24. A derailing. In support of the anti-reelection protests of May 15. *El Hijo del Ahuizote*, June 5, 1892.

benefited from this national project, arguing that foreigners, *hacendados*, industrialists, and politicians gained at the expense of the people. Opposition groups stressed the usurpation of lands, the deaths caused by accidents, the United States' domination of the economy, and the preference of U.S. railway companies to hire American workers for the majority of high-paying jobs to prove the failures of Díaz's policies, all of which connected to the railway program.

Ridiculing the presidential practice of touring the country by railroad, an exercise in promoting Díaz's cult of personality, *El Hijo del Ahuizote* offered a mock account of his travels across the nation, outlining what the dictator chose to see and not see. They noted that Díaz observed masses of people celebrating him and the peace, progress, and prosperity he had created. At the same time, he avoided touring the rural communities living in misery, their lands stolen by railway companies.[84] In another edition, they showed the newspaper's recurring character — *el pueblo*, personified as a poor rural worker — suffering a plethora of injustices. In one such example, the cover of an issue displayed a locomotive mauling *el pueblo*. From the beast's nose bursts of hot breath reading: "raised freight rates" and "derailments" blast the unfortunate victim.[85]

In 1902, the Flores Magón brothers, having taken charge of *El Hijo del Ahuizote* after Cabrera fell ill, imparted some of their most ferocious attacks against the regime. After their arrest less than a year later, Juan Sarabia took control of the newspaper.[86] While the pro-Díaz press used the language of energy and movement to promote railway development in a nation long characterized by stagnation, opposition groups inverted this discourse to point out the failings of Díaz's policies. *El Hijo del Ahuizote* juxtaposed the success of the government's ability to promote rapid and far-reaching railway construction with the plight of the people for whom economic development had done little to improve their lot. They sought to disseminate this idea with an image titled "The State of the Republic in the Light of Truth." The illustration showed the wonders of the modern age, represented by technological innovations such as the automobile, factory, streetcar, and railway, hauled away by a galleon. Above the vessel, a fearsome specter loomed with the word "hunger" printed on its robe.[87] The Flores Magón brothers sent a clear message: despite the technological advancements achieved by the Díaz regime, these innovations, while indicative of a higher level of material culture, failed to provide the basic needs of the country's poor, thus putting into question the very definition of progress. The galleon pulling away again highlighted the perception that modernization had come at the cost of national sovereignty. The image also suggested that despite the technological progress, the country languished in a state of colonial subjection to foreign powers.

In one of its final issues, *El Hijo del Ahuizote* printed a manifesto that came close to calling for revolution against Díaz and his allies. Written by members of the Ponciano Arriaga Liberal

25. Flesh and bone. *El Hijo del Ahuizote*, September 3, 1890.

Congress, an opposition group founded in 1901 in San Luis Potosí and whose members would form the PLM, it put forward a scathing indictment of the government. The writers, among a host of denunciations, contrasted the material advancements of the era with the misery of the population, stating that next to the country's railway lines hordes of poverty-stricken Indians lived an inhumane life. They contrasted the movement and energy stimulated by railroads, steamships, and factory life against the stagnation of the people who, according to the author, languished ignored and unappreciated. As in many of their other publications, *El Hijo del Ahuizote*'s writers acknowledged the railway as a positive force with socially transformative potential but disagreed with how the government had promoted its transportation policy. The manifesto's publication signified an important watershed moment in the late Porfiriato. Although its authors denied that they had called for revolution, the final lines referring to the French Revolution and how the people had sacrificed their blood to depose tyrants suggested otherwise.[88] The following month, authorities jailed the Flores Magón brothers, who had been set free after their 1902 arrest, and the Sarabia cousins after a series of scathing issues and a political protest held at the newspaper's headquarters. *El Hijo del Ahuizote* did not print another issue.[89] As demonstrated, the railway served Cabrera's opposition newspaper with a symbol that it repeatedly used to attack a variety of government policies in critiques that would play an important role in the radicalization of orthodox liberals such as the Flores Magón brothers and the Sarabia cousins. These individuals, along with other radicals such as Santiago de la Hoz and Santiago de la Vega, would become the intellectual vanguard of a growing movement within Mexico that would ultimately undertake two failed local revolts in 1906 and 1908. In 1910, they would again enter into open revolt against the government, sometimes under the banner of Francisco Madero and sometimes independent of the *maderistas*.[90]

Yet while opposition and popular periodicals might have used the railway as the central symbol with which to represent the government and criticize its policies, dissidents such as Cabrera and the Flores Magón brothers did not throw out the baby with the bath water. They recognized the transformative potential of technology as necessary for the nation's development. *El Ahuizote Jacobino* discussed railways as a regenerative force for social uplift. On one occasion the writers chided the government for failing to bring the locomotive to certain regions of the country. Discussing the backwards state of Tetela de Ocampo, Puebla, they noted that despite its valiant military contribution to the Tuxtepec Revolution, which brought Díaz to power, the government had failed to build a single bridge or railway to help that "unfortunate town."[91] A week later they even celebrated the construction of an American-owned railway that would connect Zacatlán, Puebla to Mexico City because of the commerce that it would spur.[92] The editors also used cultural mediums such as poetry to make similar claims about how the development of transportation infrastructure benefited the lives of *campesinos*. The poem, "Dos misiones" (Two missions), juxtaposed the regenerative capacity of science and technology with the stagnation the poet associated with the clergy. The anonymous writer viewed these two forces at war in the countryside, with the former now winning the hearts and minds of the peasantry:

> Oh what astonishment of those *campesinos*,
> Yesterday indifferent,
> Seeing them crisscross railways
> And tunnels and bridges!
> The quick and gentle locomotive
> Whistles with arrogance
> And the once poor village now lives
> Happy in abundance.

And today, as learned engineers inaugurate it,
What cheerful effervescence!
And to the words of missionary fathers . . .
What splendid indifference![93]

Secularization, education, and work, for the Flores Magón brothers, would allow rural people to contribute to the greater national good, an argument that matched those made by developmentalist liberals whom they regularly attacked.[94]

But it was not only the orthodox and radical liberals that espoused these viewpoints about the redemptive capacity of technology. The penny presses *El Diablito Rojo* and *El Diablito Bromista* made similar assertions. Targeting working-class audiences, these publications discussed the importance of labor in uplifting the *pueblo* through the medium of poetry, often using the railway as a metaphor for social progress and material advancement. In Francisco Celada's "En la fragua" (In the Forge), an ironworker was addressed by the very iron he kilned. The iron demanded that the stoic laborer transform it into the rail hammer, wire, and locomotive, calling on him to transform it into the powerful creative force of universal progress.[95] Another poem, written by the well-known writer and education reformer Gregorio Torres Quintero, queried what the idle had accomplished for the benefit of human progress. The poet carped about the ways that indolent men's everyday lives had been improved by the inheritances of past centuries: bridges, ports, lighthouses, and railways. Torres Quintero ended the poem as it started, rhetorically asking the indolent what they had done to deserve such material advancements.[96] *El Diablito Bromista* mirrored these sentiments when it published an editorial that likewise called on workers to distinguish themselves through their labor, using the locomotive as a symbol of progress. The writer told workers that the telegraph that "annihilated distance" and the railway that "bound the *pueblos* together like a friendly lasso" should remind them of their hardworking brethren who made "progress a reality."[97]

Conclusion

Throughout the Porfiriato a lively, vociferous opposition existed that revealed a deep critical consciousness among radical liberals, independent newspapers, and penny presses. Policymakers and the subsidized press had used the symbolic and rhetorical power of the railway to help legitimize a regime that had shed its liberal credentials and grown increasingly authoritarian. At times, opposition newspapers worked within the confines of the dominant discourse of modernity—in themes such as economic development, political progress, or social uplift—to contest the government's nation-building program and suggest alternative models for national policymaking. At other times, as with the literature printed in *Gil Blas Cómico*, they questioned the benefits of modernity altogether. The opposition and popular press exploited what the government viewed as its crowning achievement, the railway, to examine, criticize, and ridicule a variety of policies far beyond those limited to the economic realm. A wide range of groups challenged the ideological assumptions on which "order and progress" were built and, in so doing, began to erode older forms of government legitimacy. Articulating new visions about the shortfalls of modernization and what a just social contract might look like, these individuals redefined key concepts such as patriotism, civilization, and national development that had been employed decades earlier to justify a program of authoritarian modernization. The flood of criticism about the railway program that began with the widespread view that accidents had become too common reached a climax in the final years of the regime with opponents connecting transportation policy to other perceived policy failures. These voices of dissent, in the formulation of William Roseberry, reveal how the words, symbols, and images used by subordinate groups to challenge domination work within the frameworks of meaning created by the ruling elite.[98] Moreover, they demonstrate how opponents waged a "war of position" in civil society to capture the imagination of Mexicans of what a more equitable society could look like.

The railway, especially for the regime's most persistent critics, Daniel Cabrera, the Flores Magón brothers, and the Sarabia cousins, provided a perfect metaphor for the social and political wrongs they saw racking the country. At the same time, the independent weekly *Gil Blas Cómico*, more interested in art and literature than political commentary, used the railway in imaginative writings that questioned the benefits of progress and the utopian potential of modern technology to make people's lives better. These works focused on the negative aspects of progress, emphasizing chaos and loss as integral to the modern experience. *Gil Blas Cómico* and *El Hijo del Ahuizote*, as well as a number of penny presses, provided readers with different yet interconnected views of modernization. *El Hijo del Ahuizote* might emphasize the chaos that ensued from a legal system that endorsed the *ley fuga* or the irresponsible Yankee engineers who put people's lives in peril. In so doing, the regime's civilizing mission was exposed as violent and savage. *Gil Blas Cómico*, in contrast, stressed the chaos caused by the railway that made life more complicated and demanding. Yet both reflected the same expressions—sometimes in political venues, sometimes in cultural venues, and sometimes in venues that blurred both—that disseminated ideas about technological development that undermined the so-called universal truths that defined the regime's program and policies.

CONCLUSION

> In order to bring this work [economic progress] to crest, the two
> most important factors have been: peace and the wave of materi-
> al progress which has brought to the world steam with its applica-
> tion to transportation and to industry. We have seen the very skill-
> ful methods [Díaz] has used to keep the peace, one of the principal
> ones being the construction of the great railroads, but these have
> served not only for keeping peace, but they have brought about a
> marvellous development of the riches of the Nation.
>
> FRANCISCO MADERO, *The Presidential Succession of 1910*

In the months prior to the centennial celebrations of Independence on September 16, 1910, a curious letter reached the desk of
José Casarín, the secretary of the group in charge of organizing
the festivities. The letter, from an unnamed official,[1] first praised
the peace that reigned, a phenomenon the writer attributed to
the construction of railways that crisscrossed the Republic. He
stated that these lines of communication contributed to the exploitation and development of the mining and agricultural sectors, the source of the country's wealth. This material progress,
according to the author, had firmly consolidated national unity.

After his opening paragraph, the writer made no further mention of railways. In fact, the letter had nothing to do with railways whatsoever. Instead, the writer proposed a plan to purchase
10,000 pairs of pants for Mexico City's Indians, who typically
walked the streets wearing white muslin clothing (*calzón blanco de manta*) and sandals (*guaraches*). He lamented to Casarín
that, despite the country's success at becoming modern, traditional customs continued to exist that spoke poorly of the country's cultural advancements. This reality, he explained, result-

ed from the tumultuous nature of progress. He regretted that while Casarín's committee had organized the centennial festivities to highlight the decency and good name of Mexico, the indigenous people's custom of wearing what he regarded as "immoral" clothing threatened to undermine this project. People wearing such clothing in a country that had reached civilization, he argued, would appear repugnant to the entire world.[2]

This letter serves as a telling example of how people continued to associate the railway with the regime's civilizing mission. As Porfirians prepared to commemorate Independence—a month-long celebration climaxing on September 14, 15, and 16—in a series of lavish parades, fireworks, gala dances, and building inaugurations, event organizers sought to clear Indians from the streets or at least make them appear to be civilized citizens according to the elite's prescriptions. Only months before the first revolutionary armies confronted federal troops in Chihuahua, the celebration revealed the self-assuredness and confidence of government officials about the success of their mission. Yet, as the letter to Casarín confirmed, the regime's civilizing project often proved shallow, focusing on the appearance of progress rather than offering substantial improvements that would alleviate poverty and injustice. It further revealed the tensions between the government's modernizing program and the so-called traditional practices that continued in the final years of the regime. The author's use of the railway to underscore the importance of his appeal suggests that he considered it the ultimate symbol of a civilizing society, an iconic image of modernity in sharp contrast to Indians wearing their traditional garb on the city streets. This minor episode then brings together several of the themes outlined in this book.

This study has examined the interconnections of three issues: the symbolic power that the railway held for both supporters and opponents of the regime as well as elite and popular groups, the ways that this symbolic power manifested itself in cultural venues as people attempted to defend or deny the legitimacy of the government, and the ways that these cultural works revealed tensions in how various social groups understood the civilizing mission, a program intimately linked to the establishment of order and progress. It has examined particular moments of celebration and crisis when these subjects found expression in the words and works of politicians, reporters, writers, and artists. As demonstrated, the successful promotion of railway development spawned optimism among middle- and upper-class observers about the limitless possibilities of material progress. They often articulated this optimism in literature, art, and social commentaries that revealed their support for the regime's program of economic development despite its growing authoritarianism. This book has argued that the utopian hopes engendered by the locomotive as a symbol used in cultural works helped generate confidence in the regime's civilizing mission and its capacity to transform society along cosmopolitan guidelines. Supporters of Díaz consented to sacrificing representative democracy for material advancement made possible by large-scale infrastructural improvements, the most ubiquitous and far-reaching of those being the nationwide railway network. Officials at all levels used pageantry to highlight the locomotive's capacity to civilize the country as it represented the material incarnation of the government's mantra of order and progress as well as an unparalleled tool in forging national unity. Furthermore, in a country where the elite drew connections between cosmopolitanism and modern nationalism, the railway also proved an important marker of national identity.

Porfirian literary and artistic expressions homed in on the topic of technology to describe the elite's experiences, emotions, and intellectual outlooks about the regime's ability to civilize and modernize the country. Yet moments of technological crisis, especially train wrecks, undermined the utopian vision of progress promoted by officials and espoused by elite groups. The

common perception that accidents resulted from a transportation network that was foreign owned and operated allowed critics to promote their own definition of nationalism, one that saw
the regime's pandering to outside economic interests as unpatriotic. These moments of crisis opened the door for a series of
attacks against the manner in which the government had guid-
ed the nation. Opposition groups, especially orthodox liberal
and working-class presses, made use of cultural venues to com-
mandeer the symbolic power of the railway and criticize policymakers. Popular sources such as *corridos* and the penny presses reveal shared concerns with intellectuals—such as Francisco
Montes de Oca, Daniel Cabrera, or the Flores Magón brothers—about the failures of Porfirian progress to benefit people's
lives. Together they show a growing disillusionment articulated by cultural producers that worked to erode the legitimacy of
the regime. This symbolic "war of position" reshaped the hegemonic language of the elite and exposed the social antagonisms
that came to define the failures of Porfirian rule.

The growing tensions in Porfirian society about the nature
and implementation of the government's transportation policy
echoed broader social and political divisions that eventually led
to the outbreak of the Revolution (1910–20). While the visions
of what constituted a civilized country may have appeared as a
natural and universal truth to many contemporary observers,
a closer look at the multiple expressions of how exactly civilization and progress should be defined reveals something else.
The cultural works examined in this study highlight the many
ways that government officials and dissident intellectuals, as
well as elite and popular groups, understood how the rewards
of modernization could be attained. Far from outlining a set of
universal truths about what constituted progress and national
unity, these sources demonstrate that different sectors of society defined these ideas in ways that corresponded to their values, beliefs, and socioeconomic positions. The representations

of the railway in cultural mediums likewise make known that the categories of "modern" and "traditional" could be blurred and by no means defined one social group or another. Elites who celebrated the iron horse at times lamented the social and cultural changes that modernization spurred and looked back to the past with nostalgia. Conversely, popular sources that most often highlighted the destructive capacity of the railway could also rejoice at its arrival that heralded the possibility of work and prosperity. Thus this study has sought to reveal the intricate arena where different groups articulated their perceptions of what modernization could mean, revealing these ideas as amorphous, elastic, contingent, and ever-shifting.

In the government's attempts to fashion a modern, civilized society, a wide range of views emerged that conformed and competed with this project. Above all, the construction of the railway system came to represent the supreme symbol of the government's program to build a country that would stand alongside the pantheon of modern nations and, in so doing, allow its citizens to enjoy the splendors of material progress. Yet, by roughly 1895, opposition emerged questioning how Porfirian officials such as the *cientificos* had defined progress. These attacks continued and became more vociferous in 1907, when a severe economic depression exposed the failings of Porfirian-styled modernization, especially its dependence on the well-being of the U.S. economy. Francisco Madero, a wealthy native Coahuilan whose infectious charisma surpassed his small stature, came forward to provide an alternative view of what constituted a modern, civilized country.

In *The Presidential Succession of 1910*, Madero outlined his views of the ways that the country could better reap the rewards of Porfirian progress. He argued that a return to democracy and state and local autonomy would put an end to peasant and worker grievances, a belief encapsulated in his famous statement that the Mexican people wanted liberty and not bread. While Madero submitted a condemnation of Díaz's centralization of power, his treatise did not indict every aspect of Porfirian policymaking. In fact, he lauded the advancements made under Díaz, citing the railroads as the foundation of agricultural, mining, and industrial development.[3]

Yet despite his accolades for the longtime dictator and his success at improving the economy, he also shared concerns regarding railway policy that opposition groups had long articulated. When outlining the general principles of his National Democratic Party and why the Mexican people needed to hold out hope for a better future, Madero began by lamenting the foreign domination of the country's railway lines.[4] He bemoaned how native workers had received poor treatment from U.S. bosses and employees, maintaining that the government had failed to correct those grievances. Madero then praised the country's railway workers who, through their own efforts and without the support of the government, managed to secure better treatment from foreign companies.[5]

In contrast to the developmentalist liberalism of the Porfirian ruling elite, Madero understood democracy, and not just economic progress, as an ontological necessity for the attainment of civilization. He described absolute power as a form of political organization characteristic of antiquity and compared Díaz's arbitrary authority to African and Asian despotism, which he identified as backward.[6] Madero thus expressed his own beliefs about what defined civilization and a stronger foundation for national development. As he toured the states championing an open political system, setting up political clubs, and attracting followers, Madero's vision resonated with a considerable number of his countrymen. By the time Díaz took his opposition seriously, it was too late. Yet, after the octogenarian dictator had boarded a steamship and fled to Paris in May 1911, Madero failed to control the powerful forces of social, political, and economic grievances that had been kept more or less under restraint by Porfirian rule. His view that a truly democratic government would cure the ills of the country proved illusionary as the economic hardships that many people faced could not be remedied by ballot counting alone. As it turned out, the people needed more than liberty; they needed bread, too. The revolution he started unleashed a wave of violence that would consume the country for the next ten years and ultimately take the life of the tiny Coahuilan with big dreams.

In the wake of Madero's assassination in February 1913, various factions fighting in the name of the revolution he initiated would turn on each other, dividing themselves into the camps of the Constitutionalists and Conventionists and sending the country down the path of a bloody civil war. These revolutionary factions expressed their own visions of national policy that would become enshrined in the 1917 Constitution, a document that likewise reveals a diverse set of beliefs about what exactly constituted civilization, progress, and national identity. Even after the military phase of the Revolution (1910–20) and the consolidation of a new central political authority, violence continued to erupt as different sectors sought to implement their own ideas about what constituted proper government policymaking. Indeed, such debates resurfaced as revolutionary leaders attempted to establish their own authority after years of turmoil.

Even in the 1930s and beyond, government officials found difficulty in clearly articulating what constituted a civilized nation in a manner that incorporated marginalized rural and indigenous groups. To do so, they tried to strike a balance between tradition and modernity and countryside and city and create a so-called authentic national identity.[7] Revolutionary policymakers, in an attempt to forge a unified set of national beliefs, implemented the lessons learned during the Porfiriato. Individuals such as Education Minister José Vasconcelos recognized the importance of using art to disseminate political ideas among a largely illiterate population, a strategy used decades earlier by oppositional groups to challenge Díaz's legitimacy. The use of didactic images to teach lessons about nationalistic versions of history, identity, and philosophy—made famous by the muralist movement of Diego Rivera, José Clemente Orozco, and David Siqueiros—at times revealed the same skepticism about technology's civilizing potential. In the wake of the Revolution and World War I, their work highlighted the negative aspects of modern machinery, emphasizing its destructive potential rather than its utopian promises. These ideas first emerged during the Porfiriato when people's consciousness about how technology defined the boundaries between savagery and civilization awakened with the arrival of the railroad.

NOTES

Introduction

1. "Sister of the sun and the dark night, / With space and time at war, / The hills pressing on the earth, / It advances majestically across the plain. / Amongst the incense of the vapor it gleams / Rays of light, and with the rocks it closes upon, / It sinks into the heart of the mountains, / Seeking there a path or a grave. / Today it parts from the western coasts, / Tomorrow the Indian Ocean in its grasp / It will go to temper the red horizon. / On its wings it carries the fertile seeds / Of industry, of art, of progress.... / Make way for the breath of God that drives the world!" The original read: "Del sol hermana, y de la noche oscura, / Con el espacio y con el tiempo en guerra, / Los lomos oprimiendo de la tierra, / Avanza majestuosa en la llanura. / Entre el incienso del vapor fulgura / Haces de luz, y con las rocas cierra, / Y se hunde en las entrañas de la sierra, / Buscando allí camino ó sepultura. / Hoy parte de las costas de Occidente, / Mañana del mar Índico en el beso / Irá á templar la enrojecida frente. / Sobre sus alas va el gérmen fecundo / De la industria, del arte, del progreso. ... / Paso al soplo de Dios que empuja el mundo!" *El Mundo (Semanario Ilustrado)*, December 2, 1894.

2. "If a desperate person wants / To have his baptism ruined / Travel in a rail-cataclysm [railway], / As that will surely be the result; / It is true that certain machine-nihilists [engineers] / Tighten their grip so well [shake hands], / *You pay in Mexican / And they'll kill you in English.* / We no longer fear typhus, / Neither cholera, nor the fever; / That is a swindle / And backward you get your fears: / The real scare is had / In a train, plain and simple, / *You pay in Mexican / And they'll kill you in English* / The manager of the joke / Of dispatching the traveler, / Tends to be a son of a bitch / Thick as a cow, / Is as strong as a brute, / And begging him is so useless, / *You pay in Mexican / And they'll kill you in English* / —Mr. Yankee (he pleads) / Do not break our rib. / —Me no understand Spanish / He says, looking at him sideways; / But when it comes to savagery / He is such a doyen, / *You*

NOTES TO PAGES 3-5

will pay in Mexican / And they'll kill you in English." The original read: "Si quiere un desesperado / Que le estrellen el bautismo, / Viaje en ferro-cataclismo, / Que el efecto seguro es; / Pues ciertos maqui-nihilistas / Tan bien aprietan la mano, / *Que paga usté en mexicano / Y lo matan en inglés.* / Ya no tememos al tifo, / Ni al cólera, ni á la fiebre; / Eso es dar gato por liebre / Y sustitos al revés: / El sustazo se recibe / En un tren, y tan de plano, / *Que paga usté en mexicano / Y lo matan en inglés.* . . . / El encargado del chiste / De despachar al viajero, / Suele ser un majadero / Macizo como una res, / Es tan fuerte como bruto, / Y suplicarle es tan vano, / *Que paga usté en mexicano / Y lo matan en inglés.* / —Señor yankee, (se le ruega), / No nos rompa una costilla. / —*Mi non tende de castilla,* / Dice él, viendo de través; / Mas en punto á salvajada / Es de tal modo un decano, / *Que paga usté en mexicano / Y lo matan en inglés.* . . ." *El Hijo del Ahuizote,* March 17, 1895.

3. Tenenbaum, *Politics of Penury*; Stevens, *Origins of Instability in Early Republican Mexico*; and Costeloe, *Central Republic in Mexico*.

4. Santoni, *Mexicans at Arms*; and Vázquez, "War and Peace with the United States."

5. J. Bazant, "From Independence to the Liberal Republic"; Costeloe, *Central Republic in Mexico*; Anna, *Forging Mexico: 1821–1835*.

6. Dabbs, *French Army in Mexico*.

7. Knapp, *Sebastián Lerdo de Tejada*; Cosío Villegas, ed., *Historia moderna de México*, vol. 1–3; Scholes, *Mexican Politics during the Juárez Regime, 1855–1872*; J. Bazant, *Alienation of Church Wealth in Mexico*; Sinkin, *The Mexican Reform, 1855–1876*.

8. Haber, *Industry and Underdevelopment*, 15.

9. Calderón, "Los ferrocarriles."

10. Calderón, "Los ferrocarriles"; Pletcher, *Rails, Mines, and Progress*; Ortiz Hernán, *Los ferrocarriles de México*; Coatsworth, *Growth against Development*; Coatsworth, "Indispensable Railways in a Backward Economy."

11. Coatsworth, "Railroads, Landholding, and Agrarian Protest in the Early Porfiriato." While not concerned solely with railway development, many studies stressed the negative consequences of railway expansion for the majority of the population. See R. Anderson, *Outcasts in Their Own Land*, 88–89, 91–92, 215, 236; Ruíz, *The Great Rebellion*, 64–66, 88, 95; Wasserman, *Capitalists, Caciques, and Revolution*, 76–77, 98, 108–12, 155; Hart, *Revolutionary Mexico*, 41–44, 165, 188; Arthur Schmidt, *The Social and Economic Effect of the Railroad in Puebla and Veracruz, Mexico, 1867–1911*; Vanderwood, *Disorder and Progress*, 89.

12. Arturo Grunstein, for example, challenges dependency economic models that argue that Mexican policymakers, as a result of international financial linkages, could not defend national interests in regard to railways. Considering the financial limitations of the regime, he argues that policymakers had limited choices. This considered, he maintains that Porfirian policymakers succeeded in accomplishing the majority of their goals concerning railway development. Most notably, he argues that without the large foreign loans procured by the government, the 1908 Mexicanization of the system would have been impossible. See Grunstein, "Railroads and Sovereignty: Policymaking in Porfirian Mexico." Likewise, Sandra Kuntz-Ficker questions traditional views of the economic effects of railway development, arguing that high freights did not necessarily undermine the development of local markets. She finds that the Mexican Central Railroad allowed regional producers to sell goods at local markets at advantageous prices for consumers. Furthermore, she maintains that in the case of transporting minerals, although destined for the country's ports, railway development nevertheless helped to develop modern, dynamic industries at the local level. See Kuntz-Ficker, *Empresa extrangera y mercado interno*; Kuntz-Ficker and Paolo Riguzzi, *Ferrocarriles y vida económica en México, 1850–1950*. Teresa Van Hoy has questioned John Coatsworth's conclusions about the negative consequences that railway development had on the nation's peasantry, arguing that small landholders successfully negotiated fair prices for the sale of their lands and that the arrival of the railway offered benefits such as wage work, surplus materials, and piped water. See Van Hoy, *A Social History of Mexican Railroads*, xviii–xix.

13. For works on the cultural, psychological, discursive, and symbolic aspects of railway development, see Leo Marx, *Machine in the Garden*; Kasson, *Civilizing the Machine*; Schivelbusch, *Railway Journey*; Richard and Mackenzie, *Railway Station*; D. N. Smith, *The Railway and Its Passengers*; Simmons, *Victorian Railway*, 195; Freeman, *Railways and the Victorian Imagination*; Carter, *Railways and Culture in Britain*; Lee, "Railways, Space, and Imperialism"; Murdock, "The Railway in Arcadia: An Approach to Modernity in British Visual Culture." For similar studies on Latin American railway development, see Foot Hardman, *Trem fantasma: A modernidade na selva*; French, "In the Path of Progress"; Cimó Queiroz, *As curvas do trem e os meandros do poder*; Clark, *Redemptive Work*.

14. In this regard, this book owes a debt to Robert Darton's pioneering study, *The Great Cat Massacre and Other Episodes in French Cultural History*.

15. E. Bradford Burns noted that nineteenth-century leaders across Latin America associated the concept of civilization with European progress, scientific knowledge, and material culture. Its outward manifestations were most often identified with the railroad and factory. See Burns, *The Poverty of Progress*, 18–21.

16. See, e.g., Beezley, *Judas at the Jockey Club*; French, *A Peaceful and Working People*; Tenorio-Trillo, *Mexico at the World's Fairs*; Buffington, *Criminal and Citizen in Modern Mexico*; Piccato, *City of Suspects*; Agostini, *Monuments of Progress*; Weiner, *Race, Nation, and Market*; Overmyer-Velázquez, *Visions of the Emerald City*; Garza, *Imagined Underworld*.

17. Tenorillo-Trillo, *Mexico at the World's Fairs*, 8–9.

18. Elias, *The Civilizing Process*, 180–82, 189, 365–79.

19. Adas, *Machines as the Measure of Men*, 219–20.

20. For a discussion of the connections between timekeeping and the inculcation of a modern capitalist work ethic, see E. P. Thompson, "Time, Work-Discipline, and Industrial Capitalism." For a discussion of how Europeans used timekeeping to regulate discipline of the body in institutional rituals (schools, factories, militaries, etc.), see Foucault, *Discipline and Punish*, 149–56. For studies dealing with these issues in the Porfirian context, see French, *A Peaceful and Working People*, and Buffington and French, "The Culture of Modernity," 422–23.

21. Hale, *Transformation of Liberalism*, 205–206.

22. Marx, *The Communist Manifesto* and *The German Ideology*, in *Karl Marx: Selected Writings*, 159–91, 221–47.

23. Benjamin, *Arcades Project*, 388, 392–95.

24. Marx, *Capital*, vol. 1, in *Karl Marx: Selected Writings*, 435–43.

25. Benjamin, *Arcades Project*, 669. Michael T. Taussig likewise provides a useful explanation of this process. See Taussig, *The Devil and Commodity Fetishism in South America*, 23–36.

26. Bourdieu, *Language and Symbolic Power*, 122–25, 203–205. This point is also made by Philip Corrigan and Derek Sayer, who maintain that the British crown used ceremony and pageantry as a means to deify themselves. See Corrigan and Sayer, *The Great Arch*, 61.

27. For an insightful analysis of this phenomenon, see Scott, *Domination and the Arts of Resistance*, 158.

28. Corrigan and Sayer emphasize that state formation represents a cultural revolution used to moralize and inculcate people with particular values, beliefs, and norms. This, in turn, allows leaders to claim their right to rule. See Corrigan and Sayer, *The Great Arch*, 163.

29. Hardman, *Trem fantasma*, 48. For a brief discussion of the Porfirian fetish of modernization and social order, see Claudio Lomnitz, *Deep Mexico, Silent Mexico*, 72–73.

30. Gramsci, *Antonio Gramsci Reader*, 200–209.

31. Lears, "The Concept of Cultural Hegemony," 568–69.

32. Gramsci, *Antonio Gramsci Reader*, 225–30.

33. Fernández-Armesto argues that a similar transition took place in Europe in regards to artists' response to the Industrial Revolution. Nineteenth-century romantic portraits of industry gave way to bleak portrayals of smog covered towns by the 1900s. See Fernández-Armesto, *Civilizations: Culture, Ambition, and the Transformation of Nature*, 179–80.

34. In his examination of France's nineteenth-century press, Richard Terdiman argues that the dialectic interaction between dominant and oppositional presses reveals a clash of ideologies and sign systems. While opposition groups critical of bourgeois society attempted to challenge and mock dominant discourse, the counterdiscursive strategies employed often worked *within* the very systems of representation that they sought to subvert. See Terdiman, *Discourse/Counter-Discourse*, 184–85.

35. Knudson, "Periodization of the Mexican Press," 749.

36. M. Bazant, "Lecturas del Porfiriato," 206; P. Smith, "Contentious Voices amid the Order," 19, 38.

37. Coerver, *Porfirian Interregnum*, 95.

38. Thompson, *The Making of the English Working Class*, 712–13.

39. Smith, "Contentious Voices amid the Order," 62–63; Bonilla, "Imágenes de Posada en los impresos de Vanegas Arroyo."

40. Turner, *Barbarous Mexico*, 159; Cosío Villegas, *La vida política interior* (segunda parte), vol. 10 of *Historia moderna de México*, 236–74.

41. Alan Knight describes the beliefs shared by Porfirian officials and the *científicos* regarding notions of time, work, progress, etc., as a "developmentalist ideology." See "El liberalismo mexicano desde la Reforma hasta la Revolución (una interpretación)," 60–61, and *Mexican Revolution*, 1:84.

1. The Discourse of Development

1. Cimó Queiroz, *As curvas do trem*, 97.

2. Clark, *Redemptive Work*, 41–42.

3. Adas, *Machines as the Measure of Men*, 221–36.

4. Tenorio-Trillo, *Mexico at the World's Fairs*, 88.

5. For a systematic discussion of how the Díaz government secured railway contracts and construction, see Powell, *Railroads of Mexico*, 1–6, 109–66.

6. Knapp, *Sebastián Lerdo de Tejada*, 203.

7. Calderón, *La República Restaurada, la vida económica*, 2:732–42; Knapp, *Sebastián Lerdo de Tejada*, 208–209; Grunstein, "Railroads and Sovereignty," 19–22.

8. Calderón, *La República Restaurada, la vida económica*, 2:741.

9. Justo Sierra, *Evolución política del pueblo mexicano*, 447–48. Likewise, writing in the immediate aftermath of the Revolution, former Porfirian governor José López-Portillo y Rojas's history of Díaz also characterized Lerdo as anti-American. See *Elevación y caída de Porfirio Díaz*, 158–59.

10. *Diario del Hogar*, May 15, 1889.

11. Hart, *Revolutionary Mexico*, 117.

12. Tenenbaum, *Politics of Penury*, 112–13.

13. Grunstein, "Railroads and Sovereignty," 14–15.

14. Most South American countries first built railway lines in the 1840s and 1850s. During the 1860s and 1870s, most experienced a rail boom demonstrated by feverish promotion, financing, and construction. See Glade, "Economy, 1870–1914," 42–43.

15. Grunstein, "Railroads and Sovereignty," 23.

16. *Boletín de la Cooperación*, October 4, 1879.

17. *El Heraldo*, April 2, 1880.

18. *El Coahuilense*, March 2, 1889.

19. Adas, *Machines as the Measure of Men*, 204, 213, 215, 219, 220, 224, 229.

20. See Tenorio-Trillo, *Mexico at the World's Fairs*, 116–17.

21. *El Monitor Republicano*, January 20, 1879.

22. *El Hijo del Trabajo*, August 7, 1880.

23. Weiner, *Race, Nation, and Market*, 14–15.

24. *El Periódico Oficial*, June 4, 1880.

25. *El Monitor Republicano*, November 7, 1878.

26. Hale, *Transformation of Liberalism*, 32.

27. *Express Mercantil Mexicano*, October 24, 1880.

28. *La Patria*, March 13, 1880.

29. Hale, *Transformation of Liberalism*, 236.

30. *El Monitor Republicano*, April 20, 1880.

31. Beezley, *Judas at the Jockey Club*, 63–64.

32. *El Coahuilense*, April 28, 1886.

33. *Diario de los Debates, 10ª Legislatura Constitucionales de la Union*, 1:368. Clark's study reveals that Ecuadorian policymakers also drew con-

nections between a healthy, energetic youth and the need for railway development. Clark, *Redemptive Work*, 49.

34. *El Correo de Chihuahua*, February 23, 1899.

35. The emphasis by both the press and policymakers on the railway's capacity to revitalize the nation has also been demonstrated by Clark in her examination of railroad promotion in Ecuador. See *Redemptive Work*, chap. 2.

36. Grunstein, "Railroads and Sovereignty," 14.

37. *La Industria Nacional*, April 15, 1880.

38. *El Sufrigio Libre*, March 9, 1880.

39. *La Patria*, April 6, 1880.

40. *Express Mercantil Mexicano*, October 24, 1880.

41. *El Correo de San Luis Potosí*, February 1, 1885.

42. *El Correo de la Tarde*, September 26, 1881.

43. *Diario de los Debates*, 1877, 2:804.

44. *Diario de los Debates*, 1877, 2:799.

45. *Diario de los Debates*, 1877, 2:790–93.

46. *Diario de los Debates*, 1877, 2:791.

47. Kuntz-Ficker, *Empresa extrangera y mercado interno*, 36.

48. *Diario de los Debates*, 1877, 2:809.

49. *Diario de los Debates*, 1877, 2:787.

50. *El Monitor Republicano*, May 24, 1878.

51. *El Monitor Republicano*, December 5, 1877.

52. *El Express Mercantil Mexicano*, October 10, 1880.

53. *El Monitor Republicano*, May 28, 1878.

54. *La Industria Nacional*, April 25, 1880.

55. Schell, *Integral Outsiders*, 113.

56. Kuntz-Ficker, *Empresa extrangera y mercado interno*, 42; Calderón, "Los ferrocarriles," 512–18.

57. Grunstein, "Railroads and Sovereignty," 28.

58. *El Monitor Republicano*, April 20, 1880.

59. *El Hijo del Trabajo*, April 25, 1880.

60. *La Tribuna*, March 10, 1880.

61. Kuntz-Ficker, *Empresa extrangera y mercado*, 41–42.

62. Garner, *Porfirio Díaz*, 89.

63. As William Schell notes, although enough capital existed in Mexico to invest in government and private projects, most individuals did not want to risk investing in their country and chose instead to invest with foreign partners or save their money altogether. See Schell, *Integral Outsiders*, xi–xii.

64. *El Cronista de México*, March 12, 1881.

65. *El Cronista de México*, March 19, 1881.

66. *Diario de los Debates*, 1877, 2:768.

67. Adas, *Machines as the Measure of Men*, 229–30.

68. González Navarro, *La colonización en México, 1877–1910*, 26.

69. *La Industria Nacional*, April 18, 1880.

70. *El Sufragio Libre*, March 9, 1880.

71. *La Industria Nacional*, September 1, 1880.

72. Justo Sierra quoted in Weiner, *Race, Nation, and Market*, 55.

73. Coatsworth, *Growth against Development*, 184.

74. Weiner, *Race, Nation, and Market*, 55–64.

75. *El Sufragio Libre*, March 30, 1880.

76. Coatsworth in *Growth against Development* emphasized that Porfirian railway development was primarily targeted at promoting Mexico's export-led growth. Kuntz-Fickers's more recent study has shown that railway development also helped to develop internal markets. See Kuntz-Ficker, *Empresa extrangera y mercado interno*, 287, 355–59.

77. *La Industria Nacional*, April 18, 1880.

78. *El Sufragio Libre*, March 30, 1880.

79. *La Voz de México*, February 20, 1880.

80. *La Tribuna*, March 10, 1880.

81. *El Sufragio Libre*, March 9, 1880.

82. *El Hijo del Trabajo*, February 1, 1880.

83. French, *A Peaceful and Working People*, 60–61.

84. *La Tribuna*, March 10, 1880.

85. *El Sufragio Libre*, April 10, 1880.

86. Indeed, as Enrique Cárdenas states, in terms of economic development, "the construction of railroads was the most important event of the last third of the [nineteenth] century." See Cárdenas, "A Macroeconomic Interpretation of Nineteenth-Century Mexico," 77.

87. Cosío Villegas, *El Porfiriato, La vida política interior* (primera parte), vol. 9 of *Historia moderna de México*, 740–58; Garner, *Porfirio Díaz*, 93.

88. Pletcher, *Rails, Mines, and Progress*, 99–100; Knapp, *Sebastián Lerdo de Tejada*, 203–205.

89. *El Monitor Republicano*, November 8, 1877.

90. *El Monitor Republicano*, December 5, 1877.

91. *El Monitor Republicano*, April 20, 1880.

92. *El Monitor Republicano*, June 8, 1878.

93. See, e.g., *El Monitor Republicano*, September 7, November 7, 1878.

94. *El Monitor Republicano*, May 28, 1878.

95. *La Voz de México*, October 3, 1880.

96. *El Sufragio Libre*, March 30, 1880.

97. *Opinion de la prensa y de los Sres. Gobernadores de los estados de la federacion así como del Sr. Presidente de la Republica acerca del Ferrocarril Internacional e Interoceanico representado por los Sres. James Sullivan, Gral. H.J. Palmer y sócios*. It should be noted that this concession would become the Mexican National Railroad, although it is referred to as the "Ferrocarril Internacional e Interoceanico" in this publication.

98. Colección Porfirio Díaz [hereafter CPD], Leg 5, caja 8, docs. 3810.

99. CPD, Leg 5, caja 9, docs. 4214.

100. CPD, Leg 5, caja 10, docs. 4499.

101. CPD, Leg 5, caja 10, docs. 4586.

102. CPD, Leg 5, caja 10, docs. 4585.

103. CPD, Leg 5, caja 10, docs. 4594.

104. CPD, Leg 5, caja 08, docs. 3952.

105. CPD, Leg 5, caja 09, docs. 4274.

106. CPD, Leg 5, caja 09, docs. 4737.

107. *La Libertad* quoted in Cosío Villegas, *La vida politica interior* (primera parte), 9:743.

108. The *Mexican Financier* quoted in Cosío Villegas, *La vida politica interior* (primera parte), 9:747.

2. De Viaje

1. Schivelbusch, *Railway Journey*, 60; Simmons, *Victorian Railway*, 195.

2. This idea corresponds to Walter Benjamin's discussion of commodity fetishism, a concept first introduced in Karl Marx's *Capital*. Looking at the interconnections between technology, art, and architecture, Benjamin posited that the ambiguities of the capitalist world had fostered an "intoxication of perception" that obfuscated how new technologies furthered human exploitation rather than alleviated it. Similarly, in his essay about the Parisian arcades, Benjamin noted that the plethora of commodities sold within the confines of the arcade offered consumers a utopian vision that forced the laws of dialectics to a standstill: the commodity and consumer in that moment became one. *Arcades Project*, 7–10, 395. Using these insights, Francisco Foot Hardman interpreted Brazilian railway development in a manner that highlighted the dialectic engagement between experiences of utopia and regression, exploring how the disastrous construction of the Madei-

ra-Mamoré railway could be transformed into romantic bourgeois euphoria over the possibilities of bringing modernity to the jungle. In so doing, Hardman stresses how elite groups underscored the utopian promises offered by railway development while ignoring its often brutal consequences, in this case the impressments, enslavement, and a high death toll that resulted from a state project to bring the railroad, and thus civilization, to the Amazon. *Trem fantasma*, 155–85. This study will likewise draw on the term "utopian" to describe how elite groups often viewed the railway as a symbol of national salvation and progress while ignoring the social, economic, and political costs that were also central to securing railway development.

3. *El Mundo (Semanario Ilustrado)*, published between 1894 and 1914, changed its name to *El Mundo Ilustrado* in 1900. This publication should not be confused with the afternoon daily *El Mundo*, another newspaper owned by Rafael Reyes Spíndola.

4. Although distribution rates for these two publications have not been studied, they have been considered two of the most popular and highly influential periodicals of the era. See Cosío Villegas, *El Porfiriato, la vida política interior* (segunda parte), 10:583; Toussaint Alcaraz, *Escenario de la prensa en el Porfiriato*, 41–42; *Diccionario Porrúa*, s.v. "Mundo Ilustrado (El)" and "Revista Moderna (La)."

5. *El Imparcial*, along with other publications produced by Reyes Spíndola such as *El Mundo*, *El Universal*, and *El Mundo (Semanario Ilustrado)*, represented the leading outlets for the Porfirian government's public relations campaign, a service that cost the government 150,000 pesos per year. See Smith, "Contentious Voices amid the Order," 102–108; Carrasco Puente, *La prensa en México: Datos historicos*, 203.

6. Pineda Franco, "El cosmopolitismo de la *Revista Moderna* (1898–1911): una vocación porfiriana," 231, 235.

7. This list included Francisco Zubieta, an art professor at the Escuela Nacional Preparatoria, and Jesús Martínez Carrión, a frequent contributor to *El Hijo del Ahuizote* whose antigovernment caricatures landed him in Belén prison on several occasions.

8. *Diccionario Porrúa*, s.v. "Cronista de México (El)."

9. Laureana Wright de Kleinhans has been described as "the most brilliant and radical defender of women's emancipation" in Porfirian Mexico. See Cano, "The *Porfiriato* and the Mexican Revolution," 112.

10. On average, most newspapers during the Porfiriato cost three centavos a copy, making the periodicals examined in this essay extremely expensive and inaccessible to a large portion of the population, as most individu-

als earned between twenty-five and fifty centavos per day. For a discussion of the price of newspaper and weeklies and average salaries during the Porfiriato, see Toussaint Alcaraz, *Escenario de la prensa en el Porfiriato*, 15–17, and Smith, "Contentious Voices amid the Order," 38.

11. Literacy rates during the Porfiriato further hampered the distribution of these weeklies to the lower class. See Smith, "Contentious Voices amid the Order," 38.

12. For a discussion of the railways as powerful symbols of material progress, see Tenorio-Trillo, *Mexico at the World's Fairs*, 116; Garner, *Porfirio Díaz*, 176–77.

13. The *científicos* represented a powerful cadre of individuals—formed in the late 1880s—who sought to govern the nation scientifically and who held important political posts within the administration, influencing political, economic, and social policies throughout the Porfiriato.

14. Weiner, *Race, Nation, and Market*, 50–51. For a discussion of the positivist emphasis on biological understandings of society, see Hale, *Transformation of Liberalism*, chap. 7.

15. Weiner, *Race, Nation, and Market*, 27–29; Hale, *Transformation of Liberalism*, 6. For an examination of the connection between "civilization" and social peace, especially self-restraint from violence, see Elias, *The Civilizing Process*, 180–82.

16. Wolfgang Schivelbusch maintains that the idea of the "annihilation of time and space" emerged as a common characterization of the effect of locomotive travel as a result of the rates of speed—about 20 or 30 mph—made possible by the railway. Since this new form of travel was three times faster than the speed achieved by stagecoaches, a traveler could reach a given destination in one-third of the customary time. As a result, the distance between two points was, likewise, *temporally* reduced by one-third. See Schivelbusch, *Railway Journey*, 41.

17. "¡Miradlo! Va tragando las distancias; / Parece apenas que la tierra toca; / Y devorado por ansias, / Nubes vomita por su ardiente boca!" *El Mundo (Semanario Ilustrado)*, December 6, 1896.

18. Schivelbusch, *Railway Journey*, 59.

19. "¿Dónde van los campos grises / En frenética carrera? / Van á lejanos países / Donde el hombre los espera!" *Jueves del Mundo*, August 21, 1902. *Jueves del Mundo* was a supplement offered free of charge to subscribers to *El Imparcial* and *El Mundo*. It also could be purchased for five centavos in the capital and six centavos in the provinces.

20. Schivelbusch, *Railway Journey*, 60–61.

21. *El Cronista de México*, July 15, 1883.

22. *Las Violetas del Anáhuac*, March 4, 1888.

23. This theme was at times expressed through descriptions of the railway's conquest over nature. The image of the railroad dominating the rugged, uncultivated terrain was also a common symbol of progress in the artwork of José María Velasco. See Tenorio-Trillo, *Mexico at the World's Fairs*, 115–16.

24. Monsiváis, *Escenas de puder y liviandad*, 176.

25. "Te saludo, del Progreso / Mensajera bendecida, / Y te doy la bienvenida, / Nuncio de prosperidad. / Antes que te conociera / Cuánto en sueños te veía! / Y cuánto anhelaba el día / Que te pudiera mirar! / Tres años ha que soñando / En verte con más empeño, / Realicé mi bello sueño, / Y qué dicha al despertar!"

26. "De Irapuato en las orillas / Te ví por la vez primera, / Y parecióme quimera / Que vendrías á mi ciudad. / Por verte aquí tanto ansiaba, / Tan ardiente era el deseo, / Que hoy que en mis lares te veo / Estoy volviendo á soñar. . . ! / ¡Que estoy despierta me dicen / Mis lágrimas de alegría, / Con que saludo este día / De santa felicidad!"

27. Ramos Escandón, "Señoritas Porfirianas: Mujer e ideología en el México progresista, 1880–1910," 150–54; Soto, *Emergence of the Modern Mexican Woman*, 11–13; Tenorillo-Trillo, *Mexico at the World's Fairs*, 150–51; Lucrecia Infante Vargas, "De lectoras y redactoras: Las publicaciones *femeninas* en México durante el siglo XIX," 193–94.

28. "Los mil vivas á Jalisco, / De entusiasmo los rumores, / Al progreso los loores, / Al bienestar y la paz, / La emoción que se retrata / De la gente en el semblante, / Y este concierto gigante, / Me traen á la realidad. . . . / Día de grata memoria / Que honor y lauros conquista, / Al gobierno progresista / Que nos trae industria y paz." *Las Violetas del Anáhuac*, May 13, 1888.

29. Toussaint Alcaraz, *Escenario de la prensa en el Porfiriato*, 39.

30. Navarro's poem supports Claudio Lomnitz's idea that elite Porfirians made a fetish of the symbols of material progress such as the railway, see Lomnitz, *Deep Mexico, Silent Mexico*, 72–73.

31. Cano, "The *Porfiriato* and the Mexican Revolution," 112–13.

32. "Despues triste y abatida / Por las injurias del tiempo: / Mas volviendo á levantarse / En las alas del progreso, / Sirviendo á la férrea via / De estación y de sustento / Soñó que se renovaba, / Soñó que tomaba aliento." *El Coyote*, October 3, 1880.

33. This was also the case in political rhetoric as policymakers and politicians used these discursive devices when arguing for the necessity of rail-

way development between 1876 and 1880. Kim Clark has also demonstrated that the language of revitalization and movement was often used in political discourse regarding railway development in Ecuador. See Clark, *Redemptive Work*, 43–50.

34. "Del sol hermana, y de la noche oscura, / Con el espacio y con el tiempo en guerra, / Los lomos oprimiendo de la tierra, / Avanza majestuosa en la llanura. / Entre el incienso del vapor fulgura / Hace de luz, y con las rocas cierra, / Y se hunde en las entrañas de la sierra, / Buscando allí camino ó sepultura. / Hoy parte de las costas de Occidente, / Mañana del mar Índico en el beso / Irá á templar la enrojecida frente. / Sobre sus alas va el gérmen fecundo / De la industria, del arte, del progreso. . . . / Paso al soplo de Dios que empuja el mundo!" *El Mundo (Semanario Ilustrado)*, December 2, 1894.

35. "Palpitando al ritmo bronco / De sus venas poderosas, / Y crujiendo de sus músculos / La broncínea urdimbre tosca, / Delirante por los campos / Las distancias cruza y borra, / Y sus alas circulares / Van y van vertiginosas." *El Mundo (Semanario Ilustrado)*, November 20, 1898.

36. "En Tampico! Estoy aquí / Recordando ahora que ayer / Contemplando el sol arder / Allá en San Luis Potosí! / La inmensidad ante mí / Pudo angostarse al acaso / Haciendo el ámbito escaso / Para el paso? . . . Nada de eso: / En un paso . . . del progreso; / Pues bendito ese gran paso!" *Periodico Oficial del Gobierno del Estado de San Luis Potosí*, April 27, 1890.

37. Alan Knight describes the beliefs shared by Porfirian officials and the *científicos* regarding notions of time, work, progress, etc., as a "developmentalist ideology." See Knight, "El liberalismo mexicano desde la Reforma," 60–61, and *Mexican Revolution*, 1:84.

38. Weiner, *Race, Nation, and Market*, 27–31.

39. Adas, *Machines as the Measure of Men*, 219–20; Adas, *Dominance by Design*; Lee, "Railways, Space, and Imperialism," 91–106.

40. *Las Violetas del Anáhuac*, March 4, 1888.

41. Hale, *Transformation of Liberalism*, 220.

42. *El Correo de las Señoras*, May 20, 1888.

43. Cosío Villegas, *La vida politica interior* (segunda parte), 10:585.

44. Beezley, *Judas at the Jockey Club*, 16; Tenorillo-Trillo, *Mexico at the World's Fairs*, 19, 37.

45. French, *A Peaceful and Working People*, 110–11.

46. *La Revista Moderna*, June 1, 1899.

47. *La Revista Moderna*, May 1, 1899.

48. For a discussion of the social and cultural dimensions of criminal-

ity, as well as the elite views regarding crime, see Buffington, *Criminal and Citizen in Modern Mexico*; Piccato, *City of Suspects*; Garza, *Imagined Underworld*.

49. *La Revista Moderna*, January 1, 1899.

50. *La Revista Moderna*, May 1, 1899.

51. Tenorillo-Trillo, *Mexico at the World's Fair*, 167–68.

52. *El Cronista de México*, June 17, 1883.

53. Mexico City taxi prices during the Porfiriato are discussed in González Navarro, *El Porfiriato*, 695–96.

54. *El Cronista de México*, June 17, 1883.

55. *La Broma*, August 23, 1888.

56. Similar themes about the ill-fated consequences that the modern city could have for provincial women were best described in Federico Gamboa's famous 1903 novel, *Santa*.

57. *El Mundo Cómico*, December 11, 1898.

58. *El Cómico*, September 24, 1899. *El Mundo Cómico* changed its name to *El Cómico* in 1899.

59. *La Revista Moderna*, June 1, 1899.

60. "Que los conductores son / Unos yankees tan groseros, / Que viajan dentro del carro / Mascando tabaco negro / Y con las patas subidas / Encima de los asientos." *El Cronista de México*, December 23, 1883.

61. Coatsworth, *Growth against Development*, 175; Hart, *Revolutionary Mexico*, 188.

62. Along similar lines, William Beezley has demonstrated that while Mexicans participated in sports and activities introduced by the foreign community, Mexicans rejected those recreations, such as American football, that they viewed as contradictory to their values. See *Judas at the Jockey Club*, 52–66.

63. Before 1888, Díaz had prohibited bullfights from the Federal District in an attempt bolster the country's international image by not offending foreigners' sensibilities regarding cruelty to animals. Beezley, *Judas at the Jockey Club*, 16.

64. *El Cronista de México*, December 2, 1883.

65. Fritzsche, *Stranded in the Present*, 2.

66. Fritzsche, *Stranded in the Present*, 53–54.

67. Tenorio-Trillo, *Mexico at the World's Fair*, 6–7.

68. "Imágen de la vida placentera / Es el tren en que voy arrebatado, / Viendo cruzar fogosos á mi lado / Cuantos seres encuentro en mi carrera. / Yo voy en un asiento de *primera*, / Del calor y del viento resguardado, / Y

el mismo tren conduce al desgraciado / Que ocupa un duro asiento de *tercera*. / Más aunque así suframos ó gocemos / Seperados los dos, cualquiera advierte / Que la misma distancia recorremos. / É igual al fin y al cabo es nuestra suerte / Pues ambos por desgracia pararemos / En la estación del término: LA MUERTE." *El Mundo (Semanario Ilustrado)*, April 17, 1898.

69. "La ventura que surje en el camino / Como sombra se va; tal es la suerte. . . . / Qué tren tan engañoso el del Destino! / Su más bella *estación* será la muerte?" *El Mundo (Semanario Ilustrado)*, September 22, 1895.

70. Lomnitz, *Death and the Idea of Mexico*, 381.

71. Vieyra Sánchez, "La circulación de las obras de Julio Verne en la prensa mexicana del siglo XIX."

72. *El Mundo (Semanario Ilustrado)*, February 17, 1895.

73. Coatsworth, "Railroads, Landholding, and Agrarian Protest." Beyond this, Porfirian newspapers frequently reported on cases of people tampering with equipment, placing rocks on tracks, and throwing objects at passing trains.

74. "Y de Fouriér y Saint Simón delante: / Frente á la voz del Karl Marx, temida, / La creación magnífica, radiante, / Derramando calor y luz y vida, / —Del infinito incognoscible al beso;— / La universal fraternidad del justo, / Augusto Compte [sic] y su apotegma augusto: / AMOR, ORDEN, PROGRESO! . . . / —Tú— "obrero" de las sombras que pasaste / Tu juventud en honda catacumba / Y, al són del mismo golpe, noche y día, / Debajo de la tierra te incrustaste / Como en tu propia tumba; / Oye el rugir inmenso / Del vapor que la máquina conmueve, / Para exhumarte á ti: quema tu incienso / En la ara del Siglo Diez y Nueve!" *El Mundo Ilustrado*, December 30, 1900.

75. Hale, *Transformation of Liberalism*, 20, 34–36, 83.

76. *El Cómico*, September 10, 1899.

77. *El Mundo (Semanario Ilustrado)*, September 19, 1897.

78. There is considerable literature on this subject. See, for example, Thompson, "Time, Work-Discipline, and Industrial Capitalism," 56–97.

79. *El Mundo Cómico*, April 17, 1897.

80. *El Mundo (Semanario Ilustrado)*, October 24, 1897.

81. French, *A Peaceful and Working People*, 64, 84–85.

82. For example, the high-profile murder of Chief Justice Poinsot in a French railway car led to a redesign of the locomotive compartment with railway officials creating a means of communication between compartments in an attempt to avoid similar incidents. See Schivelbusch, *Railway Journey*, 84–86.

83. *El Mundo (Semanario Ilustrado)*, August 7, 1898.

84. *El Mundo (Semanario Ilustrado)*, August 23, 1896.

85. As has been demonstrated in the context of the United States' railway development, women traveling alone became objects of public scrutiny whose respectability was compromised. Likewise, women traveling at night were characterized as dangerous under the prevailing social codes in the nineteenth century. Indeed, special ladies' cars were introduced in the United States as a means for women to retain their propriety while traveling alone. See Welke, *Recasting American Liberty*, 60, 281–82.

86. *Crónica Mexicana*, June 28, 1896.

87. Schivelbusch, *Railway Journey*, 83.

88. Schivelbusch, *Railway Journey*, 197.

89. Maines, *The Technology of Orgasm: "Hysteria," the Vibrator, and Women's Sexual Satisfaction*, 89–91.

90. For a discussion of Victorian notions regarding the public sphere as a dangerous place for women, see Walkowitz, *City of Dreadful Delight*, 80, 84.

91. *El Mundo (Semanario Ilustrado)*, December 31, 1899.

3. Festivals of Progress

1. Cárdenas, "A Macroeconomic Interpretation of Nineteenth-Century Mexico," 77.

2. For a discussion of the inaugural celebrations of streetcars during the Porfiriato, see González Navarro, *El Porfiriato*, 694–95.

3. Marshall Berman argues that because the railroad operated on a more or less fixed schedule and on a prescribed route, it came to represent the nineteenth-century paradigm of order. See Berman, *All That Is Solid Melts into Air*, 159.

4. Ozouf, *Festivals and the French Revolution*, 276.

5. Lane, *The Rites of Rulers*, 2–3; Curcio-Nagy, *Great Festivals of Colonial Mexico City*, 146–51.

6. Hobsbawm and Ranger, eds., *Invention of Tradition*; Beezley, Martin, and French, eds., *Rituals of Rule, Rituals of Resistance*; Seed, *Ceremonies of Possession in Europe's Conquest of the New World, 1492–1640*; Viqueira Albán, *Propriety and Permissiveness in Bourbon Mexico*; Curcio-Nagy, *Great Festivals of Colonial Mexico City*; Beezley and Lorey, eds., *¡Viva Mexico! ¡Viva la Independencia!*

7. For a discussion of the limits of national symbols espoused by positivist republicans on popular groups, see Carvalho, *A Formação das Almas*, 141–42.

8. Anne-Marie Lecoq demonstrates that the use of symbols by the French monarchy to make known its legitimacy and authority also reminded onlookers of the king's responsibilities to the people. See Lecoq, "The Symbolism of the State," 235.

9. Beezley, *Mexican National Identity*, 61–65.

10. For a discussion of the mechanisms used to promote this "cult of personality," see Cosío Villegas, *La vida politica interior* (segunda parte), 10:165–67; Garner, *Porfirio Díaz*, 127–30.

11. Pierre Nora discusses the importance of monuments and ceremony in fostering a shared sense of group membership in society. See Nora, "Between History and Memory," 12.

12. Garner, *Porfirio Díaz*, 129.

13. Cosío Villegas, *La vida politica interior* (segunda parte), 10:167.

14. Esposito, "The Politics of Death," 86.

15. *El Monitor Republicano*, June 4, 1880.

16. *La Patria*, June 5, 1880.

17. *Exposición en Querétaro al Inaugurarse el Ferrocarril Central*, 3–4.

18. Powell, *Railroads of Mexico*, 128–29.

19. *Two Republics*, May 4, 1884.

20. *El Hijo del Trabajo*, May 18, 1884.

21. *El Telégrafo*, June 21, 1881.

22. *El Cronista de México*, December 3, 1882.

23. Pletcher, *Rails, Mines, and Progress*, 68–70; Powell, *Railroads of Mexico*, 109–11.

24. Van Hoy, *A Social History of Mexican Railroads*, 8, 11.

25. *Las Violetas del Anáhuac*, June 3, 1888.

26. *El Municipio Libre*, November 2, 1888.

27. *El Partido Liberal*, November 8, 1888.

28. Garner, *Porfirio Díaz*, 124.

29. *El Partido Liberal* November 7–11, 14, 18, and 21, 1888.

30. *El Partido Liberal*, November 21, 1888.

31. For a study of the 1888 railway inauguration ceremonies in San Luis Potosí, see Coronado Guel., *La alameda potosina ante la llegada del ferrocarril.*

32. As Charles Hale shows, the pro-government newspaper *El Universal* understood a connection between authoritarianism and progress when it argued that railway construction had succeeded because it had been imposed on people by a "*minoría científica*" (scientifically educated minority). See Hale, *Transformation of Liberalism*, 113.

33. *El Hijo del Ahuizote*, November 11, 1888. Tenorio-Trillo discusses how publications such as *El Hijo del Ahuizote* used irony and highlighted contradictions between the regime's rhetoric and the country's social realities to make known the problems of Porfirian rule. See Tenorio-Trillo, *Mexican at the World's Fairs*, 158–78.

34. *El Partido Liberal*, August 18, 1887.

35. *El Mundo (Semanario Ilustrado)*, April 12, 1896.

36. Weiner, *Race, Nation, and Market*, 50–51; Hale, *Transformation of Liberalism*, chap. 7.

37. *El Mundo Ilustrado*, January 13, 1901.

38. Hale, *Transformation of Liberalism*, 11, 134.

39. *El Mundo Ilustrado*, December 11, 1904. *El Mundo (Semanario Ilustrado)* changed its name to *El Mundo Ilustrado* in 1900.

40. Beezley, *Mexican National Identity*, 69–70.

41. "Muchos de los caciques / Dijéronse alegrones: / ¡Caramba! siempre es bueno / Poner Ferrocarril, / Y hacer á los Caudillos / Cien mil invitaciones, . . . / Para hacer una fiesta / Ferro-presidencial: / El no quiere que vaya / Limantour ni Baranda, / Que ha de ser Don Porfirio / Por entero y cabal." *El Hijo del Ahuizote*, August 14, 1898.

42. Garner, "The Politics of National Development in Late Porfirian Mexico: Reconstruction of the Tehuantepec National Railway, 1896–1907," 340.

43. *El Mundo Ilustrado*, January 27, 1907.

44. Abrahams, "Language of Festivals," 162–77; L. Schmidt, "Commercialization of the Calendar."

45. Paul Garner discusses Díaz's use of civic ceremonies and public celebrations in the construction of nation. See Garner, *Porfirio Díaz*, 128.

46. See Tenenbaum, "Streetwise History," 127–50; Tenorio-Trillo, "1910 Mexico City: Space and Nation in the City of the Centenario," 75–104; Agostini, *Monuments of Progess*, 87–88, 91.

47. It should be noted that ceremonies for other public works and infrastructural developments such as telegraph lines, factories, penitentiaries, and steamships, also played a role in making people aware of the wider nation. Nevertheless, railway inaugurations received significantly more attention in the Porfirian press.

48. Anthony D. Smith argues that the use of collective symbols such as national flags and anthems are central to the organization of ceremonies that work to create and maintain community connections and national identity. See Smith, *Ethno-Symbolism and Nationalism*, 25.

49. Esposito, "The Politics of Death," 88–89.

50. B. Anderson, *Imagined Communities*, 9–46. Anderson places heavy emphasis on the importance of print capitalism in the dissemination of national identity. Beezley puts into question the usefulness of Anderson's thesis in a country with low literacy rates such as Mexico. Instead Beezley emphasizes the importance of performance—in theaters, street shows, civic celebrations, etc.—in the construction of national identity. See Beezley, *Mexican National Identity*, vii–x.

51. Statistics provided to the Secretary of Communications and Public Works by the Mexican Central Railroad (1895–1900) reveal that Mexicans indeed took advantage of the locomotive's new speed and scale of movement. Third-class passengers in particular made up the vast majority of individuals who rode the rails. In 1895, third-class passengers totaled 70 percent of all travelers on the main line between Mexico City and El Paso. In 1896, they totaled 66 percent. In 1897, they totaled 65 percent. In 1898, they totaled 75 percent. In 1899, they totaled 76 percent. See Archivo General de la Nación, Ramo Secretaría de Comunicaciones y Obras Públicas (SCOP), 10/3175–2, 10/3176–2.

52. *El Nacional*, November 4, 1888. Also see Coronado Guel., *La alameda potosina ante la llegada del ferrocarril*.

53. Mostkoff-Linares, "Foreign Visions and Images of Mexico," 42–67.

54. *El Mundo Cómico*, December 12, 1897.

55. Again, Benedict Anderson's emphasis on print culture does little to help explain the rise of nationalism in countries with low literacy rates. Here, then, is one example where the promotion of nationalism did not necessarily require a literate populace.

56. *El Tiempo*, April 23, 1890.

57. For a discussion of the connection between landscape and national identity, see Schama, *Landscape and Memory*, 15–16; Zimmer, "Alpine Landscape and the Reconstruction of the Swiss Nation," 637–65; Ely, *This Meager Nature*.

58. *El Mundo Ilustrado*, November 1, 1903.

59. *El Mundo Ilustrado*, December 27, 1903.

60. Tenorio-Trillo, *Mexico at the World's Fairs*, 247.

61. *El Diario del Hogar*, September 8 and 9, 1882.

62. Weiner, *Race, Nation, and Market*, 34–35.

63. Hale, *Transformation of Liberalism*, 23–24, 228–29.

64. González Navarro, *El Porfiriato*, 548.

65. Fritzsche, *Stranded in the Present*, 2, 53–54.

66. Tenorio-Trillo, *Mexico at the World's Fairs*, 66–67, 69–70, 69n15.

67. *Railroader/El Ferrocarrilero*, March 24, 1888.

68. Tenorio-Trillo, *Mexico at the World's Fairs*, 88.

69. Hale, *Transformation of Liberalism*, 252; Weiner, *Race, Nation, and Market*, 55–56.

70. Frazer, *Bandit Nation*, 131–33.

71. "Con una trompa lucida / por mayor, la pasajera, / de lejos se oye el sumbido / de la máquina extranjera. . . . / Aréchiga, mi general, / con los otros de chistera, / recibieron a los güeros / de liontina y faltriquera. . . . / Se burlaron de nosotros / los gringos ajoloteros, / porque perdimos el habla / de mirar tamaños fierros." Avitia Hernández, *Corrido histórico Mexicano*, 1:183–84.

72. "Por ahí vienen los gringos / con mucha satisfacción, / vienen echando medidas / pa' levanter su estación. . . . / Muchachitas de Jalisco, / la máquina ya llegó; / más valía que hubieran traido / la madre que les parió." Avitia Hernández, *Corrido histórico Mexicano*, 1:207.

73. Beezley, *Mexican National Identity*, 146–148.

74. This desire for immigration in order to get new blood into the nation is discussed in Hale, *Transformation of Liberalism*, 234–38.

75. Beezley, "The Porfirian Smart Set Anticipates Thorsten Veblen in Guadalajara," 177–82.

76. Beezley, *Mexican National Identity*, 93–95.

77. For a discussion of the development of new neighborhoods, see Jiménez Muñoz, *La traza de poder*; Tenenbaum, "Streetwise History," 127–50; Morgan, "Proletariats, Politicos, and Patriarchs." For a discussion of working-class neighborhoods, see Lear, *Workers, Neighbors, and Citizens*.

78. *Fiestas Inaugurales del Ferrocarril a Guadalajara*, 12.

79. *El Monitor Republicano*, May 22, 1888.

80. Beezley, "The Porfirian Smart Set," 178.

81. *El Universal*, November 3, 1888.

82. *El Mundo Ilustrado*, April 28, 1903.

83. *El Tiempo*, April 23, 1890.

84. *Las Novedades*, May 28, 1888.

85. For an astute discussion of the opposition press's use of irony to criticize and mock the failures of the regime, see Tenorio-Trillo, *Mexico at the World's Fairs*, 158–78.

86. *El Hijo del Ahuizote*, May 20, 1888.

87. Benjamin, "Paris, the Capital of the Nineteenth Century," in *Arcades Project*, 7.

88. This divide is also explored in terms of the differing musical tastes between the upper and middle classes. See Beezley, *Mexican National Identity*, 95.

89. *Exposición en Querétaro al Inaugurarse el Ferrocarril Central*, 1–10. The belief in the redemptive aspects of the railway has also been examined in the case of Ecuadorian railroad development. See Clark, *Redemptive Work*.

90. *La Sombra de Arteaga*, May 1, 1882.

91. *La Patria*, December 7, 1887.

92. "Ayer se levantaba iglesias y conventos: Recorrían las calles de San Luis Potosí ejércitos de frailes, y sus más bellas hijas se encerraban monjas. El catecismo del Padre Ripalda era toda la instrucción que recibía el pueblo. Hoy se construyen ferrocarriles y se levantan fábricas: recorren las calles manifestaciones populares; hombres y mujeres, entonando himnos al progreso y á los hombres progresistas que los han sacado de la ignorancia, que los han arrancado de su estado abyecto, educándolos é instruyéndolos." *El Correo de San Luis Potosí*, November 1, 1888.

93. Curcio-Nagy, *The Great Festivals of Colonial Mexico City*, 146.

94. James Lehning reveals a similar theme in his study of the procession routes chosen for the funeral of French labor leader Léon Gambetta. Organizers sought to create a sense of sacredness in the working-class neighborhoods in an attempt to bolster popular republicanism. See Lehning, "Gossiping about Gambetta," 242.

95. *La Sombra de Arteaga*, May 1, 1882.

96. Coronado Guel., *La alameda potosina ante la llegada del ferrocarril*, 231–37.

97. Ozouf, *Festivals and the French Revolution*, 262–82.

98. Coronado Guel., *La alameda potosina ante la llegada del ferrocarril*, 235–36.

99. Hale, *Transformation of Liberalism*, 234.

100. Scott, *Domination and the Arts of Resistance*, 158. Adas argues that Europeans promoted civilized behaviors such as punctuality and work ethic to revolutionize social organization and production. See Adas, *Machines as the Measure of Men*, 208–209. This idea builds on Norbert Elias's who, although not discussing European colonialism, maintains the civilizing process in highly differentiated societies worked to organize individuals to fulfill their social function. See Elias, *The Civilizing Process*, 367.

101. A similar point is made by Curcio-Nagy in *The Great Festivals*, 153.

4. The Price of Progress

1. See Beezley and Curcio-Nagy, *Latin American Popular Culture*, xi.

2. Cockcroft, *Intellectual Precursors*, 4; María Elena Díaz, "The Satiric Penny Press for Workers in Mexico, 1900–1910," 501.

3. Terdiman, *Discourse/Counter-Discourse*, 152.

4. Thompson, *The Making of the English Working Class*, 712–13.

5. Frazer, *Bandit Nation*, 132; Vanderwood, *Disorder and Progress*, 136; Bonilla, "Imágenes de Posada en los impresos de Vanegas Arroyo," 424.

6. While I could not find any systematic studies of railway accident rates during the Porfiriato, one published account of a foreigner's lawsuit against the Mexican Central Railroad provides a study that, reportedly, had been produced by the SCOP regarding the rate of 1897 train wrecks in Mexico vis-à-vis European nations that same year. It also provided the numbers of people killed and injured on the Mexican Central and Mexican National railroads. See *Dr. Gloner V. F. C. Central, Indemnización de Daños, Dolores Físicos y Morales: Apuntes de Alegato Al Sr. Juez de lo Civil, Lic. Angel Zavalza por el Lic. José Diego Fernández*, 48, 101. I could not find these reports in the SCOP archives.

7. Williams, *Notes on the Underground*, 63–64.

8. *El Cronista de México*, May 13, 1883.

9. Beezley, *Judas at the Jockey Club*, 31.

10. Bishop, *Old Mexico and Her Lost Provinces*, 190–91. *La Patria*, June 26, 1881, offered a more realistic number of victims, estimating 260 fatalities.

11. It should be noted that the Mexican Central was a U.S. railway while the Interoceanic was British. Nevertheless, most of the Interoceanic Company's engineers were Americans.

12. For a discussion of the dividends paid to shareholders, see Pletcher, *Rails, Mines, and Progress*, 299–305; Tischendorf, *Great Britain and Mexico in the Age of Díaz*, 55–63; Coerver, *Porfirian Interregnum*, 209–10; Kuntz-Ficker, *Empresa extrangera y mercado*, 206–208.

13. *El Monitor Republicano*, March 3, 1895.

14. *El Monitor Republicano*, March 3, 1895.

15. *El Partido Liberal*, March 16, 1895.

16. Many newspapers covered the Temamatla accident. For some of the most detailed—and graphic—accounts of the wreck, see *El Siglo Diez y Nueve*, March 1, 1895; *El Municipio Libre*, March 2, 1895; *El Partido Liberal*, March 2, 1895; *El Tiempo*, March 2, 1895; *El Nacional*, March 2, 1895; *La Bandera Mexicana*, March 3, 1895; *El Monitor Republicano*,

March 3, 1895; *El Hijo del Ahuizote*, March 3, 1895; *El Universal*, March 3, 1895; *El Mundo (Semanario Ilustrado)*, March 10, 1895. Because of its severity and magnitude, the wreck also was covered in some U.S. newspapers, including the *New York Times*, March 2, 1895.

17. *El Monitor Republicano*, March 3, 1895.

18. For example, *El Continental*, March 25, 1895.

19. *El Partido Liberal*, March 5, 1895.

20. *La Convención Radical Obrera*, March 17, 1895.

21. *El Tiempo*, March 3, 1895; *El Demócrata*, March 8, 1895.

22. *Gil Blas*, March 23, 1895.

23. *El Universal*, November 6, 1895.

24. *El Tiempo*, May 17, 1896.

25 For example, *El Hijo del Ahuizote*, November 13, 1898.

26. *El Diablito Bromista*, December 22, 1907.

27. "Escuchen, señores, esta triste historia / que traigo en el pensamiento, / de lo que hace poco pasó en Temamantla / con el descarrilamiento. . . . / El jueves veintiocho del mes de febrero / del año noventa y cinco, / todos en Ameca para la estación / iban con gran regocijo. . . . / Tres coches quedaron de los de tercera / toditos hechos pedazos, / y por dondequiera nomás se veían / cabezas, piernas y brazos." Avita Hernández, *Corrido histórico mexicano*, 1:215–18.

28. For an overview of popular antiforeign sentiments during the Porfiriato, see González Navarro, *El Porfiriato*, 153–84.

29. *El Siglo Diez y Nueve*, April 13, 1895.

30. *El Noticioso*, April 12, 1895.

31. *El Partido Liberal*, March 12, 1895.

32. *Gil Blas*, March 23, 24, 26, 27, 28, and 29, 1895.

33. *El Tiempo*, March 7, 1895.

34. *El Partido Liberal*, May 2, 1895.

35. *El Partido Liberal*, January 28, 1896.

36. Coerver, *Porfirian Interregnum*, 203–205.

37. *El Chisme*, November 16, 1900.

38. *El Mundo (Semanario Ilustrado)*, March 17, 1895.

39. For a discussion of middle- and upper-class views about workers' indulgence in vice and poor work ethic, see French, *A Peaceful and Working People*, 72–74, 100.

40. *El Mundo (Semanario Ilustrado)*, December 15, 1895.

41. "Salen hoy las Calaveras / De la ciudad de Canillas, / A cantar en peteneras / Tus gloriosas maravillas." *El Hijo del Ahuizote*, March 1, 1896.

42. *El Hijo del Ahuizote*, December 12, 1897.

43. Calderón, "Los ferrocarriles," 7:502. For other railway projects that involved Gillow, see Calderón, "Los ferrocarriles," 7:527, 536; Chassen-López, *From Liberal to Revolutionary Oaxaca*, 51.

44. *El Partido Liberal*, March 29, 1895.

45. *El Hijo del Ahuizote*, May 19, 1895.

46. *El Mundo (Semanario Ilustrado)*, February 21, 1897.

47. *El Tiempo*, July 23, 1897. Indeed, Great Britain had begun to compensate accident victims with the passing of Lord Campbell's Act of 1846, although it was not passed into law officially until 1864. See Schivelbusch, *Railway Journey*, 206n1; Simmons, *Victorian Railway*, 279. Likewise, in the United States, Barbara Welke notes that by 1865 "courts had articulated all of the basic elements of a claim for negligence," although there was no universal law for accident injury. See Welke, *Recasting American Liberty*, 83.

48. *El Popular*, June 5, 1898.

49. Secretaria de Comunicaciones y Obras Públicas, *Ley sobre ferrocarriles*, 60–61.

50. Victims in the United States also experienced paralysis after railway accidents, even in cases where they had walked away from wrecks apparently unharmed. See Caplan, "Trains and Trauma in the American Gilded Age," 58.

51. *Aplicación de la Responsibildad Civil á los Siniestros en los Ferrocarriles: Apuntes de Alegato de la Compañia del Ferrocarril Interoceanico en el Juicio Promovido por D. Joaquín Cardoso sobre Indemnificación por Perjuicios Ocasionados en el Siniestro de 28 de Febrero 1892*.

52. *Aplicación de la Responsibildad*, 39.

53. *El Demócrata*, March 8, 1895.

54. Harrington, "The Railway Accident"; Caplan, "Trains and Trauma," 55–77; Schivelbusch, *Railway Journey*, 135–45.

55. *Aplicación de la Responsibildad*, 87.

56. Cabrera, ed., *Liberales ilustres Mexicanos de la reforma y la intervención*, 372–73; *Aplicación de la Responsibildad*, 88–89.

57. *El Demócrata*, March 8, 1895.

58. Several newspapers covered Dr. Gloner's accident. See *Two Republics*, May 18, 1897; *El Mundo (Semanario Ilustrado)*, May 19, 1897; *El Universal*, May 19, 1897.

59. *Dr. Gloner V. F. C. Central*, 1–96.

60. *Dr. Gloner V. F. C. Central*, 72–81.

61. *Dr. Gloner V. F. C. Central*, 61–63.

62. *El Tiempo*, July 23, 1897, cited in *Dr. Gloner V. F. C. Central*, 30.

63. Harrington, "The Railway Accident," 32.

64. *Two Republics*, August 8, 1898.

65. *Dr. Gloner V. F. C. Central*, 94–102.

66. Schivelbusch, *Railway Journey*, 135–45; Harrington, "The Railway Accident."

67. *Dr. Gloner V. F. C. Central*, 139–45.

68. *Dr. Gloner V. F. C. Central*, 139.

69. *El Hijo del Ahuizote*, April 8, 1900.

70. "Pues si quieren en dinero / la justa indemnización, / se han de recibir primero / de abogados . . . y chitón." *El Progreso Latino*, January 7, 1906.

71. Archivo Histórico del Centro de Estudios de Historia de México-Condumex, Fondo Limantour, CDLIV, seria 2ª, Año 1900, Caja 13, Documento 18985.

72. *Mexican Herald*, February 26, 1900.

73. *Two Republics*, March 8, 1900.

74. *El Popular*, March 2, 1900.

75. *Mexican Herald*, February 12, 1900.

76. *El Universal*, February 13, 1900.

77. *La Patria*, February 17, 1900; *El Chisme*, March 3, 1900.

78. Archivo General de la Nación, Ramo Secretaría de Justicia, num. 599, exp. 775.

79. *Regeneración*, October 7, 1900.

80. R. Anderson, *Outcasts in Their Own Land*, 323–30; Ruíz, *The Great Rebellion*, 106–107; Hart, *Revolutionary Mexico*, 73.

81. *Programa y proyecto de la Gran Liga Mexicana de Empleados de Ferrocarril presentado por la presidencia*, 6–9; R. Anderson, *Outcasts in Their Own Land*, 58.

82. R. Anderson, *Outcasts in Their Own Land*, 34. It should be noted that the league's mention of "accidents" is unclear, not specifying between injuries caused by wrecks or by working on the engine or brakes.

83. R. Anderson, *Outcasts in Their Own Land*, 88–89, 91–92, 95, 117–19, 214–15; A. Schmidt, *The Social and Economic Effect of the Railroad*, 194–95.

84. While the NRM had been created by Limantour by having the national government buy a controlling interest in ten prominent railway lines, it was not an entirely Mexican company. The board of directors continued to

have significant U.S. representation. Nine of the twenty-one directors sat on a board in New York, despite the congressional decree that stated the NRM would be governed from Mexico City. For more detailed accounts of the formation of NRM, see Calderón, "Los ferrocarriles," 595–634; Grunstein, "De la competencia al monopolio"; Lewis, *Iron Horse Imperialism*, 26–32.

85. *Mexican Herald*, July 17, 1909.

86. *El Diario*, July 17, 1909; *Gil Blas*, July 17, 1909.

87. *Mexican Herald*, July 19, 1909. There is brief mention of the 1909 strike in Fernando González Roa, *El problema ferrocarrilero y la Compañía de los Ferrocarriles Nacionales de México*, 180–81.

88. *El Diario*, July 21, 1909.

89. *Gil Blas*, August 5, 1909.

90. Anderson, *Outcasts in Their Own Land*, 89–90, 215, 236.

91. *El Diario*, October 11, 1909.

92. Ortiz Hernán, *Los ferrocarriles de México*, 128; Lewis, *Iron Horse Imperialism*, 21. The preeminent railway historian Francisco Calderón considered the introduction of the Spanish language to transportation services as one of the major benefits of the nationalization program. See Calderón, "Los ferrocarriles," 7:624.

93. *El Pinche*, April 28, 1904.

94. See, for example, *El Chile Piquín*, January 19 and 26 and June 22, 1905.

95. *El Ahuizotito*, April 26, 1906.

96. *El Diablito Bromista*, August 4, 1907.

97. *El Diablito Bromista*, October 13, 1907.

98. *El Diablito Bromista*, October 20, 1907.

99. Anderson, *Outcasts in Their Own Land*, 89–90.

100. See, for example, Pletcher, *Rails, Mines, and Progress*, 305–306; Hart, *Revolutionary Mexico*, 247; Garner, *Porfirio Díaz*, 178–79; Lewis, *Iron Horse Imperialism*, 26–28. Cathryn Thorup maintains that Limantour promoted British investment to reduce the influence of the United States over Mexican policymaking. See Thorup, "La competencia económica británica y norteamericana en México (1887–1910)," 639–40.

101. Katz, *Secret War in Mexico*, 21–27; Paolo Riguzzi, "México, Estados Unidos, y Gran Bretaña, 1867–1910"; Garner, "La Compañia Pearson y el Ferrocarril Nacional de Tehuantepec (1896–1907)," 106–109; Weiner, *Race, Nation, and Market*, 55–58.

102. Limantour, *Apuntes sobre mi vida pública*, 80–84; Grunstein, "Railways and Sovereignty," 139–40.

103. Hart, *Revolutionary Mexico*, 247–48.

104. Ortiz Hernán, *Los ferrocarriles de México*, 127–28.

105. Knight, "The Political Economy of Revolutionary Mexico"; Garner, *British Lions and Mexican Eagles*, 98–99.

106. Grunstein, "De la competencia al monopolio," 99–100.

107. González Navarro, *El Porfiriato*, 309, 357.

108. Lewis, *Iron Horse Imperialism*, 30.

109. Hart, *Empire and Revolution*, 128.

110. Juan Gómez Quiñonez notes that the 1908 nationalization received overwhelming approval from nearly all sectors of the press. See Gómez Quiñonez, *Porfirio Díaz, los intelectuales y la Revolución*, 140.

111. "Y que, . . . ¡que vamos á hacer / Con estas plagas sociales, / Que tienen, para estos males / Orejas de mercader!" *El Rasca Tripas*, June 4, 1882.

112. *El Rasca Tripas*, July 9, 1882.

113. *El Mundo Cómico*, December 12, 1897.

114. *El Diablito Rojo*, June 22, 1908, quoted in Anderson, *Outcasts in Their Own Land*, 327.

115. *El Diablito Bromista*, August 17, 1908.

116. *El Cómico*, August 20, 1899. *El Mundo Cómico* changed its name to *El Cómico* in 1899.

117. *El Cómico*, November 5, 1899.

118. Smith, "Contentious Voices amid the Order," 82–88.

119. *El Hijo del Ahuizote*, January 21, 1894.

120. *El Hijo del Ahuizote*, September 4, 1898.

121. While the Valle Railway was a tram and not a railroad, it is briefly examined here because newspapers used it as an example of the problems with the country's transportation system more generally, especially the perception that U.S. employees and companies cared little about Mexican life.

122. *El Alacrán*, November 4, 1899.

123. *El Correo de México*, October 31, 1899.

124. *El Hijo del Ahuizote*, May 26, 1901.

125. "*Mi non tende*" became a running gag in *El Hijo del Ahuizote*. Illustrations and articles played on the poor Spanish spoken by Americans, especially railway employees, a criticism used to evoke nationalist sentiments from readers.

126. *El Hijo del Ahuizote*, November 12, 1899.

127. By the turn of the century, U.S. interests owned 81 percent of the mining industry's capital and 80 percent of the country's railway stock. See Hart, *Revolutionary Mexico*, 134, 142.

128. Hart, *Revolutionary Mexico*, 73; R. Anderson, *Outcasts in Their Own Land*, 323–30; Ruíz, *The Great Rebellion*, 106–107.

129. "Veinticinco tirturadas / Suicidas un montón, / Y uno que otro cabezón / Dividido á cuchilladas. / Clausuras de pulquerias, / Descarrilamiento en curva. / Así se ilustra á la turba, / Con chismes y porquerias." *Don Cucufate*, October 1, 1908.

130. "Diez coches jalaba la locomotora / número cincuenta y cuatro, / y su maquinista era un extranjero, / causa de tanto quebranto." Avitia Hernández, *Corrido histórico Mexicano*, 1:215.

131. "La orden que dada tenía / no la quiso obedecer, / y era la de esperar / en Santa María otro tren." Avitia Hernández, *Corrido histórico Mexicano*, 1:252–53.

132. "Ese maquinista Lee / a la cárcel fue culpable / y a pesar de ser güerito / difícil es que se salve. / El conductor mister Moore / en Aguas se encuentra grave, / y no es fácil, aseguran, / que el pobre mister se salve." Avitia Hernández, *Corrido histórico Mexicano*, 1:241–43.

133. *La Libertad*, July 2, 1904.

134. For studies on Posada's art and its importance and influence in Mexico, see Tyler, ed., *Posada's Mexico*; Carillo, *Posada y el grabador mexicano*; Soler and Ávila, eds., *Posada y la prensa ilustrada*; and Frank, *Posada's Broadsheets*.

135. "Cuando la empresa mata, / dice: 'las manos me lavo'; / y si alguien cobra un centavo, / pidiendo indemnizaciones, / le gritan los gringos: ¡nones! / y aquí les responded ¡Bravo!" *El Diablito Rojo*, May 11, 1908.

136. Robert Buffington shows that working-class newspapers defined their patriotism as authentic vis-à-vis the elite's in a number of arenas including the commemoration of national holidays and historic national figures such as Benito Juárez and Miguel Hidalgo. See *A Sentimental Education for the Working Man*, chap. 1.

137. See R. Anderson, *Outcasts in Their Own Land*, 326–28; Hart, *Revolutionary Mexico*, 68–73.

138. R. Anderson, *Outcasts in Their Own Land*, 327.

139. Hart, *Revolutionary Mexico*, 93.

140. See Knight, *Mexican Revolution*, 1:37–77. For example, Knight downplays anti-Americanism. His examination of opposition groups that emerged during the Porfiriato makes no mention of anti-Americanism, even in its discussion of virulently anti-American intellectuals and newspaper men such as Daniel Cabrera, editor of *El Hijo del Ahuizote*, and the Flores Magón brothers, editors of *Regeneración*.

5. La Loco-Matona

1. Throughout the chapter I have differentiated between the "popular" and "opposition" press. I define the popular press as penny presses such as *El Diablito Rojo*, *El Diablito Bromista*, and *El Chisme* that targeted working-class audiences. By opposition press, I refer to more costly independent publications, usually targeting middle-class readers, such as *El Monitor Republicano* (three cents), *El Gil Blas Cómico* (five cents) and *El Hijo del Ahuizote* (thirteen cents) that consistently questioned the regime's policies or that repeatedly suffered government censorship.

2. Knight, *Mexican Revolution*, 1:230.

3. *Diccionario Porrúa*, s.v. "*Tiempo (El)*." It is difficult to pin down Montes de Oca's political and religious leanings. While he worked for the conservative, Catholic daily *El Tiempo* early in his career, his weekly *Gil Blas* has been described by Pablo Piccato as "liberal." See Piccato, *The Tyranny of Opinion*, 244. Furthermore, while *Gil Blas* was orthodox liberal insofar as it opposed Díaz's reelections and his flouting of the 1857 Constitution, it also appeared to target Catholic readership. It regularly reported on religious pilgrimages, especially those that took place for the Coronation of the Virgin of Guadalupe in 1895, and while at times it poked fun at the pilgrims' provinciality, it never attacked the Church outright or the detente between the government and religious authorities. This is not surprising, as Montes de Oca also edited the Catholic weekly *El Tiempo*.

4. Adame Goddard, *El pensamineto político y social de los católicos mexicanos, 1867–1914*, 142. For a detailed discussion of Trinidad Sánchez Santos's Catholic ideology, see Weiner, "Trinidad Sánchez Santos: Voice of the Catholic Opposition in Porfirian Mexico."

5. Navarrete Maya, "El *Gil Blas Cómico*, publicación satírica y de humor," 264–71.

6. Opinions differ over the role played by the PLM in shaping the ideological foundations of revolutionaries and in helping to spur the outbreak of the 1910 Revolution. Cockcroft and Hart maintain that PLM publications such as *Regeneración* radicalized a worker opposition to the regime and that PLM members led important military campaigns and raids before and during the Revolution. See, Cockcroft, *Intellectual Precursors*, 138, 179; Hart, *Revolutionary Mexico*, 91–93. Anderson and Knight, in contrast, downplay the PLM's importance in radicalizing workers, as there is little documentary evidence to assess whether or not workers read the journal. Moreover, Knight argues that the only clear example of the PLM's military role in the Revolution was the taking of Mexicali, Baja California, in

1911. See R. Anderson, *Outcasts in Their Own Land*, 282; Knight, *Mexican Revolution*, 1:229–30.

7. Cockcroft, *Intellectual Precursors*, 114.

8. For a discussion of *El Hijo del Ahuizote*'s popularity and targeted audiences, see Espinosa Blas, "El Hijo del Ahuizote: Un periodic americanista," 245–62; Bringas and Mascareño, *Esbozo historic de la prensa obrera en México*, 28, 32; Toussaint Alcaraz, *Escenario de la prensa*, 35; Cosío Villegas, *Vida política interior* (segunda parte), 10:239–40.

9. *Gil Blas Cómico*, October 5, 1896.

10. *Gil Blas Cómico*, August 3, 1896.

11. *Gil Blas Cómico*, August 10, 1896.

12. *El Chisme*, November 7, 1899.

13. *El Hijo del Ahuizote*, March 10, 1895.

14. *Gil Blas Cómico*, March 8, 1897.

15. "Llegando á Veracruz. Calor muy grande, . . . / y por más que veloz este tren anda / á Veracruz llegamos ya sin luz. / En el tren muchos yanquis; casi todos / son yanquis los viajeros / llegando á ser así, por varios modos, / muchas patas y pocos pasajeros. / Las patas de los yanquis, colocadas / á los respaldos van de los asientos, / balanceándose todos / del tren con los continuos movimientos, / que en Yanquilandia existen esas modas. . . . / En todos sitios por las cuales vamos / gran unidad de miras observamos; / el ideal eterno / en el puerto es hablar mal del gobierno." *El Alacran*, January 27, 1900.

16. *Gil Blas Cómico*, July 20, 1896.

17. *Gil Blas Cómico*, October 26, 1896.

18. *Gil Blas Cómico*, November 18, November 25, December 2, December 9, and December 16, 1895.

19. "Mi carta, que es feliz, pues va á buscaros, / Cuenta os dará de la memoria mía, / Aquel fantasma soy que, por amaros, / Juró estar vivo á vuestro lado un día. / Cuando lleve esta carta á vuestro oído / El eco de mi amor y mis dolores, / El cuerpo en que mi espíritu ha vivido / Ya durmiendo estará bajo unas flores. . . . / Mas tal vez allá arriba nos veremos, / Después de esta existencia pasajera, / Cuando los dos, como el tren, lleguemos / De nuestra vida á la estación postera. . . . / ¡Adiós, adiós! como hablo delirando, / No sé decir lo que deciros quiero! / Yo sólo sé de mí que estoy llorando, / Que sufro, que os amaba y que me muero!" *Gil Blas Cómico*, March 2, 1896.

20. "Tres lustros ha . . . la niña adolscente / Fué arrebatada por la suerte impía. . . . / Marchó á Paris . . . letal melancholia / Me acompañó mientras

estuvo ausente. / Llegará hoy . . . gozoso é impaciente / La espero ya . . . ¿y esa algarabía? . . . / ¡Ah! . . . silba el tren . . . se acerca . . . ¿y mi María? / ¡Eureka! . . . viene ahí . . . me vé sonriente. . . . / Llegó mi novia enferma; enamorado / La abracé con pasión . . . me miró incierta. . . . / Puso sobre mi boca un beso helado; / Dió un grito de dolor y . . . quedó muerta: / Rodamos . . . ¡miento! desperté asustado, / Abrazando la tranca de la puerta." *Gil Blas Cómico,* May 18, 1896.

21. *Gil Blas Cómico,* October 26, 1896.

22. Weiner, *Race, Nation, and Market,* 71–73.

23. Raat, "The Antipositivist Movement in Prerevolutionary Mexico, 1892–1911," 87.

24. *Gil Blas Cómico,* October 12, 1896.

25. Lomnitz, *Death and the Idea of Mexico,* 377–81.

26. A similar argument is made by Peter Fritzsche in his examination of how nineteenth-century Europeans interpreted the modern present vis-à-vis the past. See Fritzsche, *Stranded in the Present,* 178–80.

27. P. Smith, "Contentious Voices amid the Order," 54–67.

28. Garner, *Porfirio Díaz,* 178.

29. *El Hijo del Ahuizote,* August 30, 1891.

30. P. Smith, "Contentious Voices amid the Order," 62.

31. *El Hijo del Ahuizote,* December 23, 1887.

32. "La rauda locomotiva / Que al heróico puerto arriba. / Une á esos pueblos hermanos; / Y yo tambien grito ¡vivaaa! / Y aplaudo con alma y manos. / A fuerza de subvenciones / Y gordas contribuciones, / Quedan Tampico y Sau [*sic*] Luis / En estrechas relaciones / Con el resto del país." *El Hijo del Ahuizote,* April 20, 1890.

33. *El Hijo del Ahuizote,* June 8, 1890.

34. *El Hijo del Ahuizote,* June 10, 1900.

35. Coatsworth, *Growth against Development,* 96n18.

36. In Mexico City, the literacy rate improved from 38 to 50 percent during the Porfiriato. In the rest of the country, the literacy rate improved from 14 to 20 percent. Smith, "Contentious Voices amid the Order," 38.

37. This rhetoric would become central to the PLM's discussion of what they viewed as the economic imperialism of the United States and European nations over Mexico. See Weiner, *Race, Nation, and Market,* 91–92, 95–96.

38. Coatsworth, *Growth against Development.*

39. Grunstein, "Railroads and Sovereignty," 312–13; Kuntz-Ficker, *Empresa Extrangera y Mercado Interno,* 287, 355–59.

40. Hart, *Revolutionary Mexico*, 98–99. For studies of Madero's political career, philosophy, and motivations to rebel, see Cumberland, *Mexican Revolution: Genesis under Madero*, and Ross, *Francisco I. Madero, Apostle of Mexican Democracy*.

41. Weiner, *Race, Nation, and Market*, 91.

42. Smith, "Contentious Voices amid the Order," 94.

43. *El Padre Cobos*, May 15, 1880.

44. It was widely known that González had taken advantage of railway policy to make himself wealthier by buying tracts of land along planned routes. See Coerver, *Porfirian Interregnum*, 264.

45. *El Rasca Tripas*, November 12, 1882.

46. Garner, *Porfirio Díaz*, 177.

47. *El Hijo del Ahuizote*, January 27, 1889.

48. *El Hijo del Ahuizote*, February 8, 1891.

49. *El Hijo del Ahuizote*, January 4, 1903.

50. *El Ahuizote Jacobino*, July 31, 1904.

51. *El Nieto del Ahuizote*, January 5, 1887.

52. *El Chisme*, November 20, 1899.

53. *El Chisme*, May 8, 1900.

54. *El Chisme*, September 28, 1900.

55. *El Chisme*, August 12, 1900.

56. "If a desperate person wants / To have his baptism ruined / Travel in a rail-cataclysm [railway], / As that will surely be the result; / It is true that certain machine-nihilists [engineers] / Tighten their grip so well, / *You pay in Mexican / And they'll kill you in English*. / We no longer fear typhus, / Neither cholera, nor the fever; / That is a swindle / And backward you get your fears: / The real scare is had / In a train, plain and simple, / *You pay in Mexican / And they'll kill you in English* / The manager of the joke / Of dispatching the traveler, / Tends to be a son of a bitch / Thick as a cow, / Is as strong as a brute, / And begging him is so useless, / *You pay in Mexican / And they'll kill you in English* / —Mr. Yankee (he pleads) / Do not break our rib. / —Me no understand Spanish / He says, looking at him sideways; / But when it comes to savagery / He is such a doyen, / *You will pay in Mexican / And they'll kill you in English*." *El Hijo del Ahuizote*, May 17, 1895. The original read: "Si quiere un desesperado / Que le estrellen el bautismo, / Viaje en ferro-cataclismo, / Que el efecto seguro es; / Pues ciertos maqui-nihilistas / Tan bien aprietan la mano, / *Que paga usté en mexicano / Y lo matan en inglés*. / Ya no tememos al tifo, / Ni al cólera, ni á la fiebre; / Eso es dar gato por liebre / Y sustitos al revés: / El sustazo se recibe / En un

tren, y tan de plano, / *Que paga usté en mexicano / Y lo matan en inglés.*
. . . / El encargado del chiste / De despachar al viajero, / Suele ser un majadero / Macizo como una res, / Es tan fuerte como bruto, / Y suplicarle es tan
vano, / *Que paga usté en mexicano / Y lo matan en inglés. /* —Señor yankee, (se le ruega), / No nos rompa una costilla. / —*Mi non tende de castilla,* / Dice él, viendo de través; / Mas en punto á salvajada / Es de tal modo
un decano, / *Que paga usté en mexicano / Y lo matan en inglés.*" *El Hijo
del Ahuizote,* March 17, 1895.

57. *El Hijo del Ahuizote,* April 8, 1900.

58. See, for example, *El Diablito Bromista* August 4, October 13, October 20, November 1907, and December 15, 1907.

59. *El Diablito Bromista,* December 5, 1909.

60. Buffington comes to a similar conclusion in his discussion of how
working-class penny presses portrayed the elite as "cruel, corrupt, lazy, and
unpatriotic." See *A Sentimental Education for the Working Man,* chap. 3.

61. "Volverán otra vez de Yanquilandia / Las manadas de gringos á em-
igrar / Y otra vez tan groseros é insolentes / A México vendrán. / Pero
aquellos en amos convertidos / Que en los trenes quieran imperar, / Aquellos
que mamaban á dos chiches / Esos . . . no volverán! . . . / Cantarán otra vez
el *yankee doole* [sic] / Tabaco por arrobas mercarán; / Pero lo que es tortillas
y frijoles. . . . / Ya nunca tragarán." *El Diablito Rojo,* February 21, 1910.

62. It should be noted that while discussion of railway policy revealed
intense anti-Americanism, *El Hijo del Ahuizote* also demonstrated xeno-
phobic nationalism in its discussion the country's Spanish residents, claiming that they controlled important sectors of the economy such as factories
that produced, among other things, cigars, paper, and matches as well as
holding a monopoly over cities' food production. See Pérez Vejo, "La conspiración gachupina en *El Hijo del Ahuizote,*" 1116.

63. Hart, *Revolutionary Mexico*; Anderson, *Outcasts in Their Own
Land.*

64. For an examination of the placement of governors loyal to Díaz,
the recruitment of governors powerful within their native states, and the
rotation of governors, see Cosío Villegas, *La vida política* (segunda parte); Wasserman, *Capitalists, Caciques, and Revolution*; Meyers, *Forge of
Progress, Crucible of Revolt*; and Wells and Joseph, *Summer of Discontent, Seasons of Upheaval.* For an examination of the use of city police
forces, the *rurales,* and the military, see Rohlfes, "Police and Penal Correction in Mexico City, 1876–1911"; Vanderwood, *Disorder and Progress*;
and Vanderwood, *The Power of God against the Guns of Government.*

65. See Coerver, *Porfirian Interregnum*, 264–70.

66. *El Hijo del Ahuizote*, May 16, 1886.

67. *El Nieto del Ahuizote*, November, 18, 1886.

68. *El Hijo del Ahuizote*, November 21, 1886.

69. *El Hijo del Ahuizote*, February 10, 1901.

70. *El Hijo del Ahuizote*, August 17, 1902.

71. "Doña Matona la egregia / De Tuxtepec esperenza / Con esta mejora regia / Perfecciona la estrategia / Que demanda la Ordenanza." *El Hijo del Ahuizote*, November 13, 1892.

72. *El Hijo del Ahuizote*, March 10, 1895.

73. Tenorio-Trillo, *Mexico at the World's Fairs*, chap. 10.

74. Calderón, "Los ferrocarriles," 502.

75. *El Hijo del Ahuizote*, November 13, 1892.

76. Fernando Iturribarria, "La política de conciliación del general Díaz y el arzobispo Gillow," 87–88; Garner, *Porfirio Díaz*, 117–19.

77. *El Hijo del Ahuizote*, December 10, 1899.

78. *El Hijo del Ahuizote*, September 6, 1885.

79. *El Hijo del Ahuizote*, September 17, 1887.

80. Roderic Ai Camp defines *camarilla* as a group of individuals whose political interests overlap and that work with one another in order to better their opportunities for political advancement. See Camp, *Politics in Mexico*, 103.

81. *El Hijo del Ahuizote*, October 18, 1891.

82. *El Hijo del Ahuizote*, October 28, 1888.

83. *El Hijo del Ahuizote*, June 5, 1892.

84. *El Hijo del Ahuizote*, January 30, 1898.

85. *El Hijo del Ahuizote*, September 3, 1899.

86. Cockcroft, *Intellectual Precursors*, 107–108.

87. *El Hijo del Ahuizote*, January 18, 1903.

88. *El Hijo del Ahuizote*, March 1, 1903.

89. Cockcroft, *Intellectual Precursors*, 114–15.

90. Anderson, *Outcasts in Their Own Land*, 270, 287, 289–90; Hart, *Revolutionary Mexico*, 103, 240–41.

91. *El Ahuizote Jacobino*, April 17, 1904.

92. *El Ahuizote Jacobino*, April 24, 1904.

93. "¡Oh qué asombro el de aquellos campesinos, / ayer indiferentes, / al mirarles trazar férreos caminos / y túneles y puentes! / La lijera y gentil locomotora / silbó con arrogancia, / y la aldea antes pobre, vive ahora / feliz en la abundancia. / Y hoy, al honrarla doctos ingenieros, / ¡qué alegre efer-

vescencia! / Y al anuncio de padres misioneros . . . / ¡qué Hermosa indiferencia!" *El Ahuizote Jacobino*, August 14, 1904.

94. Weiner, *Race, Nation, and Market*, 91.

95. "Make me a plow, a rail hammer, / A wire, a locomotive; / Make me a creative force / Of universal progress." The original read: "Hazme arado, / riel martillo, / Alambre, locomotora; / Hazme una fuerza creadora / De progreso universal." *El Diablito Rojo*, March 23, 1908.

96. *El Diablito Rojo*, June 6, 1910.

97. *Diablito Bromista*, December 12, 1909.

98. Roseberry, "Hegemony and the Language of Contention," 360–61.

Conclusion

1. The document's final pages have been lost, concealing the identity of its writer.

2. Archivo General de la Nación, Ramo Gobernación, 907-3-1.

3. Madero, *Presidential Succession*, 156–60.

4. Although Mexico's major railway lines were nationalized by 1908, Madero correctly noted that a bulk of the control remained in the hands of foreigners.

5. Madero, *Presidential Succession*, 236.

6. Madero, *Presidential Succession*, 105–26.

7. Sluis, "City of Spectacles"; Joseph, Rubenstein, and Zolov, "Assembling the Fragments: Writing a Cultural History of Mexico since 1940," 11.

BIBLIOGRAPHY

Abrahams, Roger. "The Language of Festivals: Celebrating the Economy." In *Celebration: Studies in Festival and Ritual*, ed. Victor Turner, 161–77. Washington DC: Smithsonian Institution Press, 1982.

Adame Goddard, Jorge. *El pensamineto político y social de los católicos mexicanos, 1867–1914*. Mexico: Universidad Nacional Autónoma de Mexico, 1981.

Adas, Michael. *Dominance by Design: Technological Imperative and America's Civilizing Mission*. Cambridge: Harvard University Press, 2006.

———. *Machines as the Measure of Men: Science, Technology, and Ideologies of Western Dominance*. Ithaca: Cornell University Press, 1989.

Agostini, Claudia. *Monuments of Progress: Modernization and Public Health in Mexico City, 1876–1910*. Calgary: University of Calgary Press, 2003.

Alba, Victor. "The Mexican Revolution and the Cartoon." *Comparative Studies in Society and History* 9, no. 2 (1967): 121–36.

Anderson, Benedict. *Imagined Communities: Reflections on the Origins and Spread of Nationalism*. Rev. ed. London: Verso, 1991.

Anderson, Rodney. *Outcasts in Their Own Land: Mexican Industrial Workers, 1906–1911*. DeKalb: Northern Illinois University Press, 1976.

Anna, Timothy. *Forging Mexico: 1821–1835*. Lincoln: University of Nebraska Press, 1998.

Aplicación de la Responsibildad Civil á los Siniestros en los Ferrocarriles: Apuntes de Alegato de la Compañia del Ferrocarril Interoceanico en el Juicio Promovido por D. Joaquín Cardoso sobre Indemnificación por Perjuicios Ocasionados en el Siniestro de 28 de Febrero 1892. Mexico: Imp. F. Díaz de León Suce, SA, 1893.

Avitia Hernández, Antonio. *Corrido histórico Mexicano: Voy a cantarles la historia*. Vol. 1. Mexico: Editorial Porrúa, 1997.

Bazant, Jan. *Alienation of Church Wealth in Mexico: Social and Economic Aspects of the Liberal Revolution, 1856–1875.* Cambridge: Cambridge University Press, 1971.

———. "From Independence to the Liberal Republic." In *Mexico since Independence*, ed. Leslie Bethell, 1–48. Cambridge: Cambridge University Press, 1991.

Bazant, Mílada. "Lecturas del Porfiriato." In *Historia de la lectura en México: Seminario de Historia de la Educación en México.* Mexico: Ediciones del Ermitaño—El Colegio de México, 1988.

Beezley, William. *Judas at the Jockey Club and Other Episodes in Porfirian Mexico.* 2nd ed. Lincoln: University of Nebraska Press, 2004.

———. *Mexican National Identity: Memory, Innuendo, and Popular Culture.* Tucson: University of Arizona Press, 2008.

———. "The Porfirian Smart Set Anticipates Thorstein Veblen in Guadalajara." In *Rituals of Rule, Rituals of Resistance: Public Celebrations and Popular Culture in Mexico*, ed. William Beezley, Cheryl English Martin, and William French, 173–90. Wilmington DE: Scholarly Resources, 1994.

Beezley, William, and Linda A. Curcio-Nagy, eds. *Latin American Popular Culture: An Introduction.* Wilmington DE: Scholarly Resources Press, 1994.

Beezley, William, and David E. Lorey, eds. *¡Viva Mexico! ¡Viva la Independencia! Celebrations of September 16.* Wilmington DE: Scholarly Resources, 2001.

Beezley, William, Cheryl English Martin, and William E. French, eds. *Rituals of Rule, Rituals of Resistance: Public Celebrations and Popular Culture in Mexico.* Wilmington DE: Scholarly Resources, 1994.

Benjamin, Walter. *The Arcades Project.* Trans. Howard Eiland and Kevin McLaughlin. Cambridge: Harvard University Press, 1999.

Berman, Marshall. *All That Is Solid Melts into Air: The Experience of Modernity.* New York: Penguin Books, 1982.

Bishop, William Henry. *Old Mexico and Her Lost Provinces.* New York: Harper & Brothers, 1883.

Bonilla, Helia Emma. "Imágenes de Posada en los impresos de Vanegas Arroyo." In *La república de las letras: Asomos a la cultura escrita del México decimonónico*, ed. Belem Clark de Lara and Elisa Speckman de Guerra, 415–36. Mexico: Universidad Nacional Autónoma de México, 2005.

Bourdieu, Pierre. *Language and Symbolic Power.* Ed. John B. Thompson. Trans. Gino Raymond and Matthew Adamson. Oxford: Polity Press, 1991.

Bringas, Guillermina, and David Mascareño. *Esbozo histórico de la prensa obrera en México*. Mexico: Universidad Nacional Autónoma de México, 1988.

Buffington, Robert M. *Criminal and Citizen in Modern Mexico*. Lincoln: University of Nebraska Press, 2000.

———. *A Sentimental Education for the Working Man: Mexico City, 1900–1910*. Forthcoming.

Buffington, Robert M., and William E. French. "The Culture of Modernity." In *The Oxford History Of Mexico*, ed. Michael C. Meyer and William H. Beezley, 397–432. Oxford: Oxford University Press, 2000.

Burns, E. Bradford. *The Poverty of Progress: Latin America in the Nineteenth Century*. Berkeley: University of California Press, 1980.

Cabrera, Daniel, ed. *Liberales ilustres Mexicanos de la reforma y la intervencion*. Mexico: Imprenta "Hijo del Ahuizote," 1890.

Calderón, Francisco. "Los ferrocarriles." In *El Porfiriato, la vida económica*, vol. 7 of *Historia moderna de México*, ed. Daniel Cosío Villegas, 483–634. Mexico City: Editorial Hermes, 1955–72.

———. *La República Restaurada, la vida económica*, vol. 2 of *Historia moderna de México*, ed. Daniel Cosío Villegas. Mexico: Editorial Hermes, 1955–72.

Camp, Roderic Ai. *Politics in Mexico*. Oxford: Oxford University Press, 1993.

Cano, Gabriel. "The *Porfiriato* and the Mexican Revolution: Constructions of Feminism and Nationalism." In *Nation, Empire, Colony: Historicizing Gender and Race*, ed. Ruth Roach Pierson and Nupur Chaudhuri, 106–20. Bloomington: Indiana University Press, 1998.

Caplan, Eric. "Trains and Trauma in the American Guilded Age." In *Traumatic Pasts: History, Psychiatry, and Trauma in the Modern Age, 1870–1930*, ed. Mark S. Micale and Paul Lerner. Cambridge: Cambridge University Press, 2001.

Cárdenas, Enrique. "A Macroeconomic Interpretation of Nineteenth-Century Mexico." In *How Latin America Fell Behind: Essays on the Economic Histories of Brazil and Mexico*, ed. Stephen Haber, 65–92. Stanford: Stanford University Press, 1997.

Carillo A., Rafael. *Posada y el grabador mexicano*. Mexico: Panorama Éditorial, 1983.

Carrasco Puente, Rafael. *La prensa en México: Datos historicos*. Mexico: UNAM, 1962.

Carter, Ian. *Railways and Culture in Britain: The Epitome of Modernity*. Manchester: Manchester University Press, 2001.

Carvalho, José Murilo de. *A Formação das Almas: O Imaginário da República no Brasil.* São Paulo: Companhia das Letras, 1990.

Chassen-López, Francie R. *From Liberal to Revolutionary Oaxaca: The View from the South, Mexico, 1867–1911.* University Park: Pennsylvania State University Press, 2004.

Cimó Queiroz, Paulo Roberto. *As curvas do trem e os meandros do poder: O nascimento da Estrada de ferro Noroeste do Brasil.* Campo Grande: Editora UFMS, 1997.

Clark, Kim. *The Redemptive Work: Railway and Nation in Ecuador, 1895–1930.* Wilmington DE: Scholarly Resources, 1998.

Coatsworth, John. *Growth against Development: The Economic Impact of Railroads in Porfirian Mexico.* DeKalb: Northern Illinois University Press, 1981.

———. "Indispensable Railways in a Backward Economy: The Case of Mexico." *Journal of Economic History* 39, no. 4 (1974): 167–87.

———. *Los origins del atraso: Nueve ensayos de historia económica de México en los siglos XVIII y XIX.* Mexico: Alianza Editorial Mexicana, 1990.

———. "Railroads, Landholding, and Agrarian Protest in the Early Porfiriato." *Hispanic American Historical Review* 54, no. 1 (1974): 48–71.

Cockcroft, James D. *Intellectual Precursors of the Mexican Revolution, 1900–1913.* Austin: Published for the Institute of Latin American Studies by the University of Texas Press, 1968.

Coerver, Don M. *The Porfirian Interregnum: The Presidency of Manuel Gonzalez of Mexico, 1880–1884.* Fort Worth: Texas Christian University Press, 1979.

Coronado Guel., Luis Edgardo. *La alameda potosina ante la llegada del ferrocarril: Espacio, poder, e institucionalización de la ciudadanía moderna en San Luis Potosí, 1878–1890.* San Luis Potosí: Editorial Ponciano Arriaga, 2009.

Corrigan, Philip, and Derek Sayer. *The Great Arch: English State Formation as Cultural Revolution.* Oxford: Basil Blackwell, 1985.

Cosío Villegas, Daniel, ed. *Historia moderna de México.* 10 vols. Mexico City: Editorial Hermes, 1955–72.

———. *El Porfiriato, la vida política interior* (segunda parte). Vol. 10 of *Historia moderna de México.* Mexico City: Editorial Hermes, 1972.

Costeloe, Michael. *The Central Republic in Mexico, 1835–1846.* Cambridge: Cambridge University Press, 1993.

Cronon, William. *Nature's Metropolis: Chicago and the Great West*. New York: W. W. Norton, 1991.

Cumberland, Charles C. *Mexican Revolution: Genesis under Madero*. Austin: University of Texas Press, 1952.

Curcio-Nagy, Linda A. *The Great Festivals of Colonial Mexico City: Performing Power and Identity*. Albuquerque: University of New Mexico Press, 2004.

Dabbs, Jack A. *The French Army in Mexico, 1861–1867*. The Hague: Mouton, 1963.

Darton, Robert. *The Great Cat Massacre and Other Episodes in French Cultural History*. New York: Vintage Books, 1984.

Diario de los Debates. Camara de Diputados, 8ª Legislatura Constitucionales de la Union. 2 vols. Mexico: Tipografia literaria de Filomeno Mata, 1877.

Diario de los Debates. Camara de Diputados, 8ª y 9ª Legislatura Constitucionales de la Union. 4 vols. Mexico: Tipografia literaria de Filomeno Mata, 1878–80.

Diario de los Debates, 10ª Legislatura Constitucionales de la Union. Mexico: Tipografia literaria de Filomeno Mata, 1880.

Díaz, Maria Elena. "The Satiric Penny Press for Workers in Mexico, 1900–1910: A Case Study in the Politicisation of Popular Culture." *Journal of Latin American Studies* 22, no. 3 (1990): 497–526.

Diccionario Porrúa: Historia, Biografía y Geografía de México. 5th ed. 3 vols. Mexico: Editorial Porrúa, S.A., 1986.

Doménech, J. Figueroa, ed. *Guía general de la república Mexicana: Historia, geografía, estadística, etc*. Mexico: Ramón de S. N. Araluce, 1898.

Elias, Norbert. *The Civilizing Process: Sociogenetic and Psychogenetic Investigations*. Trans. Edmund Jephcott. Rev. ed. Malden MA: Blackwell, 2000.

Ely, Christopher. *This Meager Nature: Landscape and National Identity in Late Imperial Russia*. DeKalb: Northern Illinois Press, 2002.

Espinosa Blas, Margarita. "El Hijo del Ahuizote: Un periodic americanista." In *La prensa decimonónica en México: Objeto y sujeto de la historia*, ed. Adriana and Pineda Soto and Celia del Palacio Montiel, 245–62. Morelia: Universidad Michoacana de San Nicolás de Hidalgo, 2003.

Exposición en Querétaro al Inaugurarse el Ferrocarril Central. Querétaro: Imp. de Luciano Frias y Soto, Flor-baja número 12, 1881.

Esposito, Matthew D. "The Politics of Death: State Funerals as Rites of Reconciliation in Porfirian Mexico, 1876–1889." *Americas* 62, no. 1 (2005): 65–94.

Fernández-Armesto, Felipe. *Civilizations: Culture, Ambition, and the Transformation of Nature.* New York: Touchstone, 2001.

Fernando Iturribarria, Jorge. "La política de conciliación del general Díaz y el arzobispo Gillow." *Historia Mexicana* 14, no. 1 (July–September 1964): 81–101.

Fiestas Inaugurales del Ferrocarril a Guadalajara: Recuerdo escrito para "El Diario de Jalisco" por Manuel Caballero, en nombre de los excursionistas que vinieron en el tren inaugural, el 15 de Mayo de 1888. Guadalajara: Imprenta del "Diario de Jalisco" de Rafael León, 1888.

Foot Hardman, Francisco. *Trem fantasma: A modernidade na selva.* São Paulo: Companhia das Letras, 1988.

Foucault, Michel. *Discipline and Punish: The Birth of the Prison.* Trans. Alan Sheridan. New York: Vintage Books, 1977.

Frank, Patrick. *Posada's Broadsheets: Mexican Popular Imagery, 1890–1910.* Albuquerque: University of New Mexico Press, 1998.

Frazer, Chris. *Bandit Nation: A History of Outlaws and Cultural Struggle in Mexico, 1820–1920.* Lincoln: University of Nebraska Press, 2006.

Freeman, Michael. *Railways and the Victorian Imagination.* New Haven: Yale University Press, 1999.

French, William E. "In the Path of Progress: Railroads and Moral Reform in Porfirian Mexico." In *Railway Imperialism*, ed. Clarence B. Davis and Kenneth E. Wilburn Jr., 85–102. New York: Greenwood Press, 1991.

———. *A Peaceful and Working People: Manners, Morals, and Class Formation in Northern Mexico.* Albuquerque: University of New Mexico, 1996.

Fritzsche, Peter. *Stranded in the Present: Modern Time and the Melancholy of History.* Cambridge: Harvard University Press, 2004.

Gamboa, Federico. *Santa.* 1903. Reprint, Ediciones Botas México, 1938.

Garner, Paul. *British Lions and Mexican Eagles: Business, Politics, and Empire in the Career of Weetman Pearson in Mexico, 1889–1919.* Stanford: Stanford University Press, 2011.

———. *Porfirio Díaz.* Harlow: Pearson Education, 2001.

———. "La Compañía Pearson y el Ferrocarril Nacional de Tehuantepec (1896–1907)." In *Don Porfirio president . . . , nunca omnipotente: Hallazgos, reflexiones y debates, 1876–1911*, ed. Romana Falcón and Raymond Buve, 105–18. Mexico: Universidad Iberoamericana, 1998.

———. "The Politics of National Development in Late Porfirian Mexico: Reconstruction of the Tehuantepec National Railway, 1896–1907." *Bulletin of Latin American Research* 14 (September 1995): 339–56.

Garza, James, *The Imagined Underworld: Sex, Crime, and Vice in Porfirian Mexico City*. Lincoln: University of Nebraska Press, 2008.

Giddens, Anthony, and Christopher Pierson. *Conversations with Anthony Giddens: Making Sense of Modernity*. Cambridge: Polity Press, 1998.

Glade, William. "Economy, 1870–1914." In *Latin America: Economy and Society, 1870–1930*, ed. Leslie Bethell, 1–56. Cambridge: Cambridge University Press, 1989.

Gómez Quiñonez, Juan. *Porfirio Díaz, los intelectuales y la Revolución*. Mexico: Ediciones El Caballito, 1981.

González Navarro, Moisés. *La colonización en México, 1877–1910*. Mexico: Talleres de impresión de estampillas y valores, 1960.

———, ed. *El Porfiriato: La vida social*. Vol. 4 of *Historia Moderna de México*. Mexico: Editorial Hermes, 1957.

González Roa, Fernando. *El problema ferrocarrilero y la Compañía de los Ferrocarriles Nacionales de México*. 2nd ed. Mexico: Liga de Economistas Revolucionarios de la República Mexicana, 1975.

Gramsci, Antonio. *The Antonio Gramsci Reader: Selected Writings*. Edited by David Forgacs. New York: New York University Press, 2000.

Grunstein, Arturo. "Railroads and Sovereignty: Policymaking in Porfirian Mexico." PhD diss., University of California, Los Angeles, 1994.

———. "De la competencia al monopolio: La formación de los Ferrocarriles Nacionales de México." In *Ferrocarriles y obras públicas*, ed. Sandra Kuntz Ficker and Priscilla Connolly, 71–104. Mexico: Instituto de Investigaciones Históiricas–UNAM, 1999.

Haber, Stephen, ed. *How Latin America Fell Behind: Essays on the Economic Histories of Brazil and Mexico*. Stanford: Stanford University Press, 1997.

———. *Industry and Underdevelopment: The Industrialization of Mexico, 1890–1940*. Stanford: Stanford University Press, 1989.

Halbwachs, Maurice. *On Collective Memory*. Chicago: University of Chicago Press, 1992.

Hale, Charles. *The Transformation of Liberalism in Late Nineteenth-Century Mexico*. Princeton: Princeton University Press, 1989.

Hall, Stuart. *Modernity: An Introduction to Modern Societies*. Oxford: Blackwell, 2000.

Harrington, Ralph. "The Railway Accident: Trains, Trauma, and Technological Crisis in Nineteenth-Century Britain." In *Traumatic Pasts: History, Psychiatry, and Trauma in the Modern Age, 1870–1930*, ed. Mark S. Micale and Paul Lerner, 31–56. Cambridge: Cambridge University Press, 2001.

Hart, John M. *Empire and Revolution: The Americans in Mexico since the Civil War*. Berkeley: University of California Press, 2002.

———. *Revolutionary Mexico: The Coming and Process of the Mexican Revolution*. Berkeley: University of California Press, 1987.

Hobsbawm, Eric, and Terence Ranger, eds. *The Invention of Tradition*. Cambridge: Cambridge University Press, 1983.

Infante Vargas, Lucrecia. "De lectoras y redactoras: Las publicaciones *femeninas* en México durante el siglo XIX." In *La república de las letras: Asomos a la cultura escrita del México decimonónico*, ed. Belem Clark de Lara and Elisa Speckman de Guerra, 183–94. Mexico: Universidad Nacional Autónoma de México, 2005.

Joseph, Gilbert M., Anne Rubenstein, and Eric Zolov. "Assembling the Fragments: Writing a Cultural History of Mexico since 1940." In *Fragments of a Golden Age: The Politics of Culture in Mexico since 1940*, ed. Gilbert M. Joseph, Anne Rubenstein, and Eric Zolov, 3–22. Durham: Duke University Press, 2001.

Jiménez Muñoz, Jorge H. *La traza de poder: Historia de la política y los urbanos en el Distrito Federal DE sus orígenes a la desaparición del ayuntamiento, 1824–1928*. Mexico: CODEX Editores, 1993.

Kasson, John F. *Civilizing the Machine: Technology and Republican Values in America, 1776–1900*. New York: Grossman, 1976.

Katz, Friedrich. *The Secret War in Mexico: Europe, the United States, and the Mexican Revolution*. Chicago: University of Chicago Press, 1981.

Knapp, Frank Averill, Jr. *The Life of Sebastián Lerdo de Tejada, 1823–1889*. Austin: University of Texas Press, 1951.

Knight, Alan. "El liberalism mexicano desde la Reforma hasta la Revolución (una interpretación)." *Historia Mexicana* 35, no. 1 (July–September 1985): 59–91.

———. *The Mexican Revolution*. 2 vols. Cambridge: Cambridge University Press, 1986.

———. "The Political Economy of Revolutionary Mexico." In *Latin America: Economic Imperialism and the State*, ed. Abel Christopher and Colin Lewis, 288–317. Cambridge: Cambridge University Press, 1985.

Knudson. Jerry. "Periodization of the Mexican Press." *Contemporary Mexico: Papers of the IV International Congress of Mexican History*, ed. James Wilkie, Michael C. Meyers, and Edna Monzón de Wilkie, 747–50. Berkeley: University of California Press, 1973.

Kuntz-Ficker, Sandra. *Empresa extrangera y mercado interno: El Ferrocarril Central Mexicano*. México, D.F.: El Colegio de México, 1995.

Kuntz-Ficker, Sandra, and Paolo Riguzzi, eds. *Ferrocarriles y vida económica en México, 1850–1950.* El Colegio Mexiquense: Universidad Metropolitana Xochimilco: Ferrocarriles Nacionales de México, 1996.

Lane, Christel. *The Rites of Rulers: Ritual in Industrial Society—The Soviet Case.* Cambridge: Harvard University Press, 1981.

Lear, John. *Workers, Neighbors, and Citizens: The Revolution in Mexico City.* Lincoln: University of Nebraska Press, 2001.

Lears, T. J. Jackson. "The Concept of Cultural Hegemony: Problems and Possibilities." *American Historical Review* 90, no. 3 (1985): 567–93.

Lecoq, Anne-Marie. "The Symbolism of the State: The Images of the Monarchy from the Early Valois Kings to Louis XIV." In *Rethinking France: Les Lieux de Mémoire,* ed. Pierre Nora and trans. David P. Jordan and Mary Trouille, 217–68. Chicago: University of Chicago Press, 2001.

Lee, Robert. "Railways, Space, and Imperialism." In *Mitteilungen des Österreichischen Staatsarchivs: Eisenbahn/Kultur,* ed. Günter Dinhobl, 91–106. Vienna: Sonderband 7, 2004.

Lehning, James R. "Gossiping about Gambetta: Contested Memories in the Early Third Republic." *French Historical Studies* 18, no. 1 (1993): 237–54.

Lewis, Daniel. *Iron Horse Imperialism: The Southern Pacific of Mexico, 1880–1951.* Tucson: University of Arizona Press, 2006.

Limantour, José Ives. *Apuntes sobre mi vida pública.* Mexico: Editorial Porrúa, 1965.

Lomnitz, Claudio. *Death and the Idea of Mexico.* New York: Zone Books, 2005.

———. *Deep Mexico, Silent Mexico: An Anthropology of Nationalism.* Minneapolis: University of Minnesota Press, 2001.

López-Portillo y Rojas, José. *Elevación y caída de Porfirio Díaz.* 2nd ed. Mexico: Editorial Porrúa, 1975.

Madero, Francisco. *The Presidential Succession of 1910.* Trans. Thomas B. Davis. New York: Peter Lang, 1990.

Maines, Rachel P. *The Technology of Orgasm: "Hysteria," the Vibrator, and Women's Sexual Satisfaction.* Baltimore: Johns Hopkins University Press, 1999.

Marx, Karl, *Karl Marx: Selected Writings.* Edited by David McLellan. Oxford: Oxford University Press, 1977.

Marx, Leo. *Machine in the Garden: Technology and the Pastoral Ideal in America.* Oxford: Oxford University Press, 1964.

Meyers, William K. *Forge of Progress, Crucible of Revolt: The Origins of the Mexican Revolution in La Comarca Lagunera, 1880–1911.* Albuquerque: University of New Mexico Press, 1994.

Monsiváis, Carlos. *Escenas de pudor y liviandad*, 7th ed. Mexico: Editorial Grijalbo, 1988.

Morgan, Tony. "Proletariats, Politicos, and Patriarchs: The Use and Abuse of Cultural Customs in the Early Industrialization of Mexico City, 1880–1910." In *Rituals of Rule, Rituals of Resistance: Public Celebrations and Popular Culture in Mexico*, ed. William Beezley, Cheryl English Martin, and William French, 151–71. Wilmington DE: Scholarly Resources, 1994.

Mostkoff-Linares, Aída. "Foreign Visions and Images of Mexico: One Hundred Years of International Tourism, 1821–1921." PhD diss., University of California, Los Angeles, 1999.

Murdock, Jill. "The Railway in Arcadia: An Approach to Modernity in British Visual Culture." In *Mitteilungen des Österreichischen Staatsarchivs: Eisenbahn/Kultur*, ed. Günter Dinhobl, 113–35. Vienna: Sonderband 7, 2004.

Navarrete Maya, Laura. "El *Gil Blas Cómico*, publicación satírica y de humor." In *La prensa decimonónica en México: objeto u sujeto de la historia*, ed. Adriana Pineda Soto and Celia del Palacio Montiel, 263–72. Morelia: Universidad Michoacana de San Nicolás de Hidalgo, 2003.

Nora, Pierre. "Between History and Memory: Les Lieux de Mémoire." *Representations* 26 (Spring 1989): 7–25.

Opinion de la prensa y de los Sres: Gobernadores de los estados de la federación así como del Sr. Presidente de la Republica acerca del Ferrocarril Internacional e Interoceanico representado por los Sres. James Sullivan, Gral. H. J. Palmer y sócios. Mexico: Imprenta de Ireneo Paz, Escalerillas 7, 1880.

Ortiz Hernán, Sergio. *Los ferrocarriles de México: Una vision social y económica.* Mexico: Secretaría de Comunicaciones y Transportes, 1970.

Overmyer-Velázquez, Mark. *Visions of the Emerald City: Modernity, Tradition, and the Formation of Porfirian Oaxaca, Mexico.* Durham: Duke University Press, 2006.

Ozouf, Mona. *Festivals and the French Revolution.* Trans. Alan Sheridan. Cambridge: Harvard University Press, 1988.

Pérez Vejo, Tomás. "La conspiración gachupina en *El Hijo del Ahuizote*." *Historia Mexicana* 54 (April–June 2005): 1105–53.

Perry, Laurens Ballard. *Juárez and Díaz: Machine Politics in Mexico*. DeKalb: Northern Illinois University Press, 1978.

Piccato, Pablo. *City of Suspects: Crime in Mexico City, 1900–1931*. Durham: Duke University Press, 2001.

———. *The Tyranny of Opinion: Honor in the Construction of the Mexican Public Sphere*. Durham: Duke University Press, 2010.

Pineda Franco, Adela. "El cosmopolitismo de la *Revista Moderna* (1898–1911): Una vocación porfiriana." In *La república de las letras: Asomos a la cultura escrita del México decimonónico*, ed. Belem Clark de Lara and Elisa Speckman de Guerra, 223–38. Mexico: Universidad Nacional Autónoma de México, 2005.

Pletcher, David M. *Rails, Mines, and Progress: Seven American Promoters in Mexico, 1867–1911*. Ithaca: Cornell University Press, 1958.

Powell, Fred Wilbur. *The Railroads of Mexico*. Boston: Stratford, 1921.

Programa y proyecto de la Gran Liga Mexicana de Empleados de Ferrocarril presentado por la presidencia. Mexico: Tip. de "El Ferrocarrilero" 2ª de Galenan núm. 2, 1906.

Raat, William Dirk. "The Antipositivist Movement in Prerevolutionary Mexico, 1892–1911." *Journal of Interamerican Studies and World Affairs* 19 (February 1977): 83–98.

Ramos Escandón, Carmen. "Señoritas Porfirianas: Mujer e ideología en el México progresista, 1880–1910." In *Presencia y transperencia: La mujer en la historia de Mexico*, ed. Carmen Ramos Escandón, 145–62. Mexico: El Colegio de México, 1987.

Richard, Jeffrey, and John M. Mackenzie. *The Railway Station: A Social History*. London: Oxford University Press, 1986.

Riguzzi, Paolo. "México, Estados Unidos, y Gran Bretaña, 1867–1910: Una difícil relación triangular." *Historia Mexicana* 41 (January–March 1992): 365–436.

Rohlfes, Laurence J. "Police and Penal Correction in Mexico City, 1876–1911: A Study of Order and Progress in Porfirian Mexico." PhD diss., Tulane University, 1983.

Roseberry. William. "Hegemony and the Language of Contention." In *Everyday Forms of State Formation: Revolution and the Negotiation of Rule in Modern Mexico*, ed. Gilbert M. Joseph and Daniel Nugent, 355–66. Durham: Duke University Press, 1994.

Ross, Stanley R. *Francisco I. Madero, Apostle of Mexican Democracy*. New York: Columbia University Press, 1955.

Ruíz, Ramón E. *The Great Rebellion: Mexico, 1905–1923.* New York: W. W. Norton, 1980.

Ruiz Sacristán, Carlos, Aaron Dychter Poltolarek, Luis de Pablo Serna, Sergio Ortiz Hernán, and Miguel Tirado Rasso, eds. *Caminos de Hierro.* Mexico: Ferrocarriles Nacionales de México, 1996.

Santoni, Pedro. *Mexicans at Arms: Puro Federalists and the Politics of War, 1845–1848.* Fort Worth: Texas Christian University Press, 1996.

Schama, Simon. *Landscape and Memory.* New York: Alfred K. Knopf, 1995.

Schell, William, Jr. *Integral Outsiders: The American Colony in Mexico City, 1876–1911.* Wilmington DE: Scholarly Resources, 2001.

Schivelbusch, Wolfgang. *The Railway Journey: Trains and Travel in the 19th Century.* Trans. Anselm Hollo. New York: Urizen Books, 1977.

Schmidt, Arthur. *The Social and Economic Effect of the Railroad in Puebla and Veracruz, Mexico, 1867–1911.* New York: Garland, 1987.

Schmidt, Leigh Eric. "The Commercialization of the Calendar: American Holidays and the Culture of Consumption, 1870–1930." *Journal of American History* 78, no. 3 (1991): 887–916.

Scholes, Walter V. *Mexican Politics during the Juárez Regime, 1855–1872.* Columbia: University of Missouri Press, 1957.

Scott, James. *Domination and the Arts of Resistance: Hidden Transcripts.* New Haven: Yale University Press, 1990.

Secretaría de Comunicaciones y Obras Públicas. *Album de los ferrocarriles correspondiente al año 1891.* Mexico: Tipografia de la Oficina de Estampillas, Palacio Nacional, 1893.

Secretaría de Fomento. *Album de los ferrocarriles correspondiente al año 1889.* Mexico: Oficina Tip. de la Secretaría de Fomento, 1891.

Seed, Patricia. *Ceremonies of Possession in Europe's Conquest of the New World, 1492–1640.* Cambridge: Cambridge University Press, 1995.

Sierra, Justo. *Evolución política del pueblo mexicano.* 2nd ed. Mexico: Fondo de Cultura Economica, 1940.

Simmons, Jack. *The Victorian Railway.* New York: Thames and Hudson, 1991.

Sinkin, Richard. *The Mexican Reform, 1855–1876: A Study in Liberal Nation-Building.* Austin: University of Texas Press, 1979.

Sluis, Ageeth. "City of Spectacles: Gender Performance, Revolutionary Reform, and the Creation of Public Space in Mexico City, 1915–1939." PhD diss., University of Arizona, 2006.

Smith, Anthony D. *Ethno-Symbolism and Nationalism: A Cultural Approach*. New York: Routledge, 2009.

Smith, David Norman. *The Railway and Its Passengers: A Social History*. London: David & Charles, 1988.

Smith, Phyllis. "Contentious Voices amid the Order: The Porfirian Press in Mexico City, 1876–1911." PhD diss., University of Arizona, 1996.

Soler, Jaime, and Lorenzo Ávila, eds. *Posada y la prensa ilustrada: Signos de modernización y resistencias*. Mexico: Patronato del Museo Nacional de Arte, Instituto Bellas Artes, 1996.

Soto, Shirlene. *Emergence of the Modern Mexican Woman: Her Participation in Revolution and Struggle for Equality, 1910–1940*. Denver: Arden Press, 1990.

Stevens, Donald Fithian. *The Origins of Instability in Early Republican Mexico*. Durham: Duke University Press, 1991.

Taussig, Michael T. *The Devil and Commodity Fetishism in South America*. 30th anniversary ed. Chapel Hill: University of North Carolina Press, 2010.

Tenenbaum, Barbara A. *The Politics of Penury: Debt and Taxes in Mexico, 1821–1856*. Albuquerque: University of New Mexico Press, 1986.

———. "Streetwise History: The Paseo de la Reforma and the Porfirian State, 1876–1910." In *Rituals of Rule, Rituals of Resistance: Public Celebrations and Popular Culture in Mexico*, ed. William Beezley, Cheryl English Martin, and William French, 127–50. Wilmington DE: Scholarly Resources, 1994.

Tenorio-Trillo, Mauricio. *Mexico at the World's Fairs: Crafting a Modern Nation*. Berkeley: University of California Press, 1996.

———. "1910 Mexico City: Space and Nation in the City of the Centenario." *Journal of Latin American Studies* 28 (February 1996): 75–104.

Terdiman, Richard. *Discourse/Counter-Discourse: The Theory and Practice of Symbolic Resistance in Nineteenth-Century France*. Ithaca: Cornell University Press, 1989.

Thompson, E. P. *The Making of the English Working Class*. New York: Vintage Books, 1966.

———. "Time, Work-Discipline, and Industrial Capitalism." *Past and Present* 38, no. 1 (1967): 56–97.

Thorup, Cathryn. "La competencia económica británica y norteamericana en México (1887–1910): El caso de Weetman Pearson." *Historia Mexicana* 31 (April–June 1982): 599–641.

Tischendorf, Alfred. *Great Britain and Mexico in the Age of Díaz.* Durham: Duke University Press, 1961.

Toussaint Alcaraz, Florence. *Escenario de la prensa en el Porfiriato.* Mexico: Fundación Manuel Buendía, 1989.

Turner, John Kenneth. *Barbarous Mexico.* Austin: University of Texas Press, 1969.

Tyler, Ron, ed. *Posada's Mexico.* Washington: Library of Congress, 1979.

Valadés, José. *El Porfirismo: Historia de un régimen.* 3 vols. 2nd ed. Mexico: UNAM, 1977.

Van Hoy, Teresa M. "*La Marcha Violenta?* Railroads and Land in 19th Century Mexico." *Bulletin of Latin American Research* 19, no. 1 (2000): 33–61.

———. *A Social History of Mexican Railroads: Peons, Prisoners, and Priests.* Lanham: Rowman and Littlefield, 2008.

Vanderwood, Paul J. *Disorder and Progress: Bandits, Police, and Mexican Development.* Lincoln: University of Nebraska Press, 1981.

———. *The Power of God against the Guns of Government: Religious Upheaval in Mexico at the Turn of the Nineteenth Century.* Stanford: Stanford University Press, 1998.

Vázquez, Josefina. "War and Peace with the United States." In *The Oxford History of Mexico,* ed. Michael C. Meyer and William H. Beezley, 339–69. New York: Oxford University Press, 2000.

Vieyra Sánchez, Lilia. "La circulación de las obras de Julio Verne en la prensa mexicana del siglo XIX." In *La prensa como fuente para la historia,* ed. Celia del Palacio Montiel, 143–52. Mexico: Universidad de Guadalajara, 2006.

Viqueira Albán, Juan Pedro. *Propriety and Permissiveness in Bourbon Mexico.* Trans. Sonya Lipsett-Rivera and Sergio Rivera Ayala. Wilmington DE: Scholarly Resources, 1999.

Walkowitz, Judith R. *City of Dreadful Delight: Narratives of Sexual Danger in Late-Victorian London.* Chicago: University of Chicago Press, 1992.

Wasserman, Mark. *Capitalists, Caciques, and Revolution: The Native Elite and Foreign Enterprise in Chihuahua, 1854–1911.* Chapel Hill: University of North Carolina Press, 1984.

Wells, Allen, and Gilbert M. Joseph. *Summer of Discontent, Seasons of Upheaval: Elite Politics and Rural Insurgency in Yucatán, 1876–1915.* Stanford: Stanford University Press, 1997.

Weiner, Richard. *Race, Nation, and Market: Economic Culture in Porfirian Mexico.* Tucson: University of Arizona Press, 2004.

————. "Trinidad Sánchez Santos: Voice of the Catholic Opposition in Porfirian Mexico." *Mexican Studies/Estudios Mexicanos* 17 (Summer 2001): 321–49.

Welke, Barbara Young. *Recasting American Liberty: Gender, Race, Law, and the Railroad Revolution, 1865–1920.* Cambridge: Cambridge University Press, 2001.

Williams, Rosalind. *Notes on the Underground.* Cambridge: MIT Press, 1990.

Young Men's Christian Association. *Guide for Tourists and Strangers in Mexico.* Mexico: Gante Press, 1894.

Zimmer, Oliver. "Alpine Landscape and the Reconstruction of the Swiss Nation." *Comparative Studies of Society and History* 40 (October 1998): 637–65.

INDEX

bullfights, 79–80, 133, 272n63
Bulnes, Francisco, 28, 116, 153
Burns, E. Bradford, 262n15
Bustamante, Anastasio, 9

Caballero, Manuel, 70
Cabrera, Daniel, 201–3, 220–24,
  227–28, 236, 238–39, 242, 242,
  250, 254, 286n140
Calderón, Francisco, 284n92
Camacho, Sebastián, 27
"El camino de ultratumba," 193.
  See also corridos
Camp, Roderic Ai, 292n80
Cañada de Metlac, 60
Cáñedo, Elvira Iñíguez de, 131
Cárdenas, Enrique, 266n86
Cardoso, Joaquín, 164–67, 171, 173
Casarín, José, 251–52
Catholic press. See media
Celada, Francisco (poet), 248
centennial of Mexican Indepen-
  dence, 120, 251–52
cerebral shock, 166. See also dolo-
  res morales; indemnification; law-
  suits; railroad accidents; "railway
  spine"
Chavero, Alfredo, 39
Chávez, Gregorio, 238
Chihuahua City, 71
El Chile Piquín, 180
El Chisme, 156, 176, 201, 203,
  207, 228–29
científicos, 56, 58, 68, 115, 125,
  126, 156, 217, 255, 269n13. See
  also Porfirian elites; positivism
Cimó Queiroz, Paulo Roberto, 24
civic ceremonies: celebration of
  Porfirio Díaz during, 11, 115–16;
  promotion of modern values and,

106, 141; promotion of national identity and, 120, 276n47. See
  also fiestas presidenciales; railroad inaugurations
civilizing mission, 11, 252; European imperialism and, 12–13, 68,
  279n100; proper behaviors and
  11–12; work ethic and 11–12. See
  also Porfirian elites
The Civilizing Process (Elias), 12,
  279n100
Clark, Kim, 24–25, 270–71n33
coaches, 7, 74
El Coahuilense, 34
Coatepec, 150
Coatsworth, John, 261n12, 266n76
Coatzacoalcos, 118
Coatzacoalcos Electric Company,
  118
Cockcroft, James, 287n6
Código de la Reforma (Gutiérrez),
  166
Coerver, Don, 18
Collantes, Pedro, 42
El Cómico, 72, 76, 77, 86, 185,
  186–87, 187
commodity fetishism, 14
Comte, Auguste, 126
El Congreso Obrero, 151–52
Congress, 27, 32, 36–40, 51
conspicuous consumption, 134
Constitutionalists, 257
Constitution of 1857, 11, 41, 110,
  111, 116, 160, 201, 218, 232,
  234, 239, 240, 241, 287n3
Constitution of 1917, 257
Conventionists, 257
Corral, Ramón, 123
El Correo de Chihuahua, 34

fiestas presidenciales (presidential festivals), 107, 115. *See also* civic ceremonies; Díaz, Porfirio

Flores Magón brothers, 177, 201–2, 220, 227–28, 239, 242, 244, 246–48, 250, 254, 286n140

Foot Hardman, Francisco, 267n2

French, William, 70

French Intervention, 9, 113

Freud, Sigmund, 95, 97, 170

Frías, Heriberto, 202

Frillo, Claudio, 157

Fritzche, Peter, 80

Gálvez, Jacobo (architect), 129

Gamboa, Federico, 57, 272n56

Garner, Paul, 182

Gil Blas, 154–55, 179, 210, 287n3

Gil Blas Cómico, 201–2, 203–7, 210, 215–20, 249–50, 287n1

Gillow, Eulogio, 159–60, 238–39

Gloner, Próspero, 167–74

Gómez Quiñonez, Juan, 285n110

González, Manuel, 4, 29, 41, 51, 52, 53, 109, 226, 241, 290n44; railroad concessions and, 233

Gramsci, Antonio: cultural hegemony, 16; "war of position," 16, 197, 250, 254

Gran Liga Mexicana de Empleados de Ferrocarril, 177–78, 180

Gran Teatro Degollado, 129

Grunstein, Arturo, 182–83, 261n12

Gutenberg, Johann, 31

Gutiérrez, Blas José, 166

Hale, Charles, 275n32

Hart, John, 182, 183, 287n6

El Heraldo, 30

Hermmann, Walter, 167, 169

Herrera, Otilia, 151

Hidalgo, Miguel, 286n136

Hidalgo and Northeastern Railway, 180, 190

El Hijo del Ahuizote, 2, 112, 133–34, *134*, 152, *158*, 161, *189*, 201–3, 217, 221–25, 222, 224, 230, 232, 234, 235, 237, *237*, 241, 243, 245, 250, 286n140, 287n1; anti-Americanism in, 227–28, 285n125; circulation of, 195, 202; critique of Church-State relations, 159–60, 238–39; economic nationalism in, 222–25, 234, 243, 244; on freight rates, 223–24; government persecution of, 202, 220, 227, 244, 246; on government-sponsored violence, 232, 236; on ley fuga, 233–34; on railroad accidents, 188, 207, 243; on railroad subsidies, 221–23; on reelection, 240–41, 242; satires of Porfirio Díaz in, 112, 116–17, 172, 233, 236, 240–41, 243; on suspension of constitutional guarantees, 160; on Temamatla railroad accident, 158–61; on U.S. railroad employees, 188, 229; use of images, 202, 221, 224, 237; xenophobia of, 227, 291n62. *See also* media

El Hijo del Trabajo, 31, 40, 47

Humboldt, Alexander von, 109

El Imparcial, 56

Imperial Railway Company, 9

indemnification, 164; companies' failure to provide, 156, 167, 168; of foreign accident victims, 172–73, 175–76; satires of, 185. *See*

media (*continued*)
  287n1; racism in, 213–14; on railroad accidents, 145–46, 147–48,
  153; on railroad safety, 154, 159,
  160, 163; on railroad's effect on
  Indians, 31–32, 124–25; suppres-
  sion of, 18, 162; U.S. immigration
  and, 42; use of images, 18, 144,
  258; women's journals, 56, 57,
  69–71, 99–100
Mena, Francisco, 157–58, 160, 223
Menocal, Francisco, 37
Mexican Central Railroad, 7, 30,
  36, 48, 50, 79, 108, 109, 127,
  129, 145, 148, 149, 168, 184,
  185, 190, 208, 261n12, 280n6,
  280n11; critiques of ticket agents,
  228–29; injury rates on, 145–
  46; poor condition of, 168; trunk
  lines of, 7, 67
Mexican Financier, 53
Mexican National Railroad, 8, 31,
  36–37, 39, 48, 49, 50, 80, 110,
  121, 123, 137, 182, 223, 267n97,
  280n6; injury rates on, 146
Mexican Railway, 9, 10, 28, 49,
  175, 182, 223
Mexican Revolution (1910), 6, 177,
  201, 231, 254, 257–58, 287n6
Mexican Southern Railroad, 236
México a través de los siglos, 125
Mexico City, 7, 18, 57
México Gráfico, 103
Ministry of Communications and
  Public Works (SCOP), 145, 158,
  169, 277n51, 280n6
"La mi non tende," 229, *230*
modernization: ambivalent view
  of, 59, 76, 98–99, 100–101; anx-

ieties regarding, 56, 58, 92–93,
  100–101, 184, 219; complexities caused by, 205, 214, 220,
  250; defined against the traditional, 78, 80–81, 100–101, 219–20,
  255; ephemeral nature of, 219;
  Europe as model of, 70; hygiene
  as representative of, 69; industry
  as representative of, 71; nationalism's link to, 123–24, 253; negative views of, 200, 250; opposition to government's program of,
  200, 244–46, 249; of provincial
  cities, 69–73; sentimental side of,
  63; social order as representative
  of, 69, 71–73; work ethic and, 69
El Monitor Republicano, 31, 32,
  33, 39, 40, 49, 149, 150, 190,
  201, 224, 237, 287n1
Monsiváis, Carlos, 62
Monterrey, 71
Montes de Oca, Francisco, 154,
  155, 201, 228, 254, 287n3
Morelos Railway, 31
Moreno, Antonio de P., 202
El Mundo (Semanario Ilustrado),
  1, 56, 57, 58, 66, 81, 82–84, 87,
  88, 89, 90, 114, *114*, 156, 157,
  162, 207, 268n3
El Mundo Cómico, 77, 87, 96, 185,
  186
El Mundo Ilustrado, 90, 91, 116,
  118, *119*, 123, *130*, *132*, 203,
  268n3

National Democratic Party, 256
nationalism: contradictions within, 44–45; economic sovereignty
  and, 37–38, 226; foreign invasion

positivism, 13, 32, 58, 61–62, 70.
  See also *científicos*
*The Presidential Succession of
  1910* (Madero), 255
El Progreso Latino, 172
provincials: media satires of, 73–
  78. *See also* modernization
pulquerias, 191

race: European imperialism and,
  12–13; railroad and, 31–32
railroad/railway: attacks against,
  85, 273n73; civilizing capacity of,
  30–31, 58, 62; economic growth
  and, 24; expansion of, 4; as fetish
  object, 14, 65; immigration and,
  42–43, 128; issue of safety and,
  178–79, 180; limits of egalitarianism and, 84–86; movement and
  energy and, 34, 51, 53, 244, 246;
  nationalization of, 36, 45, 178,
  180, 181, 261n12, 293n4; national unity and, 35; negatives views
  of, 15–16; political stability and,
  24; race and, 31–32; as regenerative force, 26, 29, 32–34, 59, 62,
  65–66, 115, 125, 247–48; symbolic power of, 1, 19, 26–27, 252–
  53, 254; as symbol of capitalist society, 13; as symbol of death, 2,
  82, 203, 215–16, 217; as symbol
  of disorder, 2, 203, 206, 210; as
  symbol of egalitarianism, 81–82,
  215; as symbol of foreign domination, 2; as symbol of nineteenth
  century, 2; as symbol of "order
  and progress," 6, 253, 270n23; as
  symbol of progress, 1–2, 116, 248;
  as symbol of regime, 242; as sym-

bol to challenge regime, 5–6; as
  symbol to legitimate regime, 5;
  U.S. investment in, 227, 285n127;
  work and, 46–47. *See also* railroad
  accidents; railroad inaugurations;
  railroad poetry; railroad stations;
  railroad travel; railroad workers
railroad accidents, 143–49, 145t,
  146t, 185, 191, 194, 196, 219,
  249, 253; changing views of, 149;
  corridos about, 191–94; European
  courts and, 169–70, 171; factors
  contributing to, 147–48; financial compensation and, 149, 153,
  154, 156, 157, 163, 168–72, 174,
  185; injuries caused by, 164, 167;
  Lechería (1882), 148–49; Morelos (1883), 148; rising incidents
  of, 149; risk taking and, 147; satires of, *186*, 186–87, *187*, *189*; as
  symbol of democracy, 146–47; as
  topic in literature, 162–63, 207,
  209, 211, 215; Zacatecas (1904),
  192–93. *See also* cerebral shock;
  dolores morales; indemnification; lawsuits; "railway spine";
  Temamatla (railroad accident)
railroad inaugurations, 14–15, 196,
  240; celebration of Mexican Independence and, 29, 106; celebration of Porfirio Díaz and, 104,
  106, 110, 111, 123–24; discussion of race and, 31–32; Durango-Oaxaca, 103, 238–39; foreign
  colonies' participation in, 138,
  140; Guadalajara, 109, 110, 121,
  129–31, 137; Mexico City-Amec-
  ameca, 107–8; Mexico City-
  Puebla, 106; political goals of, 15,

To order or obtain more information on these or other University of Nebraska Press
titles, visit nebraskapress.unl.edu.

CPSIA information can be obtained at www.ICGtesting.com
Printed in the USA
BVOW03s1549051113

335491BV00002B/2/P

9 780803 243804